Approaches to
Archaeological
Ceramics

Approaches to Archaeological Ceramics

Carla M. Sinopoli
University of Wisconsin–Milwaukee
Milwaukee, Wisconsin

Plenum Press • *New York and London*

Library of Congress Cataloging-in-Publication Data

Sinopoli, Carla M.
    Approaches to archaeological ceramics / Carla M. Sinopoli.
        p.   cm.
    Includes bibliographical references and index.
    ISBN 0-306-43852-6. -- ISBN 0-306-43575-6 (pbk.)
    1. Pottery.   2. Archaeology--Methodology.   I. Title.
CC79.5.P6S56   1991
930.1'028--dc20   91-17024
                                                             CIP

© 1991 Plenum Press, New York
A Division of Plenum Publishing Corporation
233 Spring Street, New York, N.Y. 10013

Printed in the United States of America

Foreword

More than any other category of evidence, ceramics offers archaeologists their most abundant and potentially enlightening source of information on the past. Being made primarily of clay, a relatively inexpensive material that is available in every region, ceramics became essential in virtually every society in the world during the past ten thousand years. The straightforward technology of preparing, forming, and firing clay into hard, durable shapes has meant that societies at various levels of complexity have come to rely on it for a wide variety of tasks. Ceramic vessels quickly became essential for many household and productive tasks. Food preparation, cooking, and storage—the very basis of settled village life—could not exist as we know them without the use of ceramic vessels. Often these vessels broke into pieces, but the virtually indestructible quality of the ceramic material itself meant that these pieces would be preserved for centuries, waiting to be recovered by modern archaeologists.

The ability to create ceramic material with diverse physical properties, to form vessels into so many different shapes, and to decorate them in limitless manners, led to their use in far more than utilitarian contexts. Some vessels were especially made to be used in trade, manufacturing activities, or rituals, while ceramic material was also used to make other items such as figurines, models, and architectural ornaments. The amazing qualities of ceramic materials are still being discovered today as demonstrated by their continued use in virtually every household in the world as well as their innovative uses in computers and rocketships.

Their importance to archaeologists does not rest solely in the fact that ceramics were abundant, but that they were used in many behavioral contexts while the nature of their fabrication facilitated a great diversity in details of shape, texture, appearance, and possible decorations that allowed an almost endless variety of human expression. The diversity of well-preserved material remains and the contexts in which they are found constitute the primary raw material of archaeological interpretations of the past. As potentially exciting as this information is, it requires the most diligent and innovative approaches to its study to unlock its secrets. The classification, analysis, and interpretation of ancient ceramics has been at the heart of the archaeological enterprise since its inception.

Commensurate with its importance to archaeologists have been efforts to refine existing approaches to the study of ceramics and to develop new methodologies for answering basic questions about the past as well as new interpretive questions posed by recent theoreticians. Decorative styles, utilitarian implications of form, traces of use wear, chemical composition, physical properties, and even studies of the motor habits of the makers are all part of the arsenal of tools the ceramicists apply in their investigations. Whereas in the past practical training in ceramic studies for students might have occurred in an offhand manner as part of an ongoing laboratory project, it is now imperative that students receive a broader and systematic exposure to the potential methods of ceramic analysis.

Approaches to Archaeological Ceramics by Carla Sinopoli is an excellent response to that need. This well-written and neatly organized text provides the student and professional alike with a complete overview of ceramics. The reader is given a useful treatment of the key steps in the manufacture of ceramics, providing insights essential for understanding analytical methods. From there the basic methods for analyzing ceramics are presented. The core of the volume, and its unique strength, is that Chapters 4–7 present approaches to answering various interpretive questions and examples of how they have been utilized by archaeologists. These examples make clear the advantages and disadvantages of each approach, giving the reader both the scope of available methods and a means for evaluating their relevance in each situation. A further aid to the student and professional is the Appendix, which outlines often-used statistics as they have been applied to ceramic studies.

Sinopoli concludes her volume with a discussion of new and potential approaches that will come to characterize ceramic studies in the future. These are useful directions to ponder as our discipline makes great progress with reaching the interpretive potential of our most common artifact: archaeological ceramics. This book definitely makes its own contribution to that progress by providing both a sourcebook on what has already been accomplished and a guidebook on where we might usefully proceed.

Charles L. Redman

Arizona State University
Tempe, Arizona

Preface

The past decade has seen a tremendous proliferation of literature about archaeological pottery. Recent works on ceramics include a comprehensive sourcebook on ceramic materials and analyses (Rice 1987); a view of ceramic production in ethnographic contexts from a cultural-ecological and systemic perspective (Arnold 1985); a guide to ceramic technology (Rye 1981); numerous edited volumes containing specific case studies and examples of approaches to archaeological and ethnographic pottery (Howard and Morris 1981; Olin and Franklin 1982; Rice, ed. 1984; van der Leeuw and Pritchard 1984; Nelson 1985; Kolb 1988; Kolb and Lackey 1988); and countless other monographs and articles.

This growth of literature attests to the vitality and potential of ceramic studies for archaeological analysis and to our increasing ability to use ceramics to ask and answer questions about the past. The abundance of literature on pottery, though, may prove daunting to the student seeking a general introduction to the topic. This work attempts to address this need and is intended to serve as an introductory guide and overview to the scope and potential of ceramic analysis in archaeology. I hope that it will provide a general guide to the literature of ceramic analysis, to the kinds of goals that have been and can be accomplished through ceramic analysis, and to the tremendous potential of ceramic analysis for asking and answering anthropological questions about the past.

Chapter 1 introduces some of the main concerns of the book and presents a broad overview of its organization. In Chapter 2, I consider the nature of ceramics and provide the basic vocabulary of ceramic analysis. The raw materials of ceramic manufacture and the range of techniques used in forming, firing, and decorating vessels are considered. I then present a detailed description of ceramic production in a contemporary village in India to provide a more concrete illustration of the general processes of ceramic production.

In Chapter 3, I consider the crucial first step in the study of archaeological ceramics: ceramic classification. Artifact classification, or the assignment of archaeological materials into discrete or coherent groups or classes, is an essential part of any archaeological study. The assumptions and procedures we use in ceramic classification greatly influence all later analyses and must be carefully considered. In Chapter 3, I discuss three common approaches to ceramic classification and provide examples of their use in archaeological contexts.

In Chapters 4–7, I shift attention from general approaches to documenting archaeological ceramics to the more important concerns of how archaeologists can and have used ceramics to ask questions about the past. A range of topics are discussed: ceramic ethnography and chronology (Chapter 4); ceramic use, production, and distribution (Chapter 5); ceramics and social organization (Chapter 6); and ceramics and political organization (Chapter 7). I first present a general discussion of each of these issues and then present one or more case studies, drawn from all over the world, which illustrate successful approaches to these questions using ceramic data. In Chapter 8, I consider how new techniques and new questions about the past will shape the future of ceramic research.

In preparing this manuscript, I have accumulated many debts to many individuals. Most important, I would like to acknowledge all of those researchers whose work I cite. I have learned much from them and hope that I successfully communicate a portion of what they have taught me. My research on ceramics in southern India, discussed in several sections of this work, would not have been possible without the permission and support of the Government of India, the Archaeological Survey of India, the Directorate of Archaeology and Museums of the Government of Karnataka, the American Institute of Indian Studies, and John M. Fritz and George A. Michell. I thank them all for their help in support of this work. Funds for this research were provided by the Asian Cultural Council, the National Science Foundation, the Smithsonian Institution, and the University of Michigan. I also thank the potters of Kamalapuram for teaching us of their craft, and Laura Junker and Richard Blurton for learning of it with me.

I began writing this work while a Weatherhead Scholar at the School of American Research in Santa Fe in 1986–1987. I cannot overstate my gratitude to the School of American Research and to Richard Weatherhead for their support and for the opportunity to spend a year in a wonderful place with wonderful colleagues. Following Santa Fe, this manuscript (or derivations thereof) has traveled with me to the University of Michigan in

Ann Arbor, before proceeding on to the University of Wisconsin–Milwaukee. Thanks to my friends and colleagues in both of these places for their help with the preparation and completion of this work.

A number of individuals have provided me with unpublished manuscripts and photographs. I would like to thank Cathy Costin, Barbara Mills, William J. Parry, Alison E. Rautman, and Kim Smiley for their help. My thanks, too, to the Museum of Anthropology of the University of Michigan for allowing me to photograph materials in its collections to serve as illustrations throughout the book. Especial thanks to Kay Clahassey, David Kennedy, Jill Morrison, and Henry Wright. Several individuals have read various sections or drafts of this manuscript along the way. I have not necessarily heeded all of their comments—probably unwisely—but I am grateful for their advice, critiques, and encouragement. I would like to thank Michelle Hegmon, Ed Jackson, Susan Pollock, and Virginia Vitzthum. Thanks also to the anonymous reviewers of this manuscript for their comments and criticisms, and to Eliot Werner of Plenum Press for his support and patience.

Contents

Approaches to Archaeological Ceramics

Humans differ from any other species on this planet in our extensive ability to transform the natural world in order to ease our existence in it. By shaping stone, wood, and clay we make tools that increase our effectiveness in procuring and preparing food, in securing shelter, and in producing the conditions and comforts of life that we now view as necessary for our survival. We also produce goods to ornament our homes and bodies, designed according to cultural rules of esthetics, as well as objects necessary for the acknowledgment or ritual enactment of our religious beliefs.

The transformation of clay into ceramic objects was a relatively recent innovation in human history; stone, bone, and wooden implements predate ceramics by hundreds of thousands of years. This does not mean that the beneficial properties of clay have not been recognized for nearly as long. Early humans undoubtedly recognized and exploited the ability of certain sticky sediments to be molded into shapes that could be used for a variety of purposes. The transformation of clays by fire into more durable objects must also have occurred innumerable times in the past before people began deliberately controlling and exploiting such products.

The earliest ceramic objects were fired clay figurines. These are found in large numbers in the site of Dolni Vestonice in Czechoslovakia from as early as 26,000 years ago (Vandiver *et al.* 1989). As a common class of tools though, the appearance of fired clay implements seems to coincide with the increasingly sedentary existence of societies exploiting stable and secure food sources in the early Holocene, after 10,000 years ago. These include dense maritime or wild-plant resources or agricultural crops. We, as yet, have no clear understanding of why ceramics became important when they did in human history. The process of sedentarization may have played a role, in that ceramics are difficult to transport without breaking, and would therefore have been of lesser value among mobile hunter–gatherers than among more sedentary societies. In addition, certain food-stuffs, particularly seeds and grains, may be most effectively processed and consumed when cooked with water, and ceramics are very effective for such food preparation techniques.

Ceramic use and manufacture emerged independently in many parts of the world (Figure 1.1), and undoubtedly the idea of ceramics and the knowledge of techniques for producing them spread rapidly among societies in which these vessels proved useful. Because of their ubiquity and their excellent preservation in archaeological contexts, ceramics are among the most common materials that archaeologists recover in research on ancient cultures of the past 10,000 years.

Ceramics have been tremendously important in archaeological research for well over a century. Archaeologists and antiquarians quickly recognized that variations in ceramic forms and decoration were restricted in space and in time. Spatial variations could, therefore, be used to distinguish between different prehistoric regions, and temporal variations could help in the important process of defining chronological sequences within those regions. As new theoretical perspectives, research interests, and increasingly sophisticated analytic techniques have been developed in archaeology, the range of ceramic research has also expanded to pursue a much broader range of research questions. The development of the fields of ethnoarchaeology and ceramic ethnography has also contributed to new ways of looking at ceramic technology and at ceramic production and use in their social context.

This work does not seek to explain the reasons for ceramics. Rather, we will examine a variety of ways in which archaeologists can and have studied ceramics in order to learn about the past. I will focus on a number of topics in ceramic research: ceramic raw materials and production, ceramic classification, and on the sorts of questions that anthropological archaeologists can ask about the past through the study of ceramics. These include questions on chronology, production and distribution systems, ceramic use, and questions on social and political organization and relations of the past. In each chapter, I will discuss basic theoretical or methodological issues and then illustrate various successful approaches to ceramic analysis through one or more case studies.

Chapter 2 will begin this discussion through a consideration of what ceramics are and how they are made. We will examine the nature of the raw materials necessary for ceramic production, clays, inclusions, water, and fuel. Next, we will focus on how ceramics are made and pursue the process from the acquisition and preparation of raw materials, through a variety of

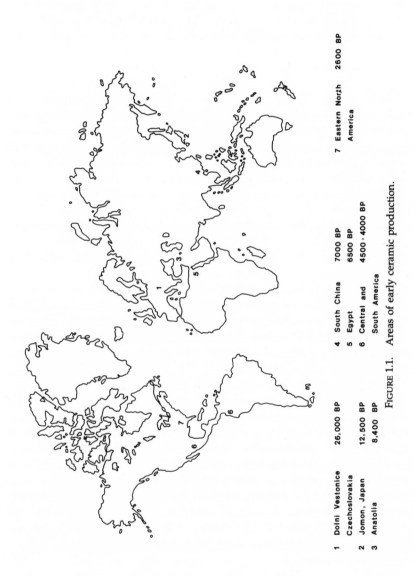

1	Dolni Vestonice	26,000 BP		4	South China	7000 BP		7	Eastern North	2600 BP
	Czechoslovakia			5	Egypt	6500 BP			America	
2	Jomon, Japan	12,500 BP		6	Central and	4500 - 4000 BP				
3	Anatolia	8,400 BP			South America					

FIGURE 1.1. Areas of early ceramic production.

hand-building and wheel-making techniques, on to ornamentation and surface treatment, and finally look at the range of techniques involved in ceramic firing. Following a general introduction to these issues, I will present a more detailed discussion of traditional ceramic production in southern India, in order to more precisely define the process of ceramic production in a specific context. This background on ceramic production and materials, derived largely from ethnographic contexts, is crucial to being able to place materials from archaeological sites in their proper context.

In Chapter 3, the focus will switch to a more explicit concern with archaeological ceramics, with a focus on ceramic classification. The classification of material culture, or placing objects into more or less discrete categories on the basis of similarities and differences, is a key aspect of human behavior and is essential to all archaeological analysis. In daily life, our classifications of contemporary material culture draw on a large body of mostly unquestioned cultural knowledge on how things should look and what they mean. We do not have to consciously reason to recognize, for example, that paper plates and gold-plated bone china are different in more than raw material. They are different in their context of use (e.g., picnics vs. formal dinners), and they are different in their value, both in terms of the prestige or status they embody and their economic cost. Which of the differences between these types of serving vessels we choose to emphasize will vary considerably in different contexts and for different people. We need not all use the exact same categories or assign the exact same meaning to them. But the importance of goods and their classification into categories is a crucial aspect of human behavior in creating and understanding the world we live in.

The classification of archaeological materials is equally critical for understanding the past. In prehistoric contexts we do not have direct access to how ancient peoples interpreted or classified their material world. Classifications of archaeological materials typically rely on a variety of factors, including raw materials, spatial and temporal distributions, and patterns of formal similarities and differences in size, shape, decoration, and so on. There have been numerous debates on the nature of archaeological classifications or typologies; whether they can or should replicate ancient classifications, whether they are real and objective or a creation of the researcher, and how best they should be carried out. In Chapter 3, we will examine three approaches that have been commonly used to classify archaeological ceramics.

The first approach to ceramic classification I term *intuitive typology*. This approach is based on the recognition and division of materials on the basis of perceived patterns of similarities and differences. Intuitive typologies typically involve a process of sorting ceramic sherds or vessels into groups, so that members of each group more closely resemble each other than they do members of other groups. The second approach to classification that I consider is the *type–variety method*. This method involves a more explicit and hierarchically defined sorting of vessels into broad groups, or types, and finer groups, or varieties, usually on the basis of raw materials, or clays and tempers, and decorative treatment.

The third method of classification that is discussed in Chapter 3 is a *quantitative*, or statistical, approach to ceramic classification. This approach is based on explicitly defining and measuring a number of attributes or traits of ceramics and using a variety of statistical techniques to examine their distributions and divide the vessels into objectively verifiable categories. As will be discussed in Chapter 3, the nature of the attributes selected and the categories defined may vary considerably in response to the goals of the classification and research project. I will examine a range of attributes that are frequently used in quantitative classification and discuss how they may be measured. The appendix presents an introduction to some basic statistical techniques useful in ceramic classification and analysis.

In Chapters 4 through 7, focus will shift away from what ceramics are and how we can classify them to a concern with how archaeologists can use ceramics to answer a range of questions about the past. Chapter 4 focuses on the importance of ethnographic information and analogical arguments in studying past societies. The field of ceramic ethnoarchaeology (or ceramic ethnography) will be introduced. Ceramic ethnoarchaeologists focus on several aspects of ceramic production and use in contemporary societies. Traditional production techniques, patterns of learning and transmission of the ceramic craft, the social and economic status of potters, systems of ceramic distribution, and ceramic use have all been studied. In addition, questions of specific concern to archaeologists, on ceramic use life, breakage patterns, and discard practices among contemporary pottery users have also been studied. The rich body of knowledge that has been developed through these studies provides an important framework for considering the production, use, and archaeological deposition of ceramics in prehistoric contexts. Chapter 4 concludes with a discussion of the use of ceramics in constructing chronologies, with a focus on the technique of seriation. A case study from the Moundville region of West–Central Alabama is presented to illustrate a sophisticated approach to ceramic seriation.

Two aspects of ceramic analysis will be considered in Chapter 5. The first concerns the study of how ceramics are used, and the second, the nature of ceramic production and distribution systems. Ceramics are tools, goods used for particular purposes. The most common uses of ceramics involve the storage, preparation, and serving of foodstuffs, though ceramics serve many other purposes as well. The identification of ceramic use and the distribution of functional classes across sites and regions can provide a tremendous amount of information on the nature and distribution of past activities. Two case studies focusing on the uses of ceramics are presented: The first is work by Barbara Mills in New Mexico, and the second examines ceramic use and spatial organization in an urban context in medieval South India.

The remainder of Chapter 5 focuses on the organization of ceramic production and distribution systems. Techniques of ceramic production are discussed in Chapter 2. In Chapter 5, I examine the organization of ceramic production, including questions of the scale of production and the nature of ceramic-producing workshops. Distribution systems ranging from production for personal use to large-scale exchange networks are described. Four case studies dealing with ceramic production and distribution systems are presented. Van der Leeuw's study of the manufacture of beakers during the Dutch Neolithic considers the nature and continuity of regional traditions of ceramic production. The second case study deals with the scale and organization of production in three Indus Valley sites of Pakistan during the late third millennium B.C.. The third study documents long distance trade and ceramic movement during the Roman Empire, and the final study looks at ceramic production and distribution in northern Mesopotamia during the sixth millennium B.C.

Chapter 6 focuses on how ceramics may be used to examine social relations and social systems of the past. I begin the chapter with a general overview of various approaches to ceramic analysis and social organization that have been taken over the past three decades. General models of the social meanings of goods are considered, along with more specific views on how the nature of ceramic use, largely in food systems, plays a role in the significance of ceramics in expressing, reflecting, and actively defining social relations. Four case studies that present somewhat different approaches to the study of ceramics and social organization are presented. These include work by Pollock on Susiana ceramics from fifth-millennium-B.C. southwestern Iran; work by Braun on decorated ceramics from Middle and Late Woodland periods in the eastern United States; a study by Hodder of changes in decorative treatment of Neolithic Beakers from The Netherlands, and an ethnographic study by Miller of ceramic use and hierarchical social relations in Central India.

Chapter 7 focuses on how ceramics have been used to study ancient political systems, in particular, the relation between centralized administration in early states and empires and systems of ceramic production and distribution. Direct control of some aspects of the economy is an important strategy of many early states. I consider the reasons for this and how control of ceramic production or distribution may be manifested in the archaeological record. Three case studies that have focused on this topic are presented. The first is a study by Feinman and colleagues of ceramic production and distribution in the Valley of Oaxaca, Mexico, from *ca.* 1500 B.C. to 1500 A.D.. The second study, by Johnson, examines ceramic production in southwestern Iran during the period of initial state formation. The final study by Costin and colleagues looks at ceramic production, distribution, and use in the Mantaro Valley of Peru before and after the conquest of the region by the Inka empire.

The various approaches to ceramic analysis presented in this book are not meant to be a catalogue of all possible approaches to the study of archaeological ceramics nor to represent the only ways that ceramics can be studied. Rather, I hope to accomplish two things with this book. First, I hope to provide a general overview of what ceramics are and why they are important in archaeological analysis. Second, I hope to provide frameworks for some of the anthropological and historical questions we can ask of the past through ceramic analysis. Many more approaches to ceramic classification and interpretation exist than could be presented in this brief volume; additional references on various topics are presented at the end of each chapter.

Ceramics, of course, are only one sort of remains that archaeologists recover from archaeological sites. Because ceramics endure whereas other remains frequently do not preserve well in archaeological contexts and because ceramics are abundant in many archaeological sites, they are extremely important for archaeological analysis and interpretation. As with all classes of material culture, the technology, economy, and social importance of ceramic production and use allows us to do much more than simply document their presence or absence in a site or region.

We can best use ceramics to ask questions of the past when we work with carefully collected and well-provenienced samples of materials from sites and regions and when we consider them in their broader archaeological and cultural context. We must also recognize that although ceramics are abundant and important, they are not necessarily always relevant or well suited to answering all of the questions we are interested in asking. We must carefully consider both our research questions and the nature of our database before commencing any archaeological analysis.

The approaches and case studies presented in this book represent some of the current approaches being taken to ceramic analysis. As both analytical techniques and theoretical interests of archaeology continue to expand, so shall the nature of the questions that archaeologists ask of the past. In Chapter 8, I will consider some of the directions that ceramic analysis may take in the future.

2

Defining Ceramics

Ceramics, produced by the transformation of clay through heat into hard and durable products, can take many forms and be characterized in many ways. A geologist might view ceramics in terms of the mineralogical and chemical constituents of their basic raw materials—clays and inclusions. Chemists view ceramics in terms of the chemical composition of their raw materials, the nature of the ionic bonds between chemical elements, and the chemical transformations that result from the application of heat, whereas potters may define ceramics on the basis of their form and the techniques involved in their manufacture. Archaeologists studying particular aspects of prehistoric ceramics use each of these and other characterizations of ceramics: to examine raw materials and their sources, manufacturing techniques, firing processes, and the uses of ceramics in specific prehistoric contexts. In this chapter, I will examine some of the relevant definitions and characteristics of ceramics and their constituent materials, and the techniques involved in ceramic manufacture.

RAW MATERIALS

Ceramics are composed of three basic raw materials: (1) clay, a sticky fine-grained sediment that becomes plastic or moldable when wet; (2) non-plastic inclusions, mineral or organic materials found naturally in clays or deliberately added to them that help make clays more easily workable and also help to limit shrinkage; and (3) water, added to the clays and inclusions to make them plastic and lost during vessel drying and firing. Other raw materials are also involved in ceramic production: pigments or coloring agents used in vessel decoration and the fuels used in firing the vessels.

Clays are the basis of all ceramics, and like ceramics, may be defined or classified in a number of ways, according to the size of the particles that comprise them, their source or point of origin, their chemical composition, mineralogy, or behavior as a plastic material. In general terms, a clay is a very fine-grained sediment, with particle sizes of less than two-thousandths of a millimeter. These small particles become plastic and sticky when combined with water, permitting the material to be molded into a range of shapes. The molded forms maintain their shape as they dry and when heated to high temperatures are hardened into durable objects.

As sediments, clays are derived from rocks. They are formed by the chemical or physical weathering of their parent raw material, igneous rocks. The mineralogical composition of the parent rock determines the mineralogical content of the clay. The location of clays relative to their parent rock defines whether they are *primary* clays, found close to their parent rock, or *secondary* or *transported* clays, found far from their parent rocks, transported by water or wind. Most naturally occurring clays are not composed solely of clay particles but contain a mixture of clay particles, larger soil particles, rock fragments, and organic materials. These naturally occurring clays are the ones used by early potters (Arnold 1985:21–32). Clay sediments are very common throughout the world, though they vary considerably in their mineral content and quality as pottery-making materials. Variations in production techniques and vessels of ancient and modern potters should be viewed as having been conditioned in part by the quality and nature of the raw materials available to them.

Chemically, most clays are composed of a small number of elements and compounds, mainly silicates, aluminum, and water joined in a crystalline structure. Other elements, including potassium, sodium, calcium, and iron, among others, occur in smaller quantities (Rice 1987:40). These rare or trace elements are particularly important in the identification of clay sources of archaeological ceramics, as will be discussed in Chapter 3.

Types of clays are distinguished by their mineral composition, and the patterns of arrangement of their various mineral constituents and many kinds of clays have been defined. Most are constructed of layered crystalline sheets and include both two- and three-layer clays (see Table 2.1). Two-layer clays include kaolinites, a very common clay mineral that in its purest form is used in the manufacture of porcelain vessels. Three-layered clays include smectites and illites, frequently used by potters as paints or for decorative coatings (known as slips) on vessel surfaces. The strength of the bonds between layers in different clays determines their ability to absorb water, affecting their plasticity. In addition, each of these clays responds somewhat differently to heat, resulting in variations in vessel color, vessel strength, shrinkage, and in the temperatures required during firing.

TABLE 2.1. Common Clay Minerals

	Kaolinite	Smectite	Illites
Type	2 layer	3 layer	3 layer
Particle size	Large	Very small	Small
Plasiticity	Low to good	Very good	Good
Shrinkage	Low	High	—
Fired color	White-variable	Cream, red, light brown	Variable

(After Rice, *Pottery Analysis*, 1987:44). Reprinted by permission of the University of Chicago Press.

To the potter, the most important features of any clay concern its ability to be shaped. Is it plastic or easy to manipulate, while at the same time being firm enough to hold its form once shaped in a particular way? How will it behave as it dries or is heated; will it shrink significantly as water is lost? Will the vessel produced be strong enough to serve its intended use? Will it be an attractive color? Each of these features is affected by a range of factors, including the clay itself, the inclusions in the clay, as well as manufacturing and firing techniques.

Plasticity, the ability of the clay to be molded and maintain its shape, is determined by the interactions of clay particles with water. Plastic clays consist of individual clay particles surrounded by a film of water (Rice 1987:53). The water acts as a lubricant and permits the clay particles to glide over each other and over nonclay inclusions, allowing the clay to be shaped into a variety of different forms. Typically, the most plastic clays are those with the smallest particle sizes. Small particles have a proportionately larger surface area relative to their mass than do larger particles, providing greater areas that can be exposed to and lubricated by water. High quantities of organic materials in a clay also lead to increased plasticity.

A clay must be combined with water in order to make it plastic. A second important characteristic of a clay of concern to potters is how the clay reacts when water is lost, first through evaporation and second through chemical transformations that occur during firing. As water is lost through evaporation, the vessel will decrease in size and lose its plasticity. The higher the water content in the vessel and the smaller the clay particles, the greater the extent of shrinkage and the slower the process of water loss. Shrinkage rates are determined by the mineralogical structure of the clay, in particular, the size and placement of capillaries through which water present in the vessel body's pores can reach the vessel's surface (Rye 1981:21). Irregular rates of shrinkage within a single vessel will result in distortion of the vessel's shape and, if severe, in breakage.

The initial stages of drying a vessel must therefore be carefully controlled to permit a gradual and uniform loss of moisture content from the vessel. This can be achieved by drying vessels in the shade, in a specially constructed drying chamber, or in indirect sun, taking care to turn the vessels periodically so that warming and consequent water loss is even on all sides of a vessel. All pots will shrink as water is lost. They vary considerably, though, in their ability to resist cracking or warping as they dry (Rice 1987:69). The addition of nonplastic materials to a clay can act to limit the extent of shrinkage. Water loss that occurs in firing will be discussed in the later section on vessel firing.

As noted earlier, most naturally occurring clays contain a proportion of nonclay particles, including organic materials, rock fragments, sand, and so on. These particles, whether naturally occurring or added to the clays as *temper*, have an impact on a range of aspects of clay's behavior—its workability, shrinkage, and its responses to firing and conditions of use. Potters frequently add materials to natural clays in order to improve and alter their characteristics. Commonly used tempering materials include sand; organic materials, such as chaff, seeds or seed husks, or ash; lime or shell; mica; and so on. Small fragments of fired ceramic vessels, known as grog, may also be added to clays as temper.

A number of characteristics of fired ceramics are determined by the nature of their raw materials and the interactions between the clay(s) and the nonplastic inclusions or tempering materials that comprise them. These characteristics include appearance, strength, and thermal stress or thermal shock resistance.

Potters select clays and tempering materials on the basis of the appearance of the finished product. Color and texture are two important aspects of a vessel's final appearance that are partly determined by the raw materials used. The color of a fired vessel is determined by a number of factors, including the chemical composition of the clay and the atmosphere in which the vessel is fired (see later discussion). In particular, the amount and distribution of iron minerals and organic materials in clay are important determinants of its color when fired. If neither of these materials is present, clays will fire to a white or cream color.

The color of fired clays that contain both organics and iron minerals varies with the temperatures attained during firing and with the nature of the firing atmosphere, whether oxygen rich (oxidizing) or oxygen poor (reducing). Iron inclusions will lead to red or brown colors if oxidized and black or gray colors when reduced (Rice 1987:333). Organic inclusions, if not fully oxidized, result in dark brown, black, or gray surface or body colors. Often, organic materials found near the interior or exterior surface of a vessel wall will be burnt away during firing, leaving a dark core in the center of the vessel wall (see Figure 2.1; Rye 1981). In many traditional firing contexts, the firing atmosphere is neither constant nor uniform throughout a firing facility, and vessels from a single firing often exhibit considerable variation in color; individual vessels may also exhibit broad variations in body and surface colors.

Ceramic strength, the ability of vessels to resist breakage when subjected to use and associated stresses (Mabry *et al.* 1988:830), is determined by a variety of factors. These include the raw materials used, manufacturing techniques, vessel form, and firing conditions (Rice 1987:357). A number of methods have been developed to measure the strength of fired and unfired ceramics in response to a variety of stresses or mechanical forces that may impinge upon a vessel in one way or another. In ceramics vessels, these stresses can include the pressure on a vessel that results from stacking heavy vessels, such as full storage pots, one on top of each other (known as compression stresses). Other stresses may include sudden stresses that occur when a vessel is dropped or banged (known as impact stresses).

In general, ceramics fired at low temperatures (that is, less than 1000 degrees Celsius) are less strong than ceramics fired at higher temperatures. The porosity of a vessel, referring to the size and number of pores in a fired vessel, is inversely related to ceramic strength: the more and larger the pores, the weaker the vessel, though pores may also help to prevent or

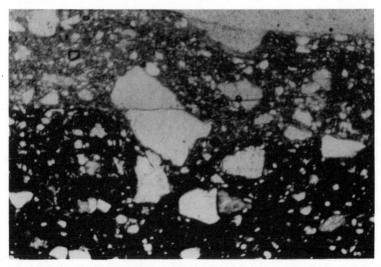

FIGURE 2.1.   Firing core as seen in ceramic petrographic thin section (6× magnification; photo by Alison E. Rautman). Reprinted by permission.

delay vessel breakage by acting to inhibit the spread of incipient cracks. Vessels composed of fine-grained materials with homogeneous composition are less vulnerable to stresses than vessels of coarse-grained heterogeneous pastes, with a mixture of large and small inclusions.

A very important aspect of ceramic strength involves the ability of a vessel to resist cracking or weakening when exposed to rapid heating and cooling. Because, as will be discussed in Chapter 6, an important use of many pots is in food preparation, the reaction of cooking vessels to heat is an extremely important characteristic that potters must consider in their selection of clays and tempering materials. A vessel's ability to withstand repeated heating and cooling is known as its *thermal stress resistance*. When a vessel is heated, it expands. Because ceramics are generally poor conductors of heat (and, as a result, are good insulators), the outside of a vessel will expand faster than the inside, resulting in irregular stresses on the clay body. These stresses can lead to cracks in the vessel body and, over time, to vessel breakage.

Potters can reduce the impact of thermal stress on their products in a number of ways: by selecting raw materials that are resistant to thermal stress; by increasing vessel pore size and number; and by producing cooking vessels in shapes that conduct heat efficiently. The particle size and porosity of a clay affect its ability to resist thermal stress (Rye 1976; Rice 1987:367–368). Clays with small particle size conduct heat at a slower rate than large-particle-size clays. Therefore, when a pot made of clays with small particles is heated, the outside surface of the vessel will warm up and reach high temperatures more rapidly than the vessel interior. These temperature differentials contribute to high thermal stress in vessels made of these clays as compared to vessels of large-particle-size clays, which absorb heat more rapidly and evenly. However, vessels composed of fine-particle clays are much more resistant to cracking than those composed of coarse-particle clays, and therefore the problem of temperature differentials may be mitigated somewhat.

The number and size of pores or voids are also important to thermal stress resistance. Cracks that form in response to thermal stress are stopped from spreading when they reach large pores. Pores can be increased in size and number by adding organic materials such as straw or seeds to clay. These organic tempers burn out during firing, leaving the large pores that are most effective in thermal stress resistance. The presence of other inclusions in clays in more problematic because these may expand at different rates than the clay body, leading to additional stresses on the vessel. Certain minerals that have expansion rates similar or lower than those of the clays are most suited for avoiding thermal stresses (Rye 1976:117; Arnold 1985:24). These include plagioclase and other feldspars, hornblende, and calcite. Quartz, a common natural and deliberate inclusion in many ceramic vessels, has a very high rate of thermal expansion and is therefore poorly suited for use in cooking vessels (Rye 1976:118).

Many of the features of raw materials discussed have been identified through chemical analysis and mineralogical studies. Such techniques are not available to the traditional potter. Nonetheless, traditional potters throughout prehistory and to the present have accumulated a tremendous amount of knowledge about available raw materials. Recipes for preparing clays are passed from generation to generation, and potters often combine more than one clay type in particular proportions in order to produce vessels with certain characteristics. A variety of tempering materials are added in different quantities until the clay has the right "feel," and the potter can be sure that his or her materials are appropriate for producing the desired end. The experience of pottery making and use, its failures as well as successes, has played a key role in enabling potters to understand the characteristics and behavior of their raw materials and to make the best use of locally available resources.

FORMING CERAMIC VESSELS

The social organization of ceramic production will be discussed in Chapter 5. In this section, I will focus on the range of techniques involved in forming ceramic vessels. In general, these techniques may be divided on the basis of tools and equipment used in their manufacture into two basic categories: hand-building and wheel-building techniques, each of which is discussed later. Often, more than one technique is used in the construction of a single vessel.

Raw-Material Acquisition

The first step of ceramic manufacture is acquiring the necessary raw materials and preparing the clays. Potters typically obtain their raw materials from sources close to home, usually 1 to 6 kilometers from the manufacturing site (Arnold 1985:51–52). Transportation techniques used in bringing materials from their sources to manufacturing areas may vary considerably and play a role in how far potters are willing to transport their bulky raw materials. Not surprisingly, for example, potters who transport their materials by boat may move them much greater distances than those who carry their materials on their back.

Clays are found abundantly in many areas of the world. Collection of clays involves travel to the sources and the excavation and transport of clay deposits. Tempering materials are often transported much longer distances than clays, though readily available materials such as chaff or small fragments of fired vessels may also be used. Other raw materials that must be acquired include pigments for decorating painted or glazed vessels, fuel for firing the vessels, and the materials needed for the tools used in vessel manufacture. A number of factors affect raw-material acquisition; the spatial distribution of the materials, their cost and accessibility, the quantity of materials needed, the cost of transport, and the culturally perceived value of the goods, all play a role in determining what sources potters will exploit.

Preparing Raw Materials

Few clays are ready to be formed into vessels in their natural state; most must be cleaned and prepared for use. Most naturally occurring clays contain a range of large and small impurities, including stones, pebbles, and organic debris, that must be removed before the clays are suitable for ceramic manufacture. The extent to which a clay must be cleaned varies with the manufacturing technique used in vessel forming. In wheel-built vessels, the presence of large impurities in the clay would tear the potter's hands and the vessel wall while forming, whereas for many hand-built vessels much coarser clays are perfectly suitable.

Impurities may be removed from clays by picking them out by hand or by drying the damp clays and then pounding them and passing them through a coarse screen. Alternatively, the clays may be combined with water to form a suspension, with the coarse particles eventually sinking to the bottom and the fine-grained clay particles remaining on top. An elaboration of this technique is known as *levigation*, which involves passing a suspension through a series of traps or channels. This technique is most common in fairly large-scale ceramic production industries.

Nonplastic inclusions, or tempers, often added to clays in order to improve their workability and to achieve desired effects in fired vessels, must also be acquired by potters and prepared for use. Nonplastic inclusions can include organic materials, such as ash, seed husks, or ground straw, as well as inorganic materials, such as sand and crushed rock or lime, grog, and so on. These materials must be ground to appropriate size and then mixed in suitable proportions with the clay.

The proportion of tempering materials added to clays varies with the nature of the clay, especially the ratio of nonplastics that occur naturally in the clay and the desired end product. The proportion of nonplastics in a prepared clay typically ranges from 20 to 50% of the total volume (Rye 1981:39). In addition to adding tempering materials to a clay, potters may combine more than one type of clay in order to produce a paste suited to particular vessel types or uses.

Once the raw materials are combined, the clay(s) or clay–temper mixture must be made plastic by adding water and carefully blending the mixture. This blending serves to make the paste homogeneous as well as to eliminate air pockets within the material. Potters may prepare their clay by kneading it with their hands or feet, or by wedging it, slicing through the clay with a cord or wire and repeatedly recombining the sliced sections (Rice 1987:119). Once the clay is well mixed, with desired plasticity and moisture content, the potter is ready to begin forming vessels, using either hand-building or wheel-building techniques.

Hand-Building Techniques

Among the simplest of the hand-building techniques used in ceramic manufacture is known as *pinching*. Pinched pots are made by holding a ball of clay in one hand and shaping it with the other hand by making a hole in the center and then thinning the vessel walls by drawing the clay out from the base with thumb and forefingers (see Figure 2.2). Pinching is well suited to forming small vessels or for forming the bases of larger vessels that can be added on to with other techniques.

Slab building is the technique of forming vessels of two or more flat slabs of clay that are pressed together into the desired vessel shape (see Figure 2.3). The slabs can be joined together by hand or with a wooden paddle or other tool. This technique is well suited for forming irregularly shaped (i.e., nonround) vessels or for building very large vessels.

Among the most common of the hand-building techniques is *coiling*. The potter shapes the prepared clay into long narrow coils, by rolling it against a hard surface or squeezing it between her/his fingers. The coils can be used to form a base or can be added on to a base formed by another technique. The walls of the vessel are gradually built up by successively adding on more coils (see Figure 2.4). The potter may moisten or score the tops of the coils to help them adhere to each other more strongly. The joints between coils can be left visible or smoothed over with fingers or with the help of a wooden tool or a smooth stone. It is very important for the coils to be securely joined together, as these joints are the weakest areas on coiled vessels and are vulnerable to breakage during drying, firing, or use.

Another common hand-building technique involves the use of *molds*. In preparing mold-made vessels, prepared slabs of clay are pressed into or over a prepared mold. The mold may be constructed of plaster, stone, fired clay, or may be simply the base of a broken vessel. Mold-made vessels may be made in a single piece or may be composed of two or more molded sections joined together. The joining of molded sections to form a single vessel is sometimes identifiable archaeologically by a seam visible on the vessel interior. Molds are either convex, with the clay applied over the exterior, or

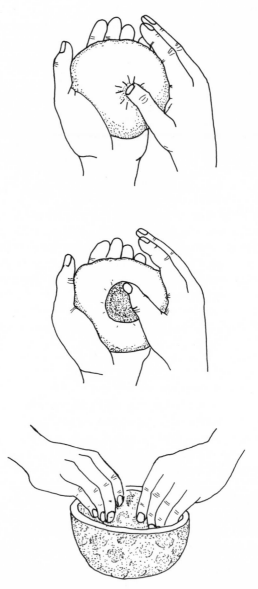

FIGURE 2.2.   Hand-building techniques: pinching (after Rye 1981:70). Reprinted by permission of Taraxacum.

FIGURE 2.3.   Hand-building techniques: slab technique, joining slab base to coiled rim
(photo by William J. Parry). Reprinted by permission.

concave, with the clay pressed into the mold interior. In order to prevent the
clay from sticking to the mold, the mold may be coated with fine sand, ash,
or powdered clay. Given the ease of forming mold-made vessels, mold
building is an effective technique for rapidly producing large numbers of
nearly identical vessels.

Molds are well suited to making constrained vessel forms, such as
canteens or bottles, where it is difficult for the potter to reach inside a
narrow opening to smooth coils or use other techniques. In many cases,
only certain portions of vessels may be constructed with molds. For example, molded bases may be added on to by coiling or slab-building techniques to form large vessels. Decorative patterns can also be carved into
plaster or stone molds, resulting in a raised design on the finished vessels.

FIGURE 2.4.   Hand-building techniques: coiling (photo by William J. Parry). Reprinted by
permission.

In forming and finishing hand-built vessels, potters may employ a
number of tools. Along with molds, stones, wooden spatulas, or damp
cloths may be used to smooth the surface of the vessel and conceal junc-
tures between slabs or coils or to impress decorations into the surface of a
pot. Pots may be placed on turntables so that the potter can slowly spin
them about to work on all sides of the vessel. In general, though, the
construction of hand-built vessels, as the name implies, involve a minimum
number of tools. With a small investment in tools and facilities, potters can
easily produce hand-built vessels for household use or for exchange.

Wheel-Building Techniques

The potter's wheel is an innovation with considerable impact on the organization of pottery production. The wheel, a rotating platform that allows the potter to exploit the principles of centrifugal force, permits the rapid production of large numbers of vessels. As such, the potter's wheel is typically associated with large-scale workshop-level production (see Chapter 5). Clays used in wheel throwing must be softer and wetter than clays used in hand building, in order to be easily drawn up by the potter's hands and in order to keep from drying out too rapidly on the rapidly rotating wheel (Rice 1987:128–129).

A variety of types of wheels are used by potters worldwide; some consist of two platforms, an upper one on which vessels are formed, and a lower one that is spun by the potter's feet; others consist of a single platform, turned by hand or with a pole by the potter or by an assistant (see Figure 2.5). Contemporary potters often use electric wheels that can maintain a continuous and constant rate of rotation. In most wheel-forming techniques, wheels typically rotate at speeds between 50 and 150 rotations per minute (Rye 1981:74).

Wheel-made or wheel-thrown vessels are formed in a number of steps. A ball of clay is placed on the throwing platform, and pressure is exerted on it with both hands in order to center it, so that the ball revolves concentrically with the wheel (Rye 1981:74). The clay must be kept moist throughout the throwing process, and potters moisten their hands frequently in order to keep the clay moving freely through their hands. The centered ball of clay must next be *opened up*; a hole is made by forcing the

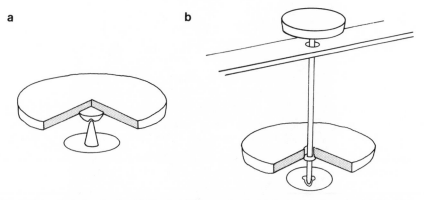

FIGURE 2.5. Potter's wheels. (a) Single platform wheel; (b) dual platform wheel (after Rye 1981:74). Reprinted by permission of Taraxacum.

thumbs into the center of the rotating ball of clay. Next, the walls of the vessel can be *lifted*, by placing one hand inside the vessel and the other on the outside, and exerting even pressure in an upward direction, to slowly thin and raise the walls of the vessel. The vessel may be *shaped* at the same time, by applying pressure on the vessel interior or exterior to push certain areas of the vessel wall out or in from the central axis (see Figure 2.6).

As the vessel is pulled up, the top may become uneven; it can be leveled by cutting off the top of the rotating vessel with a sharp tool, such as a needle or wire. The rim of a thrown vessel may be formed by simply smoothing the upper surface or by folding it over on itself to form a thick rim that can then be shaped into the desired form. When this initial stage of vessel forming is completed, the vessel must be removed from the wheel.

FIGURE 2.6.   Wheel-building techniques: shaping vessel and throwing from the hump.

This can be accomplished by passing a wire between the base of the vessel and the wheel platform, and removing the vessel, taking great care to not distort the vessel shape. Often potters will attach a small ceramic or wooden platform to the top of the wheel, on which the vessel is thrown. In this way, the entire platform can be removed, and the potter can avoid touching and potentially deforming the wet pot.

An alternative approach to wheel throwing is known as *throwing from the hump*. In this technique, a large mass of clay, sufficient for several vessels, is placed on the wheel, and vessels are formed and removed from the upper portion of this large hump. Vessels cut from a wheel while it is still in motion have a characteristic spiral pattern on their bases. Throwing from the hump allows several vessels to be formed from a single block of prepared clay and is an efficient technique for producing many similar vessels.

Finishing Ceramic Vessels

The forming techniques discussed give the vessel its basic shape. The potter may stop the forming process at this stage or may use a variety of other techniques to finish shaping the vessel and to decorate its surface. Finishing techniques that alter the shape of the vessel include paddle and anvil or beating techniques, scraping, trimming, shaving, and turning (Rye 1981:84–89).

The *paddle and anvil method* involves the use of a wooden paddle and a stone or ceramic anvil. The anvil is held inside of the vessel, and, directly opposite the anvil the exterior of the vessel is beaten with a paddle (see Figure 2.7). Paddle and anvil work thins and compacts the walls of the vessel while increasing vessel diameter (Rye 1981:84). The initial forming stages of vessels finished with the paddle and anvil technique may have involved a range of techniques, including coil or slab-building as well as wheel-building techniques (see later example).

Paddle and anvil techniques are usually performed when the vessel has dried somewhat, to what is known as a *leather-hard* state. In this leather-hard state, a vessel is still malleable, but it has lost much of its plasticity and will therefore be able to maintain a thinner shape. The paddle and anvil method is very well-suited to producing round-based vessels, often used as cooking vessels, in part because they lack the sharp carinations that are often fracture points on vessels subject to thermal stresses.

In many building techniques, it is necessary to leave the base and lower walls of a vessel quite thick, in order to support the upper portions of the vessel while the clay is still wet and highly plastic and thus prevent the vessel from sagging. Once the vessel has dried somewhat, these portions

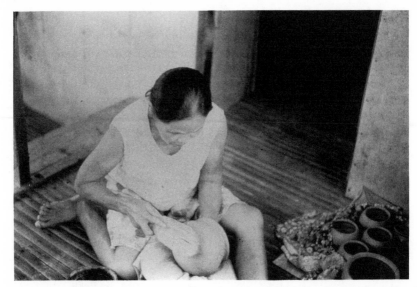

FIGURE 2.7. Finishing techniques: paddle and anvil method (photo by William J. Parry). Reprinted by permission.

can be removed and the vessel walls thinned by employing a variety of techniques. *Scraping* involves removing excess clay with a tool held perpendicular to the vessel surface. In the *trimming* technique, excess clay is cut away with a tool, such as a knife, held at an acute angle to the vessel wall. A tool similar to a wood plane may be used to *shave* excess material from a vessel exterior and to form angular facets on the vessel surface (Rye 1981:87). Vessel thinning may also take place while a vessel is rotating on the wheel. In this method, known as *turning*, the vessel is inverted on the a rapidly rotating potter's wheel. A cutting tool is held at an acute angle against the rotating vessel, symmetrically trimming away excess wall thickness. Each of the trimming techniques discussed leaves distinctive traces on the vessel wall that if not smoothed over by other techniques can be recognized by archaeologists working with sherds or whole vessels (see Figure 2.8).

The finishing techniques that I have discussed thus far serve to shape the vessel into its final form. The techniques presented later are primarily decorative, affecting the surface appearance and ornamentation of the vessel. Decorative techniques may involve applying color to a vessel, either to the entire vessel as a slip or a glaze, or to portions of it. Other decorative techniques involve altering the body of the vessel itself through a variety of

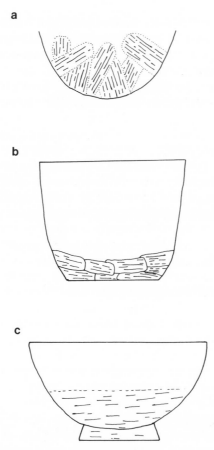

FIGURE 2.8.   Traces of thinning techniques: (a) scraping, (b) trimming, (c) turning (after Rye 1981:86–88). Reprinted by permission of Taraxacum.

plastic techniques. As with the techniques already discussed, most decorative techniques are performed when the vessel is partly dried, or leather hard.

Techniques that do not involve the application of color and that can affect the entire surface of the pot include *smoothing, burnishing,* or *polishing* (Rye 1981:89–90). In each of these techniques, a hard tool, often a stone or a broken and smoothed potsherd, is rubbed against the surface of the pot. This serves to conceal irregularities on the vessel's surface and to alter the vessel's appearance. Smoothed surfaces have a uniform texture and a matte, nonglossy appearance. Burnished surfaces are more lustrous than smoothed vessels, but the luster is irregular, and it is possible to identify lines left by the passage of the polishing tool over the vessel. Polished vessels have a uniform and highly glossy surface, and no traces of the tool used remain (see Figure 2.9).

A range of plastic techniques are used in pottery decoration (see Figure 2.10). Patterns may be *incised* into vessels with a pointed tool; a comb may be run along the surface of the vessel to produce *combed* designs, portions of a vessel may be cut away, either *perforating* the wall of the vessel or *carving* out portions of the clay, without penetrating the vessel wall. *Impressed designs* are formed when a tool is pressed into the soft clay of the vessel wall. Tools used in impressed designs may include unmodified objects such as sticks or pebbles or may be decorative stamps, with patterned designs. Textiles or basketry may also be pressed into the vessel surface to form a continuous patterned design over the vessel surface. Molded clay may be added on to vessel to form *appliqué* decorations.

Techniques for the application of color to a vessel include slipping, glazing, and painting. A *slip* is a liquid mixture of clay that is applied to a vessel as a thin coating before the vessel is fired. Slips are often a different color than the vessel body and are usually easily identifiable. Slipped vessels may be subject to further finishing techniques; they may be smoothed, burnished, or polished, and plastic or painted decorations may

FIGURE 2.9.   Decorative techniques: surface treatments. (a) Smoothed, (b) burnished.

Figure 2.10.   Decorative techniques: plastic designs—(a) impressed, (b) punctate, (c) carved and impressed, (d) incised (collections of Museum of Anthropology, University of Michigan). Reprinted by permission.

be added. Like slips, *glazes* may also be applied over an entire vessel. Glazes are composed of silica, fluxes (materials such as ash that lower the melting point of the glaze), and metallic oxides that provide color. Glazes become vitrified, or glasslike, when fired at high temperatures (see Figure 2.11). The production of glazed vessels typically involves multiple firings. The first firing before the application of glaze produces vessels known as biscuit or bisque ware. Following this initial firing, the glaze solution is applied, and a second firing takes place.

Painted designs are formed by applying a pigment to a vessel's surface (see Figure 2.12). Both inorganic and organic pigments are used in traditional pottery making. Carbon is the most common organic pigment used by traditional potters, whereas inorganic pigments include iron and manganese oxides (Rice 1987:148). These colorants are typically mixed with clay and water to form a liquid paint that can then be applied with a twig, brush, finger, or other tool. Paints may be applied to vessels before or after firing. Glaze paints may also be used in ceramic decoration; these are applied before firing, so that vitrification can occur.

Firing Ceramic Vessels

The final stage of the ceramic-forming process is the firing of the formed and dried vessels. Firing, the application of heat to vessels, results

FIGURE 2.11.   Decorative techniques: glazed vessels (collections of Museum of Anthropology, University of Michigan). Reprinted by permission.

in chemical transformations of the clay body, producing a hard and durable product that has lost the plasticity essential for its original forming. Firing may take place in a number of contexts: in the open air, in small pits or bonfires, or in permanent facilities, such as ovens or kilns. The appearance and structure of a vessel at the end of the firing process is determined by three main factors: the maximum temperature attained, the duration of firing, and the firing atmosphere (Rice 1987:81).

In general, fired ceramics are distinguished on the basis of temperatures attained during firing (see Table 2.2). Vessels fired at low temperatures are more porous and coarse than those fired at higher temperatures. Terracottas are vessels fired at low temperatures, below 900 degrees Celsius. Earthenwares refer to ceramics fired at somewhat higher temperatures, ranging from 900 to 1200 degrees Celsius. Next are stonewares with harder and partially vitrified bodies, fired at temperatures ranging from 1200 to 1350 degrees Celsius. Porcelains, white, fully vitrified ceramics, are fired to very high temperatures of more than 1300 degrees Celsius. Along with differences in firing temperatures, these different ceramic wares are also distinguished by the raw materials used in their production. For example, porcelain vessels are made of relatively pure kaolin clays, whereas earthenware clays are primary clays with high iron content that fire to red or brown colors (Rice 1987:5–6).

FIGURE 2.12.   Decorative techniques: painted designs (collections of Museum of Anthropology, University of Michigan). Reprinted by permission.

The chemical transformations that clays undergo during firing are dependent on temperature and mineralogy. Clay minerals and water, as well as nonclay inclusions, are affected in different ways by heat. For example, water held on the surface of clay particles will be converted to a steam, a gas, at temperatures of 200 to 300 degrees Celsius. Water that is chemically bound to the clay particles is lost at somewhat higher temperatures. A number of other materials found in many clays or added to them as tempers are also lost as gases at temperatures of 500 to 600 degrees Celsius. These include carbon, salts, carbonates, sulfides, and sulfides. As gases are lost, vessel shrinkage begun in the drying process continues, and vessels can lose as much as 15 percent or more of their original mass during firing.

TABLE 2.2.   Fired Ceramics

Type	Firing temperature (degrees Celsius)
Terracottas	Below 900 degrees
Earthenwares	900–1200 degrees
Stonewares	1200–1350 degrees
Porcelains	Above 1300 degrees

If vessels are heated too rapidly and if they were not sufficiently dried before firing, the rapid emission of steam and other gases can prove catastrophic, resulting in vessel fracturing or explosion.

At temperatures of 500 degrees Celsius and above, clay minerals undergo major irreversible structural alterations. If temperatures of higher than 900 degrees Celsius are achieved, the clay minerals lose their structure completely and form new silicate minerals. At these high temperatures, vitrification can occur as the silicates and oxides melt or fuse to form a glassy material (Rye 1981:104). The inclusions and impurities in the clays also undergo transformations during firing. For example, quartz undergoes major structural changes at temperatures of 573 degrees, 867 degrees, and 1,250 degrees Celsius. Each constituent of ceramic vessels undergoes specific changes at specific temperatures. By examining the mineralogical structure of a fired vessel, archaeologists can estimate the firing conditions, including temperature, duration, and atmosphere.

The duration of firing refers both to the total time span between the initial heating and final cooling of vessels and to the length of time that vessels are at their maximum firing temperature. As noted earlier, heating vessels gradually will aid in limiting explosions due to overly rapid loss of water and other volatiles in the clay body. The rate of cooling also has an impact on the final vessel form. Too rapid cooling may be as dangerous as too rapid heating in leading to vessel cracking and breakage. Depending on the firing technology, cooling may take from minutes or hours to as long as a week (Rye 1981:110). Firing durations can range from as short as 15 minutes in open-air firings to as long as several days.

Differences in firing atmospheres are defined on the basis of the presence or absence of air circulation, and especially, the presence of oxygen in the firing chamber. When oxygen is present, an *oxidizing* atmosphere exists; if little oxygen is present, a *reducing* atmosphere exists. The firing atmosphere affects vessel color, hardness, porosity, and shrinkage (Rice 1987:81).

Firing atmosphere can be controlled by potters in a number of ways. Firing facilities may be sealed so that little oxygen enters the chamber, or they may be open, allowing free flow of oxygen. In addition, firing atmospheres may change throughout the course of a firing with difference in heating and cooling atmospheres controlled in order to affect vessel color. Where abundant oxygen is available, carbon present in the vessel body and fuels is fully consumed, and the vessel will be light in color. Black or dark-brown vessels are typically produced in a reducing atmosphere. In these oxygen-poor atmospheres, the carbon in the vessel body is not lost, and carbon from fuels may be deposited on the vessel surface, producing a pot that is dark in color. Vessel color may differ from the core to the surface depending on the firing and cooling conditions and the degree to which organic materials were fully oxidized. In addition, surface color may vary in a single pot, if some areas of the firing facility were exposed to greater oxygen than others.

Firing Contexts

As noted earlier, ceramics may be fired in a variety of contexts, from impermanent open-air firing to firing in permanent facilities. Open-air firing may take place in hearths or in pits. *Hearth firing* is the simplest of the open-air techniques. Fuels, such as wood, brush, grass, or dung, are placed under and around the vessels that are placed in a pile. Often, only a few vessels are fired at any one time, though in some cases, considerable numbers of vessels may be fired at once (see Figure 2.13). The firing atmosphere is difficult to control in this type of firing once the fuel has been lit. Potters may add more fuel to the fire as it burns (Rye 1981:98). In *pit firing*, pots and fuels are set into a depression that may be partly covered with stones or earth in order to produce a reducing atmosphere and black pots. Heat can be retained somewhat longer in pits than in hearth firing, and pit firing is therefore more efficient and requires less fuel.

An *oven* is a more permanent firing facility that functions similarly to a firing pit. Ovens are circular or rectangular enclosures, made of stone or

FIGURE 2.13.   Open-air firing: hearth firing with dung fuel (photo by F. E. Smiley). Reprinted by permission.

clay. These enclosures typically do not have permanent roofs but are sealed anew each time vessels are fired. As in the firing techniques discussed above, fuels and vessels are placed together in an oven. Larger numbers of pots may be fired with ovens than with the other open-air techniques. These more permanent constructions are typically reused many times.

The most sophisticated kind of firing facility is the *kiln*. Kilns are characterized by separate chambers for fuel and vessels, with flues for heat transport connecting the two (see Figure 2.14). Kiln temperature and atmosphere are much easier to control than in the open-air facilities discussed, and much higher firing temperatures can be attained. The simplest kilns are known as updraft kilns. These are two-level kilns, with the chamber holding vessels located directly above the firing chamber. The heat from the firing chamber rises through holes to reach the chamber containing the vessels. A permanent or temporary roof may seal the

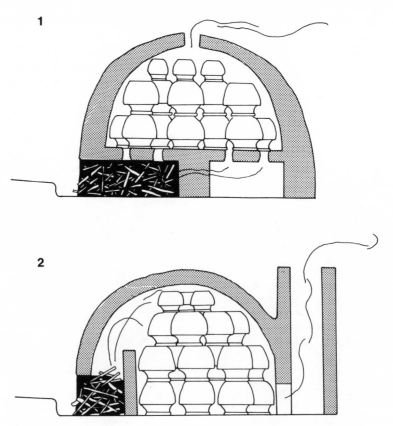

FIGURE 2.14.   Kilns. (1) Updraft, (2) downdraft (after Hodges 1964:36–37).

chamber. Air holes in the kiln walls or roof may be sealed or opened to alter the firing atmosphere. A second kiln type is the downdraft kiln. These kilns can attain higher temperatures than updraft kilns. In downdraft kilns, the firing chamber and vessel chamber are located adjacent to each other, sometimes on a slope, and the heat from the firing chamber passes over a wall or barrier and into the vessel chamber from above (Rye 1981:100).

The firing technology used by potters affects the type of fuel that can be used in a firing. The opposite also holds; the fuels available affect the type of firing technology that can be used. Fuel availability is a common problem faced by potters, particularly in areas where deforestation is occurring and little wood is available. In open-air firing, a great variety of fuels may be used: dung, grass, straw, and other waste materials, as well as wood and charcoal. In kiln firing, where high firing temperatures are desired, wood is the most suitable fuel, as the other materials combust too rapidly to produce the consistently high temperatures needed. The availability of fuels is often a major constraint on ceramic production, especially in areas where deforestation is occurring. Modern potters also use gas to heat their kilns.

In all firing techniques, some vessels break during firing due to too rapid heating or cooling or imperfections in the vessel body. Vessels may also blister and warp, forming distorted sherds or *wasters* that are easily recognizable in the archaeological record and are often found in the vicinity of firing areas (see Figure 2.15; Stark 1985). Broken or overfired sherds may be used to cover or separate vessels during firing to produce a reducing atmosphere or to facilitate air flow between vessels.

After the vessels have cooled and been removed from the firing facility, they may be subject to some further treatment of their surface. Ashes and other materials that may cling to them are brushed off, and the vessels are cleaned. In addition, some fired vessels may be painted or coated with graphite for decoration. Once-fired vessels may be coated with glaze and subjected to a second or even a third firing. Water vessels may be coated with tar or bitumen to make them watertight. Once finished, ceramic vessels may be used by their producers or distributed more widely, through barter or in marketplaces. I will consider the organization of ceramic distribution in some detail in Chapter 5.

POTTERY MANUFACTURE IN RURAL SOUTH INDIA: A CASE STUDY

Throughout many regions of the world, traditional potters continue to make ceramics in much the same way that their ancestors have for many hundreds of years. In this section, I will examine a traditional pottery-

FIGURE 2.15.   Ceramic wasters from Tepe Farukhabad, Iran (collections of Museum of Anthropology, University of Michigan). Reprinted by permission.

making workshop operating in a large village of southern India. The pottery-making process from raw-material acquisition to the sale of finished pots in the village market will be described in some detail in order to provide a better understanding of the range of materials, activities, and skills involved in pottery manufacture.

Pottery making in India is a specialized activity, carried out by individuals who are born into hereditary pottery-making groups. In the village of Kamalapuram, located in the state of Karnataka in southern India, a single family of related potters are still practicing their traditional craft (see Figure 2.16). This extended family, of four men, four women, and their children, work together in the range of tasks involved in the production and distribution of earthenware ceramics.

Approximately once a week the potters travel to clay sources where they collect clay with simple picks and shovels. Clay is gathered from locations near water sources, at distances of 3 to 5 kilometers from the workshop. The clay is loaded into sacks and transported to the workshop using donkeys or carts pulled by oxen. Fine-grained sand, used as temper, is dug from nearby pits. Ash collected from the debris of earlier pottery firings is also added to the clay. Graphite, used to coat the fired vessels to give them a metallike sheen, is purchased in a town some 15 kilometers from the village. Fuel for pottery firing is the most expensive material that

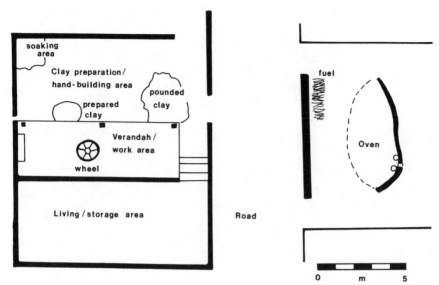

FIGURE 2.16.   Plan of the potter's workshop in Kamalapuram, India.

the potters must acquire. A variety of fuels are used by the Kamalapuram potters, including dung, coconut husks, plant stalks from harvested agricultural fields, and wood. The last two of these fuels must be purchased, and the family spends a considerable amount of time collecting animal dung and other waste products to minimize fuel costs.

Once the raw materials are brought to the workshop, they must be prepared for use. The moist clay is placed in the sun and allowed to fully dry. Once dried, the clay is pounded into a fine powder, using a wooden paddle or large stone (see Figure 2.17). The clay is usually prepared by the women of the workshop or by men who do not work on the potter's wheel. The powdered clay is then passed through a fine screen to remove any large impurities, and it is mixed with water and allowed to soak overnight. The next day, the clay mixture is kneaded with the feet and hands. The potters then place the prepared clay under damp sacks and store it within their house until needed.

The Kamalapuram potters employ a number of techniques in forming vessels, including the hand-building techniques of pinching and slab building as well as wheel-building and paddle and anvil techniques. They produce a variety of earthenware vessel forms, including round-bottomed cooking and storage jars, water jars, lamps, lids, and small cooking stoves, or braziers. Most of the vessels are made using a combination of wheel-

FIGURE 2.17.   Clay preparation: pounding (note piles of prepared clay and potter's wheel in background).

throwing and paddle and anvil work. In this region of India, the potter's wheel takes the form of a large spoked wheel with a central platform on which the vessels are formed. A stone socket is embedded in the base of the wheel that spins on a stone pivot set on the workshop floor. The wheel is spun using a large bamboo pole, wielded by the man forming the vessels (and in India, only men work at the potter's wheel) or by an assistant. In the Kamalapuram workshop, the potter's wheel is stored against the back wall of the roofed veranda of the home/workshop and is only set up for use as needed. When not in use for pottery manufacture, the work area is used by the family for dining, sleeping, tending children, and other activities of family life.

In Kamalapuram, as elsewhere in India, pottery production begins with a prayer, as the potter bows before the clay and his potter's wheel. The prepared clay is once again kneaded, and sand and ash are added until the desired consistency for working is reached. The clay is then formed into a long cylinder, which is placed on the already spinning wheel. The potters practice the technique of throwing off the hump, and this large cylinder of clay produces between five and twelve vessels. The potter works in a crouched position, standing above the wheel and using the weight of his body to center the clay (see Figure 2.18).

FIGURE 2.18.   Forming vessels on the wheel (note partially formed vessels in foreground).

Once the clay is centered, the potter can begin to form the first vessel. This is accomplished by shaping the upper portion of the clay into a cylinder and then using the thumbs to open up a hole in the middle of the cylinder. The potter uses his palms and fingers to elongate the open cylinder and shape the upper portion of the vessel. Once the vessel is roughly shaped, he forms the vessel's rim with his fingers, smoothing it with a damp cloth. The process of forming a vessel on the wheel takes approximately three minutes.

The pots are cut from the wheel using a wire spoke and left to dry. At this point, the rim and shoulder of the vessel are fully formed. The lower part of the vessel has been left unformed; it is an open cylinder with walls approximately 2 to 4 cm thick. This mass of clay provides the material for the next stage of production, the paddle and anvil process, in which the base of the vessel is formed and the vessel takes its final shape (see Figure 2.19). Triangular or rectangular wooden paddles and several sizes of stone anvils (ranging from 5 to 15 cm in diameter) are used in the paddle and anvil work. The anvil is held against the inside of the vessel and used to push out and thin the wall of the pot, against the pressure applied by the beating of the paddle.

Paddling takes place in two stages, separated by a period of drying. In the first stage, the base of the vessel is closed and the pot is roughly formed.

FIGURE 2.19. Shaping vessels with the paddle and anvil method.

In the second stage of paddling, the pot takes its final form; the walls are thinned, and the base is symmetrically rounded. Paddling, excluding time for drying, takes between 25 and 30 minutes, roughly ten times the time needed for throwing the upper portion of the vessel. After the vessels are fully formed, they are placed in the storeroom and allowed to dry for 10 to 15 days before firing. Other vessels produced in the workshop are entirely hand-made. These include small, shallow saucers used as lamps, larger saucers used as lids, and large ceramic ovens and storage jars. The lamps are made using pinching techniques, whereas the others are formed with the slab technique.

Once a large number of pots have been produced and have sufficiently dried, a firing can take place. The Kamalapuram potters typically fire between 200 and 350 vessels at a time. Firing is carried out across the road from the workshop in a simple oven facility. The oven consists of a shallow pit, enclosed on one side by a permanent semicircular stone wall. Layers of fuel are placed along the floor of the oven, and the vessels, which have been warmed in the sun for several hours, are carefully stacked above them.

Wasters, or misfired and broken pots from earlier firings, are used to separate and support the pots as they are stacked in the oven. Large vessels are placed on top of each other, with small pots used to fill in gaps between the larger vessels (see Figure 2.20). Once all the pots have been stacked, circular vents made of the lids of broken vessels are placed along one side and on top of the pile of vessels.

When all the vessels are arranged, the top of the oven is covered with several layers of broken potsherds. These are used to hold the vessels in place and keep them from shifting as the fuel is consumed during the firing process. The sherds are then covered with more fuel, taking care to leave the vents exposed, and finally the entire oven is covered with a thick coating of ashy soil. The fuel in the base of the oven is lit through a stoke hole in the stone wall and gradually ignites. During the firing, more fuel may be added through this hole (see Figure 2.21). Firing lasts for approximately 3 hours, after which all of the vents are closed using ceramic lids. Once the vents are sealed, the flow of oxygen into the oven is limited, and the vessels cool in a reducing atmosphere, resulting in a dark brown or black surface color. When the potters wish to make red vessels, they leave the vents open and may remove some of the earth covering the oven in order to create an oxidizing cooling atmosphere.

Once heating is completed, the pots are left to begin cooling in the

FIGURE 2.20.   Loading the firing facility (photo by T. Richard Blurton).

Figure 2.21. Adding fuel during firing (note mounded earth over oven; photo T. Richard Blurton).

oven for the night. Early the next morning, the kiln is opened, and the still-warm pots are removed (see Figure 2.22). The precariously stacked vessels often break during this stage, and much care must be taken in their removal. Failures or broken vessels range from about 15 to 20 pots per firing in the dry season. In the wet season, when vessels may not be fully dried before firing, failure rates may be as much as 50 percent of each oven load.

Finished pots are distributed to consumers in a number of ways. Some are purchased by professional merchants who take them by truck to sell in nearby towns. Others are sold at the weekly market in Kamalapuram. Some pots are produced on commission for individual customers. Commissioned pots include pots used in wedding and funerary rituals and other special events. And pots are sometimes sold directly from the workshop to customers who come in need of a particular kind of vessel.

Pottery vessels remain widely used throughout rural India for cooking and food and water storage within the house. Pots are also carried to local wells and fountains where drinking water is obtained. Ceramic vessels are, however, rapidly being replaced by inexpensive metal and plastic alternatives. In 1986, the potter in Kamalapuram reported that he was producing roughly half the number of vessels per year than he had 20 years earlier. The use of ceramics in ritual context and their preferred use with certain

Figure 2.22.   Fired vessels.

foodstuffs (for example, local people say that yogurt made in earthenware pots is much tastier than yogurt produced in metal or plastic vessels) assures that the pottery-making industry will persist in India, though probably in a much diminished form as time goes on.

Defining Ceramics: Discussion

The definition and characterization of ceramics can be carried out at many levels. In this chapter, we have examined some of the ways of defining ceramics and their constituent raw materials. Traditional potters, both prehistoric and contemporary, did not have access to the sophisticated chemical and mineralogical knowledge available to us. Yet they had a tremendous wealth of knowledge based on many years, or often, generations of experience; knowledge on what materials worked well under what conditions, on how to form and fire vessels that were effective in heating food or cooling water or in any of the other myriad uses to which vessels were put. As archaeologists, there is much we cannot know about the individuals who produced the vessels we recover. Yet the vessels themselves provide eloquent testimony to the skills, knowledge, and aesthetics of the peoples who made and used these vessels. In the remainder of this book, we will examine ways in which archaeologists can study and understand the ceramics that we recover in our field research, and, in so doing, we will consider how we can study and understand the cultures in which the ceramics were produced and used.

SUGGESTED READINGS

For detailed discussions of ceramic raw materials, characteristics, and manufacturing techniques, see Rice (1987), Rye (1981), Shepard (1961). For discussions of clays, Grim (1968).

Descriptions of traditional pottery manufacture can be found in the following sources: Arnold (1975, 1976, 1978, 1985, 1989), David and Hennig (1972), Rye and Evans (1976), Saraswati and N. Behura (1966), Kolb (1988), Roux (1989), van der Leeuw (1976, 1977); DeBoer (1974, 1984, 1985), Franken (1971); Haaland (1978), Longacre (1985), and others (see bibliography and Kramer, 1985, for additional references). Expanded discussions of the Kamalapuram pottery workshop can be found in Junker (1985) and in Sinopoli and Blurton (1986).

3

Studying Archaeological Ceramics

The first step in any study of archaeological materials is, necessarily, ordering the material into some sort of classificatory system. A pile of undifferentiated sherds can tell us nothing about their producers other than that they made pottery. Classifications may vary considerably, both in how they are generated and in their level of specificity. Bowls versus Jars or Plain versus Decorated are simple binary typologies that provide one way of ordering a body of material. Classing a bowl as a Plain Bowl with Out-turning Rim and Shell Temper provides a more detailed and inclusive definition of a group of vessels.

Approaches to ceramic typology are, and should be, varied. An archaeologist studying the evolution of ceramic technology is interested in very different aspects of vessels than an archaeologist interested in ceramic decoration. The former will focus on evidence for construction techniques and the identification of raw materials, whereas the latter will consider color, the placement and shape of designs, and so on. The variables or characteristics of a vessel that we choose to focus on depend to a large amount on what we ultimately wish to learn from the vessels (Hill and Evans 1972). However, to be effective, a typology should reflect actual modes or patterns in the data, and in so doing will reflect, to a greater or lesser extent, conscious decisions of the artifacts' producers.

Neither the archaeologist interested in ceramic technology, nor the one interested in decoration is in any sense providing a "complete" character-ization of the vessels he or she studies. By focusing on specific interests, both are ignoring vessel size, shape, rim form, and other characteristics that we typically use to distinguish one vessel from another. If a typology is to be useful to archaeologists other than the original researcher, that researcher must provide some information on these aspects to his or her colleagues.

Just how much information and how it should be presented and used in constructing a typology is an open question and one that is subject to intense debate in the archaeological literature. There are potentially an infinite number of characteristics or variables that can be recorded for each vessel, and in that sense a "complete" characterization is impossible. Deciding how much information to provide depends in part on accepted practices and on the nature and scale of previous research in a particular region, whether the same body of material has already been studied from other perspectives, and on the accessibility of the material for future studies.

There is and can be no formula governing the definition and identification of traits relevant to constructing a typology of a particular set of data. If, for example, all pots in a particular inventory are black, color will not be useful or relevant in distinguishing groups of vessels within that inventory (though color may be useful in contrast to other sites or periods). But, if 20% of the sherds are black, 30% are brown, and 50% are red, the variable color will record some meaningful variation between vessels. And, if the vessels grade from light gray through dark gray to black, with no discrete cutoff points, the archaeologist must attempt to identify why such a continuum exists and whether distinctions between light gray and black represent random or patterned variation in the inventory (e.g., are certain vessel forms always one shade or another, or do all forms vary continuously). Traits that exhibit patterns of measurable variation or that can occur in different states are known as *variables*.

While the definition of relevant variables requires serious consideration, so does the issue of how best to measure them. For the pots that are black, red, or brown, it may be adequate to record those *qualitative* or *nominal attributes* of the variable color (i.e., black, red, brown) to classify them. For the sherds that vary along a continuum, we may be interested in defining their color more accurately by placing it on a scale of "grayness" and then looking at the distribution of points along that scale. Such a scale might be a relative or *ordinal* ranking of sherds as, for example, into the categories pale gray, light gray, medium gray, dark gray, or black. Or the scale may be numeric of *quantitative*, employing techniques to more precisely quantify the color of each sherd.

Another example of qualitative versus quantitative measurement scales is the classing of vessels into small-, medium-, or large-sized classes versus measuring size by means of rim-diameter measures, vessel volumes, or other appropriate quantitative measures. Again, if there are neat and consistent size classes, for example, if all small bowls range from 4 to 6 cm in rim diameter, all medium bowls from 10 to 13 cm, and all large bowls from 20 to 24 cm, with no bowls in between, then qualitative measures adequately and efficiently characterize bowl size. If, however, rim diameter varies along a continuum from 4 to 24 cm, then quantitative measures will permit us to identify the overall distribution of the variable rim diameter and to look for size classes within that distribution (see Figure 3.1).

Along with deciding what variables to use and how to measure them, an additional problem exists in that many of the *dimensions* that we wish to consider, such as size or shape, are not directly measurable by just one variable. Total vessel volume may be the most accurate way of assessing size, but rarely do we recover enough whole vessels to be able to calculate volumes. Vessel shape is even more complicated, as the shape of a vessel depends on a variety of factors, such as the curvature of the vessel at various points, orientation of the neck, height at maximum diameter, and so on. Again, how one will approach such problems will depend in large part on the nature of the assemblage and the specificity of the classification one wishes to construct. This latter question itself depends on why one is

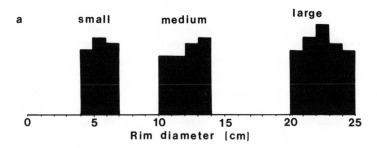

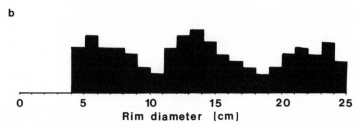

FIGURE 3.1. Histograms of vessel rim diameters: (a) discrete size classes, (b) continuous distribution.

constructing the typology, that is, the research questions one is asking in the first place.

Two important requirements of archaeological typologies are: (1) they should be replicable, and (2) they should be verifiable. An explicit statement of the defining criteria of the typology is critical to the fulfillment of both of these requirements. By replicability, I mean that other scholars working with the same or similar bodies of materials should be able to produce the same classification using the same criteria. In this way, archaeologists working on contemporary materials from sites within a broad region can utilize published or unpublished analyses to consider intersite variation and to situate their own material in a broader regional context.

By verifiability, I mean that however the typology is derived, it should be possible to support it statistically. That is, whether the typology is derived through intuitive sorting or sophisticated computer-assisted analytical techniques, it should be possible to express the defining variables and to support and justify their use through analyses using statistical techniques. Some basic statistical techniques will be considered in the appendix.

Throughout this discussion, I have deliberately skirted some of the issues that have been the subject of intense and often heated debate in the archaeological literature on typology over recent years: whether types are monothetic (defined by a small number of attributes that are both necessary and sufficient for the definition), or polythetic (defined by a large set of attributes, such that no individual attribute is either necessary or sufficient for the type definition); and whether qualitative (Spaulding 1982) or quantitative variables should be used in constructing typologies. Rather, I have tried to stress that there is and can be no absolute formula for constructing typologies (see Whallon and Brown [1982] for recent discussions of these and other issues concerning typology).

Each dataset is different and imposes certain constraints on what techniques are appropriate and what variables will be significant in distinguishing between types. In addition, the specific goals and interests of the researcher and the nature of the available sample will necessarily condition both the approaches taken and variable selection. In the subsequent sections of this chapter, we will consider some of the varying approaches used by archaeologists for constructing typologies.

OBTAINING CERAMIC SAMPLES FOR ANALYSIS

Before turning to the question of ceramic typologies in more detail, it is important to consider the nature of the ceramic collections or samples that we use to construct our typologies. As archaeologists, we are almost always working with limited collections of a site, a region, or a class of materials, such as ceramics. A concern with the nature and representativeness of our data is therefore extremely important in all stages of archaeological research and analysis.

Archaeologists use a variety of methods to recover materials for analysis, including excavation, collection of materials from the surface of the ground, and the study of existing museum collections. The ways in which data are collected in each of these contexts has a clear impact on the content and representativeness of the ceramic assemblages that we study and base our interpretations on. It is therefore important to consider some of the general approaches to archaeological sampling that play a role in determining the structure and limitations of our ceramic data sets. In this section, I will outline some of the most common approaches to sampling in archaeology that are relevant to the study of ceramics.

As archaeologists, we always excavate or analyze only a portion or sample of a population (where a population is defined as the total set of possible sites or materials of the time period under study). In most cases, we study that sample not only to develop a description of the sample itself but also to make inferences about the population from which our sample is derived. Archaeologists may at times choose to treat a collection from a site or region as a complete population for analytical and interpretive purposes. Whichever approach is taken, the size and nature of our collections are extremely important in insuring the accuracy of our interpretations of the population under study, be it a site, a regional phase, or a ceramic industry.

A number of approaches may be taken in selecting a sample for excavation or analysis. In general, sampling techniques may be divided into random or judgment techniques. In all techniques, the total set of sampling units, be they potential excavation or surface collection units at a site, or all sherds in a collection, must be identified before a sample of them can be selected. A researcher must also decide how many units, or what *sampling fraction*, of the total set of possible units will be selected.

The sampling fraction is usually a compromise, mediated by a desire to select as many units as possible so as to achieve an accurate representation of the archaeological population, while at the same time meeting the logistical goals imposed by constraints of available time, labor, and facilities for fieldwork and analysis. Given the painstaking detail of most contemporary fieldwork, archaeologists typically sample only a very small fraction of most sites or regions, often 10% or less. Probability statistics can help us evaluate the sampling fraction needed to allow accurate estimates of a population's parameters (Hole 1980).

Once sample units are defined and sampling fraction determined, sample units can be selected, using random or judgment techniques. In *random sampling,* the selection of any one unit is independent of the selection of all other units, such that each unit has an equal probability of being selected. The units are numbered, 1 to *n*, and selection is accomplished by use of a random numbers table, by picking numbers from a hat, or other random method, until the desired number of units is selected. This method, called *simple random sampling,* incorporates no prior knowledge about the sampling universe into its designs. That is, all units have an equal probability of being selected, with no units or sorts of units favored over any other.

In many instances, we may wish to incorporate our knowledge of the region, site, or cultural period, into sample selection. A *stratified random sample* permits the incorporation of prior knowledge into the sampling design, while maintaining the desirable unbiased features of a random sample. In stratified sampling, the total set of sampling units is divided into distinct strata defined on the basis of particular and explicitly defined characteristics, and samples from each stratum are selected independently. At the site or regional level, characteristics considered in defining strata may include environmental or topographic factors, as well as information on site structure (e.g., inside town walls vs. outside town walls), and so on.

Judgment samples are samples defined and collected without incorporating randomness into sampling design. Rather, the researcher uses his or her own knowledge and experience to define and select the sampling units to excavate, collect, or analyze. Judgment samples have some advantages over random samples, in that they enable the researcher to focus exclusively on particular areas or aspects of a site that are of interest. Conversely, they also can allow a researcher to attain even coverage of a site or region by laying out evenly spaced units over a grid. In addition, judgment samples are often simpler to lay out and execute than random samples. Judgment samples have some disadvantages, however. Many statistical tests that archaeologists use to analyze data require the assumption that the samples used were randomly selected from a population. Judgment samples clearly violate this basic assumption.

An additional limitation of judgment sampling is that in selecting judgment samples a researcher is imposing a structure on the data that can be recovered. This structure may prevent the researcher from discovering patterns that contradict his or her research goals. As an example, let us consider an archaeologist who is interested in ceramic decoration, and in particular, in the importance of decorated ceramics in food-serving activities in a particular period and region. That is, the researcher argues that decorated vessels are most important in activities associated with food serving. The researcher then defines criteria for identifying food-serving vessels (i.e., size, shape, volume, etc.) and selects a judgment sample defined as all of the decorated vessels from a particular site. He or she then classes all of the vessels into two classes, food serving and nonfood serving, and demonstrates that 75% of them belong to the food-serving class. Therefore, the researcher claims, the hypothesis of decoration being differentially linked to food-serving vessels is correct.

In selecting for analysis the total sample of decorated ceramics from a population that includes both decorated and undecorated vessels, however, the archaeologist failed to evaluate the structure of the population from which the sample was selected. We can imagine, for example, a population in which serving vessels accounted for 75% of the ceramics, and nonserving (i.e., cooking, storage, etc.) vessels for 25% of the ceramics. If this were the case, then the frequency of decorated serving vessels is directly proportional to the total frequency of serving vessels, decorated plus undecorated, in the population, and therefore there appears to be no evidence for differential importance of decorated serving vessels. By selecting a judgment sample that included only decorated ceramics, the researcher was thus unable to evaluate other factors that contributed to the high frequencies of decorated serving vessels.

Despite the potential risks of judgment samples, they have advantages as well. They are often much easier to execute than random samples. In addition, in cases where researchers have very explicit and limited research goals, judgment samples can be most effective in attaining these goals. Effective sampling designs are often hierarchical and incorporate both judgment and random sampling techniques, depending on their suitability for particular research goals.

APPROACHES TO TYPOLOGY

Once ceramic samples have been obtained, through whatever set of techniques applied, the first step of ceramic analysis is classification. In this section, I will examine three important approaches to ceramic classification or typology: intuitive or traditional typologies; the type–variety system; and quantitative or statistical typologies.

Intuitive Typology

The most prevalent and in many cases the most successful approach to ceramic typology used in archaeology is *intuitive typology*. By intuitive typology, I refer to the common practice of laying out sherds on a table and sorting them into piles of more or less similar sherds. Although definite criteria are used in this sorting, they are seldom made explicit during the sorting process. The sorting criteria are sometimes defined in retrospect as the analyst tries to characterize each pile. Intuitive typology is very successful because it depends upon complex processes of human perception: our ability to see and detect patterns even though we cannot always explicitly define what factors contribute to the patterns we perceive. For example, despite the difficulty in defining the variables that determine a vessel's shape, we can readily perceive differences in shape between a group of vessels. Intuitive typologies are most successful when the researcher has a lot of experience working with ceramics in general and with a specific industry in particular.

In a study of Owasco pottery from Central and East New York State (A.D. 1000–1300), Robert Whallon (1972) attempted to examine the unstated rules that underlay the long-standing and reliable traditional typologies developed by Ritchie and MacNeish (Ritchie 1944:29–100; Ritchie and MacNeish 1949). Whallon found that there were indeed specific rules underlying this classification, but that they were very different than the rules stated *post facto* by the analysts themselves.

For Ritchie and MacNeish, a type, following Krieger (Ritchie 1944), was defined as a "cohesive combination of features," implying the co-occurrence of a series of associated variable states. Whallon's analysis showed, however, that there was a hierarchy of importance among the attributes used. In this typology, not all traits were equal; some were considered before others in sorting the vessels into groups. Whallon also observed that the criteria for type definition shifted from one type to another, depending on where one was in the hierarchy (see Figure 3.2; Whallon 1972:15). The classification system was thus a "tree classification" with attributes considered sequentially, rather than simultaneously. At each level in the classification process, a single variable, with two opposing attribute states, was necessary and sufficient to define the type. Whallon next developed a computer program to generate classifications on similar principles as those used in the traditional typologies and proposed that this "monothetic subdivisive method" was a useful quantitative approach to ceramic typology (Whallon 1971).

The details of Whallon's program do not concern us here. What is important to note is that the success of this and presumably other traditional typologies rests in their dependence on some very specific principles and rules. With effort, these rules can be identified and applied to other sets of data. Such typologies do have their limitations, however, not the least of which is that they are very rarely made explicit or evaluated and are therefore difficult to impossible for other scholars to replicate or verify. They are also bound, to a greater or lesser extent, to the perceptions, experience, and implicit biases of the individual researcher. Ideally, such

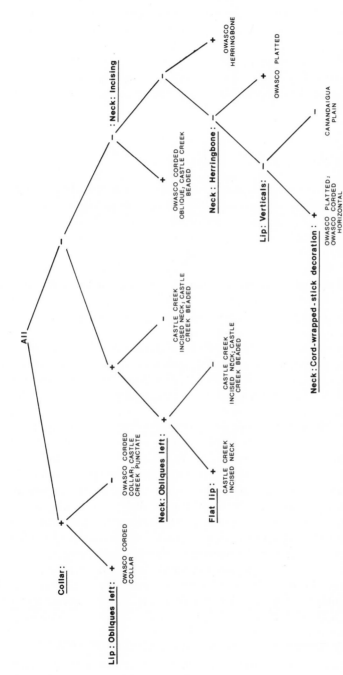

FIGURE 3.2.   Hierarchical structure of the Owasco classification. The distinguishing variables for each level of the classification are underlined;
Ritchie and MacNeish's type names are in lighter print (after Whallon 1972:25).

perceptions will be shared by researchers, so that two individuals approaching the same set of materials would produce similar classifications. This is not necessarily the case, however, as individual experience and interests could lead to rather different hierarchies of importance. In addition, traditional typologies are "general-purpose" typologies. They are particularly suited to examining certain questions, such as chronological change, but are less suited to questions concerning technology, style, the organization of production, and so on.

The Type–Variety Method of Typology

The type–variety method of ceramic classification was first proposed by Gifford, Wheat, and Wasley in 1958 as a response to the rapid proliferation of ceramic types in the southwestern United States occurring at that time. As the intensity of archaeological research increased in that area, so did the tendency for each archaeologist to classify and name the materials from his or her particular site, without regard to broader regional classifications. This problem is not exclusive to any area of the world, and the type–variety system is one solution to developing a uniform nomenclature. Wheat, Gifford, and Wasley were not particularly concerned with issues that would later become important, concerning what a type is or how it should be defined. Types, for them, should look different, should be restricted to limited time periods, and should be spatially bounded (Wheat, Gifford, and Wasley 1958:34). The type–variety system was an attempt to link a multiplicity of localized designations into a single coherent framework.

In the type–variety framework, the "type" refers to a broad class of ceramics defined on the basis of a small number of diagnostic traits. Varieties differ from the broader type to which they are related in one or more minor details. A variety must occur within the spatial and temporal range of the type, although it may be more bounded in either space and/or time. The variety cannot differ significantly in surface finish, decorative treatment, or paste from the type. A type together with its varieties is called a "type cluster" and represents a regional manifestation of similar ceramics. Type clusters can themselves be grouped into "ceramic systems" that reflect broader, though weaker, similarities. The similarities of ceramics within the type cluster and ceramic system are conceived as the product of shared ideas or normative concepts concerning ceramic form, decoration, and production techniques and also result from high intensity of interaction between potters (J. Gifford 1960).

From its initial statement in 1958, the type–variety system has become very influential in New World archaeology, particularly in the southeastern United States and in the Maya region of lowland Mesoamerica. This framework has, however, had relatively little impact in the Old World. The important contribution of the type–variety system lies not in its impact on the concept of typology but rather in its emphasis on creating a regional framework for ceramic description. Within this framework, ceramics from a variety of sites can be compared, and spatial and/or temporal changes can be considered.

Within the type–variety system, types are generally designated with a binary terminology (Phillips 1970). The first term refers to its region of occurrence, either a broad area or the site where the type was first identified. The second term refers to some characteristic of surface treatment or decoration, for example, polished, incised, stamped, red slipped, and so on. The variety designation typically consists of a single term that refers to a specific defining characteristic of the variety. This can be a site or regional name, a decorative attribute, or a technological trait (e.g., shell temper). Vessel shape, production techniques, and details of vessel morphology are not considered in type–variety identifications.

An example of the type–variety approach is the classification developed for late prehistoric ceramics from the Moundville site of West-Central Alabama (Chapter 4 and Steponaitis 1983). Three variables are used to define the type categories: tempering material, surface treatment, and decorative motifs (see Figure 3.3). At the broadest level, the Moundville ceramics are distinguished on the basis of tempering materials, into shell or grog-tempered ceramics. The shell-tempered ceramics are further subdivided on the basis of surface treatment into burnished and unburnished ceramics. The nature of ceramic decoration is the third variable used to distinguish ceramic types. Ceramic varieties within these types are defined on the basis of minor variations in inclusions or in decoration.

Like the intuitive types discussed, a major strength of the type–variety system lies in its temporal and spatial specificity. The consistency of criteria used in defining types and varieties within a region, and the detailed descriptions of those criteria in publications makes this system easier to replicate and verify than typical intuitive typologies where sorting criteria are seldom explicitly defined. Ceramics types and varieties are most useful in the construction of regional and local sequences and in identifying interconnections between sites, that is, defining regional "culture areas." Other classificatory schema must be used to consider questions of vessel use, fine-scaled technological or stylistic variation, and so on.

Quantitative Typology

By *quantitative typology*, I refer to typologies that are constructed and evaluated using statistical techniques in the analysis of two or more variables. Both the techniques used and the types and number of variables

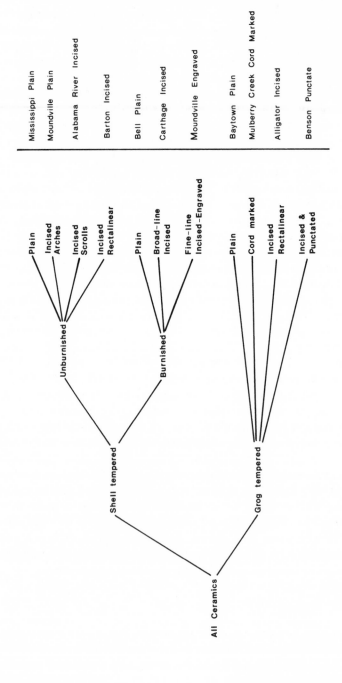

FIGURE 3.3. Type–variety classification of Moundville ceramics (after Steponaitis 1983:51).

employed in constructing the typology will vary as the goals and levels of specificity desired vary and with different ceramic inventories. As discussed earlier, the most important step in quantitative typology is variable selection. Variables chosen may be measured on nominal or ordinal (qualitative) scales or may be measured on numerical (quantitative) scales.

Variables selected should be whole or partial measures of the dimensions in which the investigator is interested. Partial measures of vessel size, for example, may include the variables *rim diameter, maximum diameter, vessel height, height to maximum diameter*, and so on. To the extent that these variables are measures of the same dimension, they will be closely *correlated*, such that as rim diameter increases, so does vessel height, and so on. These correlations will not be absolute, however, because variables are typically partial measures of more than one dimension, including, in this example, vessel shape.

The selection of qualitative or quantitative measurement scales should be linked to the degree of variation in the data. For example, when size modes are discrete and not overlapping, it may be sufficient to sort vessels into qualitative categories such as small, medium, and large. Even in such a case, it is still useful to measure a representative sample of vessels to make sure that one's perceptions of discrete vessel classes coincide with actual patterns. Variable selection, definition, and measurement will be discussed in more detail later. In any construction of a classification, and particularly when using statistical techniques, it is extremely important to have a sample of ceramics that is sufficiently large and is representative of the greater population that one is classifying.

As discussed earlier, it is, of course, usually impossible for any archaeologist to examine the total set of extant ceramics from any period or site, much less to consider the total set of ceramics that existed in the past. But if a sample has been carefully selected, using either judgment samples or random sampling methods, then it should be representative of the general range of variation found at a site or in a region. In large sites, excavations often focus on only a small portion of the site, not necessarily representative of the overall site. In such cases, as well as in collections from special-purpose sites, such as cemeteries or campsites, ceramics recovered cannot be assumed to be representative of the inventory as a whole.

This does not mean that we cannot use these ceramics to study the past, just that we must be aware of the potential limitations in our sample in terms of its representativeness of the ceramic industry overall. For example, if one excavates in elite residential areas of an urban site and recovers high frequencies of elaborately decorated ceramics, one cannot assume that these occur in all areas of the site in similarly high frequencies. The differential access to goods such as decorated ceramics by various segments of a population can itself become a very important question in considering the social or political organization of the culture under study.

Just how large a sample is sufficient for typology construction is difficult to say. In principle, the more sherds or whole vessels the better, though when one is working with samples of thousands or tens of thousands, analysis is very time consuming, and calculations become impossible without the use of a computer. Certain classes of vessels will be rare in any ceramic industry, and it will be difficult to accumulate any substantial sample of them. Adequate sample sizes also depend upon the nature of the artifacts under study—if clear discrete boundaries between "types" are present in the data, these may be detected with relatively small samples. If, however, the types are "fuzzy," without discrete boundaries, larger samples might be necessary before patterns can be distinguished.

VARIABLE SELECTION AND DEFINITION

Although an infinite number of potential variables can be recorded on ceramics, some are more important and useful than others in ceramic classification. In this section, I wish to consider how we select and measure particular variables for study and the relation of individual variables to dimensions of ceramic variability, including technological dimensions, size, shape, and decoration.

The category *technological variables* includes variables related to raw materials, production and firing techniques, and the mechanical functioning of ceramic vessels. Raw materials may be identified through a variety of techniques, including macroscopic or microscopic examination as well as chemical identification. As discussed in Chapter 2, the raw materials used in ceramic production include clays, tempers or nonplastic inclusions, and paints or pigments. Identifications of clays used in ceramics can be accomplished in a variety of ways (see Table 3.1). Clay crystals or particles are too small to be seen with the naked eye; they can be identified using a variety

TABLE 3.1. Some Techniques for Identifying Ceramic Raw Materials

Technique	Identification
Electron microscopy	Structure of clay minerals
X-ray diffraction	Crystalline structure of clay minerals
Neutron activation analysis	Trace elements
Atomic absorption spectroscopy	Trace elements
Petrographic analysis	Nonplastic inclusions, pores

of techniques that include, among others, the scanning electron microscope and x-ray diffraction techniques (Grim 1968:126–164; Rye 1981:30).

The electron microscope makes it possible to view the structure of clay particles. A ceramic sample is first bombarded with a stream of electrons. The electrons bounce off of the specimen, and the pattern of their response is recorded photographically or on a fluorescent screen. This pattern records the structure of the clay particles, allowing the identification of specific clays and slips (Rice 1987:402–403). X-ray diffraction techniques make possible the identification of the crystalline structure of clay minerals. X-ray diffraction proceeds by bombarding a ceramic specimen with x-rays. Each clay mineral has a different crystalline structure, and each diffracts or reflects the rays in a different manner. The pattern of diffracted rays is recorded by a detector, which allows recognition of the minerals present (Rice 1987:383–386). X-ray diffraction works best when only focusing on a small number of minerals, as looking at too many can create a very confused diffraction pattern that is difficult to identify.

Although most clays are mineralogically similar, the rare minerals or trace minerals, which occur in minute proportions in clays, can be very important to identifying clay sources and differences between raw materials. Trace minerals may also be identified using a number of different techniques. These include neutron activation analysis, atomic absorption spectroscopy, or x-ray fluorescence (Rye 1981:47).

Neutron activation analysis is one of the more common methods used in trace-element identification. In neutron activation analysis, finely ground ceramic materials are bombarded with neutrons, a class of subatomic particles. The neutrons interact with the elements in the clay and emit short-lived gamma rays. Each mineral has a particular gamma-ray signature that can be measured, and the major constituents and trace chemicals present in the sherd can be identified. Because, unlike the primary mineralogical constituents of clays, trace minerals are relatively rare and localized, the identification of trace minerals is particularly important in the identification of clay sources of archaeological ceramics. The composition of tempers and pigments can also be identified through neutron activation analysis. The analyst must be wary of the problem of mixing clays, temper, and pigments in individual samples (Bishop 1980; Bishop et al. 1982). Techniques for examining clay composition are costly and time consuming. Their use should follow the use of less expensive macroscopic or microscopic studies, and pilot studies of small samples, when there is reason to believe that significant variation in raw materials might be present.

The nonplastic inclusions and tempers found in ceramics can sometimes be identified by eye or by using a hand lens, but mineralogical identification often requires the use of a petrographic microscope in the analysis of thin sections. Thin sections are slices of pottery cut to a precise thickness of three microns (see Figure 3.4). Polarized light is passed through the thin sections. Different minerals react to and transmit polarized light in different ways. Color and other characteristics can be used to identify the mineralogy of the large inclusions in ceramics. Organic inclusions are often fully oxidized or burnt away during the firing of the vessels and must be identified by the impressions or voids they leave in the vessel wall. Microscopic analysis also allows the identification of the size and shape of inclusions, allowing, for example, the distinction of rounded river sand from more angular sand inclusions. The size and shape of particles can thus provide evidence for what kinds of locations and sources were being selected by ancient potters.

The known responses of clay minerals and nonplastic inclusions to heat are important tools in the study of the temperature at which vessels were fired. Different clay minerals decompose at specific temperatures, and inclusions also decompose, are combusted, or alter their state at certain temperatures. Quartz, for example, undergoes a change in crystalline form at 573 degrees Celsius. The identification of the composition states of the various mineral components of a vessel provides information on the temperatures attained during firing. The study of firing temperatures contributes to the identification of firing techniques—whether vessels were fired in open pits or in enclosed ovens or kilns, where higher temperatures are typically attained. Surface and core color can provide information about the firing atmosphere, whether oxygen rich (oxidizing), in which case carbonaceous minerals will be fully burnt and the vessel will be light in color, or oxygen poor (reducing), which will produce blackened vessels (see Rye 1981:114–118). Core colors will also provide information on cooling after firing (Rye 1981:114–118).

Thermal stress resistance can be measured experimentally, by replicating clay and temper combinations and subjecting them to controlled temperatures (Steponaitis 1983). Vessel strength may also be measured experimentally. Pore size and frequency can be evaluated by counting the number and size of pores per square centimeter in a thin section.

Variables that provide measures of the dimensions of *vessel size* and *vessel shape* are, as has been noted earlier, often interrelated. I will therefore consider them in tandem. Qualitative measures, such as small, medium, or large, or bowl, cup, or jar need little consideration, except to say that if used they should be explicitly defined descriptively and/or numerically, and they should be verifiable. In ceramic industries where such neat categories cannot be easily defined or where we want to quantify precisely what is meant by each category and examine variability within it, quantitative

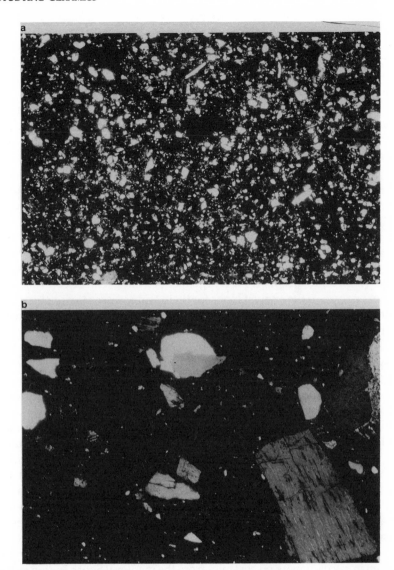

FIGURE 3.4.   Petrographic thin sections: (a) fine-grained inclusions, (b) coarse inclusions, feldspar and quartz (cross-polars, 6× magnification; photo by Alison E. Rautman). Reproduced by permission.

measures of size and shape are useful. Numerous measures can be taken on a single rim sherd or whole vessel (see Table 3.2). Variable selection should be made on the basis of their relevance to desired ends: If I want an assessment of size, what variables will best provide it, or of rim form, or of variation within bowl classes, and so on.

Table 3.2 and Figure 3.5 illustrate a selection of commonly measured variables. Undoubtedly other variables will prove useful and can be defined in the analysis of specific data sets (for example, lip angle, ring-base diameter and thickness, etc.). If one chooses to use quantitative measures of variables, it is important that they be defined precisely and measured consistently. If one researcher measures rim diameter on the interior of the vessel and another measures it on the vessel exterior, they are not recording comparable information.

Even when two individuals are recording the same information, subconscious measuring biases may potentially distort their results. For example, certain individuals may even select rim-diameter measures over odd values (e.g., 14, 16, 18 cm vs. 15, 17, 19 cm). Such biases can be controlled for in later analyses if the analyst looks for them and assesses their nature. The biases in diameter measures can be dealt with by examining rim-diameter distributions at intervals of two or more centimeters. Individual variation in measurements can be minimized by repeated checking of consistency between the analysts and the tools used and by limiting the number of individuals involved in data recording.

The analysis of quantitative data is useful both for distinguishing among broad classes of vessels and for assessing the range of variation within such classes. That is, vessels can first be sorted into broad morphological or shape classes—shallow bowls, cups, necked vessels, and the like. Quantitative measures can then be used to identify divisions within these classes, thus permitting a much finer-scaled classification of vessel forms. The recognition and quantification of variation within vessel classes may be significant in identifying chronological changes, interworkshop variation, or stylistic variations within broadly consistent categories of vessels.

An example of this quantitative approach to ceramic classification can be seen in my own work on ceramics from the medieval South Indian city of Vijayanagara (see Chapter 5). In approaching the classification of the Vijayanagara ceramics, I first sorted them into broad categories on the basis of overall vessel form. Vessels were divided into unrestricted vessels or bowls and restricted or necked vessels. These categories were further subdivided on the basis of secondary attributes or rim form or general vessel characteristics. A large number of quantitative measurements were taken on vessels in each of these categories, and statistical distributions of variables

TABLE 3.2. Quantitative Measures of Ceramic Variation

Variable	Scale	Definition and measurement
Rim diameter	cm	Circumference of vessel at rim, measured with rim diameter chart, should have at least 3 cm of rim for accuracy
Neck diameter	cm	Circumference at neck, measured with diameter chart
Maximum (body or vessel) diameter	cm	Circumference at point of maximum diameter, measured with diameter chart
Rim height	cm or mm	Vertical height from rim base to rim top, measured with vernier calipers
Neck height	cm or mm	Vertical height from rim top to neck inflection, measured with vernier calipers
Height to maximum diameter	cm or mm	Vertical height from rim top to point of maximum vessel diameter, measured with vernier calipers
Vessel height	cm or mm	Total vertical height of vessel, measured with vernier calipers
Lip thickness	cm or mm	Thickness of vessel at lip, measured perpendicular to line of vessel at point of maximal lip thickness, measured with vernier calipers
Rim thickness	cm or mm	Thickness of vessel at rim base or point of maximal rim thickness (definition must be consistent), measured with vernier calipers
Neck thickness	cm or mm	Thickness of vessel at neck inflection, measured with vernier calipers
Body thickness	cm or mm	Thickness of vessel at consistent point along vessel wall, e.g., 2 cm below neck inflection, 5 cm below rim top, measured with vernier calipers
Base thickness	cm or mm	Thickness of vessel at base center or specified point below base carination, measured with vernier calipers
Rim angle	Degrees	Measurement of orientation of vessel at rim, measured from horizontal, measured with goniometer (to nearest 5 degrees)
Body angle	Degrees	Measurement of orientation of vessel at specified point, e.g., below neck inflection on a jar, measured with goniometer (to nearest 5 degrees)

Note. These variables represent only a sample of possible measures that can be made. Many other measures and different definitions of these variables are possible. It is most important that however variables are defined, they be measured consistently on all sherds.

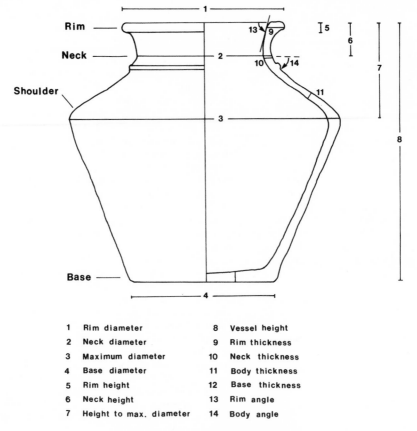

1	Rim diameter	8	Vessel height
2	Neck diameter	9	Rim thickness
3	Maximum diameter	10	Neck thickness
4	Base diameter	11	Body thickness
5	Rim height	12	Base thickness
6	Neck height	13	Rim angle
7	Height to max. diameter	14	Body angle

FIGURE 3.5.   Some quantitative variables.

were examined in order to subdivide the broad vessel classes into finer typological categories. For example, the unrestricted Vijayanagara vessels were divided on the basis of size and general form into the categories of saucerlike vessels (used as oil lamps), shallow carinated bowls, and other bowls (see Figure 3.6). Within the category of shallow carinated bowls, two variables, vessel diameter and rim orientation, were used to further subdivide the vessels into finer size and shape classes. The distribution of the variable rim angle was used to sort the vessels into three types, those with inturning rims, those with roughly vertical rims, and those with sharply outturning rims (see Figure 3.7). With this relatively fine-scaled classification, it was then possible to examine variations in size and vessel form within a single broad class of ceramic vessels in order to look at a variety of

Unrestricted Vessels

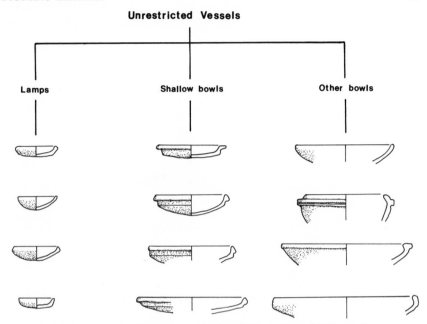

FIGURE 3.6.   Vijayanagara ceramic classification: unrestricted vessels.

research questions, including temporal change, interworkshop variations, vessel use, and the spatial distributions of the different bowl categories.

Decoration and surface treatment are other dimensions of ceramic variability that can be examined. Ceramic industries vary greatly in the degree of attention paid to the most visible part of the vessels: the exterior surface of jars and interior surface of bowls. As discussed in Chapter 2, surface treatments can range from none, to casual smoothing of the vessel, to elaborate burnishing, or painted, incised, or other decoration. The treatment of a vessel's surface may tell us something about the scale of production and labor investment, that is, whether a vessel was hurriedly and casually produced or carefully and intensively finished, and may also provide information about vessel use or its ritual or symbolic significance. Some studies of ceramic decoration that consider some of these issues will be presented in Chapter 5.

Surface treatment may be divided into several categorical attributes. These can include smoothed, polished, burnished, slipped, glazed, roughly finished, or coarse surfaces, and so on. Individual vessels may be characterized by one or more of these attributes. Slips can be identified by a color contrast with the vessel paste, though they are often difficult to

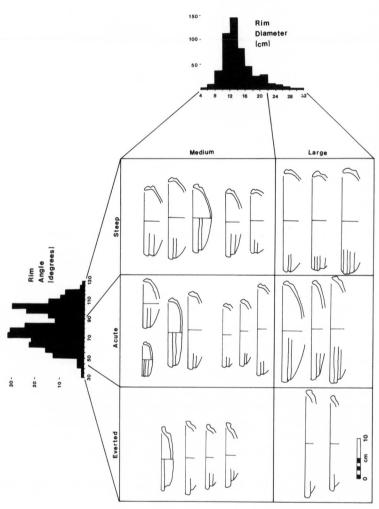

FIGURE 3.7. Vijayanagara shallow bowls: variable distributions and final classification.

identify when they are close in color to the paste. Hand lenses are useful in examining slips, as they often appear as a separate layer and sometimes flake off and separate from the vessel body. Glazes are characterized by a glassy surface and are typically a different color than the vessel wall.

Vessel surface and paste color can be recorded using either broad categorical categories or a color chart developed for more precise measurements of color hue, value, and chroma. The Munsell Soil Color chart is the most popular chart of this kind used in archaeological research, both for recording soil colors in excavations and for measuring the color of artifacts. The mineralogical content of slips and glazes can be assessed through chemical analytic techniques, such as neutron activation analysis.

Ceramic decoration includes painted and plastic ornamentation. Information on the technique of application and the constituent elements and layout of designs can be recorded. For analytical purposes, a design may be defined as a combination of decorative *elements* organized into a pattern or *design configuration*. Design elements may be defined as the smallest portion of a design that can stand alone. Design elements are combined into a structured set known as a design configuration. The organization and layout of design configurations follow specific cultural rules or norms governing what constitutes an appropriate design (Kintigh 1985:40–41). These rules govern the placement of specific elements or configurations on a vessel (Friedrich 1970), the symmetry and orientation of elements (Washburn 1977, 1989), and how elements can be linked together into a configuration.

The analysis of painted decoration includes the definition of design elements, their placement on a vessel and in configurations, their color (including, perhaps, chemical identification of the pigments used). Other information on "micro-element" variation, such as line width, distance between lines, brush stroke, and the like may also be recorded, and may reflect individual variation in design application (Friedrich 1970; Hill and Gunn 1977). Information recorded on plastic designs can include the technique, element, and configuration form, size and repetition, and placement on a vessel.

DATA ANALYSIS

Once information about ceramics is recorded, either in qualitative or quantitative form, the next step is to use the raw data to accomplish the analytical goals: to define types, search for stylistic patterning, or answer other questions of interest. Data analysis is, in its essence, a search for patterning. The techniques used in analysis may vary from simple graphic displays of single variables to more complex multivariate methods such as cluster or factor analysis.

As a general rule, the first stage of data analysis should be the use of simple display techniques and descriptive statistics to summarize information on individual variables. Simple graphic descriptive techniques include the construction of histograms or scatter plots to assess variable distributions and interrelations. The computation of means, modes, variance, and standard deviations are also basic techniques for describing quantitative variables.

Once individual variable distributions are assessed, pairs of variables may be examined and inferential tests used to compare two variables or different subsets of a single variable. Some simple statistical tests include the students' t-test and analysis of variance tests for quantitative data, and the chi-square test for qualitative data. If these tests reveal meaningful patterned variation that allow vessels or groups of vessels to be distinguished, it may be sufficient to stop the analysis there. If the data are more complex, such that no single variable or pair of variables suffices to account for the dimensions of interest to the researcher, then more complicated analytical methods may be necessary.

A thorough discussion of statistical techniques for ceramic analysis is beyond the scope of this book. In the appendix, I present a brief introduction to the use of a number of simple statistical techniques in their classification. For more detailed discussions of statistical techniques, there are several very good books available that focus on statistical techniques in the analysis of archaeological data in general, with considerable relevance to ceramic data. These include works by Doran and Hodson (1975), Hodson (1970), Orton (1980), Shennan (1988), and Thomas (1976, 1986).

There is a saying that has gained considerable popularity among statisticians and computer scientists—"Garbage in, garbage out." These four words have great relevance to the analysis of archaeological data as well and not merely because much of what we analyze is prehistoric garbage. They mean that the results of our analyses are only as good as the raw data we put into them. In archaeological analysis, the quality of our data is affected by sampling procedures, which affect the representativeness of our collections; sample sizes; variable definition—the selection of variables relevant to our research questions; and variable measurement. In addition, errors can arise when coding and transforming our raw data into analytical quantities for computer analysis or manipulation by hand.

At each stage in any analysis, it is necessary to check one's data and approaches and consider how these data are relevant to one's research questions. There are undoubtedly some basic criteria for competent archaeological analysis and recording techniques. However, there can and should be no recipe book for exactly how sites will be examined and collections made or for what information and measurements should be recorded and how they can be analyzed. The analysis of archaeological data is, at its best, a reflective process, which although time consuming, can yield fruitful and significant results for our understanding of cultures and societies of the past.

SUGGESTED READINGS

An overview of approaches to archaeological classification and typology is presented in Whallon and Brown (1982). Discussions of sampling techniques in archaeology include Hole (1980), Mueller (1975), Ragir (1972), Redman and Watson (1970), Redman (1973), and Whallon (1983). Technological analyses of ceramic raw materials are described in Bishop (1980), Bishop *et al.* (1982), Olin and Franklin (1982), Rice (1987), and Rye (1981).

4

Using Ceramics to Answer Questions

I. Ethnographic Data, Ceramic Ethnoarchaeology, and Ceramic Chronologies

The classification of ceramics into meaningful types is the first necessary step in using ceramic data in archaeological analysis. The next and ultimately more important step is to use those data to answer questions about the past. These questions can focus on differences between past societies or the ways that societies changed over time and space. Temporal changes in ceramic forms can be used to construct chronological sequences. Ceramics can also be examined to consider the spatial distribution of activities in which pots are used within or between sites or regions. Because, as the products of human action, ceramic forms represent the cultural choices of people living in specific historical contexts, ceramic analysis can also inform on the structure of past social, political, or ideological structures. A further topic that can be approached through ceramic analysis is the study of the organization of ceramic production and distribution. Approaches to some of these various questions are the focus of the remainder of this book.

The consideration of such questions about the past involves moving one step back from the sherds themselves to examine how they are linked to their broader context. These connections are made through "linking arguments." Linking arguments necessary for using ceramics to answer questions about the past fall into two basic categories. The first set of linking arguments concerns the material implications of a variety of characteristics of ceramics in particular contexts, including their production, technology, use, and meaning. These arguments attempt to assess the range of potential roles played by ceramics in past societies and the kinds of material patterning that we would expect as a result of those differing roles.

The second set of linking arguments are those that attempt to consider the impact of cultural and noncultural factors in producing the archaeological record from which ceramics are recovered. Archaeologists do not recover past cultures, or even past behaviors. What we recover are the partial remains of the by-products of those behaviors, the broken and distorted material residues of human activity. In evaluating archaeological ceramics, it is therefore necessary to consider how their present state relates to their past uses. Questions relevant to these considerations include human discard practices in specific cultural contexts as well as information on ceramic breakage and a variety of other factors affecting the formation of archaeological sites.

Archaeological analysis proceeds by evaluating models about the past, through a process of feedback between our frameworks or models for how past societies were structured or changed and the material remains of the archaeological record. The sources of models about the past can be multiple; they can be derived from ethnographic studies, historical information, archaeological studies, general anthropological knowledge, or inspiration. The important characteristics of such models are, however, that they be internally consistent and logical and that they be testable and tested with archaeological data, rather than accepted merely because they "seem to fit." Although we may never be able to conclusively demonstrate that our model is the correct one, we should be able to demonstrate whether it is supported or refuted by archaeological data.

In the remainder of this book I will consider how ceramics may be used to answer specific questions about the past. For each category of questions, I will first present the general issues and assumptions involved and discuss some broad methodological approaches. Second, some successful case studies will be presented. Many of the studies presented involve the use of ethnographic evidence in the construction of models about the past. Ethnographic studies have been used by archaeologists to develop general frameworks of ceramic production and use, and for considering ceramics in particular sociocultural contexts. Before turning to specific archaeological case studies, I wish to consider the broader question of the relevance and use of ethnographic data in the interpretation of archaeological ceramics.

USING ETHNOGRAPHIC INFORMATION IN THE ANALYSIS
OF ARCHAEOLOGICAL CERAMICS

The use of ethnographic information in archaeological analysis is not new. In the past, however, ethnographic data were often not collected with archaeological goals in mind and were therefore often inappropriate or insufficient for use in archaeological studies. Recently, a new discipline has developed within archaeology—*ethnoarchaeology*. Ethnoarchaeological studies systematically examine contemporary cultural and material systems in order to develop frameworks relevant to archaeology.

The links between present ethnographic cases and past archaeological cases are made through *analogical* arguments. Philosophers of science define analogical arguments as arguments that take a particular form. The structure of analogical arguments depends upon identifying and testing similarities between analogs, objects or phenomena that are formally similar.

Analogies involve the recognition and identification of similarities between two objects or phenomena. The recognition and identification of a set of similarities between objects and the nature of the interrelations of the similar traits are used in analogical arguments to predict information about the lesser known of the objects. If, for example, objects A and B are both characterized by traits 1–20, and A also contains trait 21, we want to be able to predict whether object B also possesses trait 21. Predicting the presence of trait 21 in object B requires the argument that there is a necessary link between traits 1–20 and 21, such that when the former occur, the latter would also be found. Such arguments are difficult to make because of the complexity of defining the nature of the relations between a set of traits and their necessary association in all cases.

In archaeology, analogical reasoning involves making connections from known contemporary phenomena to past phenomena. Typically the past phenomena we study, whether a class of artifacts, subsistence behavior, or political organization, are only partially represented in the archaeological record. We observe only the material or physical by-products of past societies, and these are distorted by conditions affecting site formation and material preservation. Ethnographic data provide a means for linking contemporary behaviors to their material implications and, by extension, help us to consider relations between materials and behaviors of the past. The extension of processes we observe in the present to occurrences in the past is a key principle of all archaeological studies. We can only study the past if we make the basic assumption that the same processes we can observe in the present world also occurred in the past, with similar material consequences.

Physical similarity between modern and archaeological examples is, however, not in itself a sufficient criterion for assuming functional similarity or similarities in valuation and symbolic import. One cannot say that just because two pots share some external or formal similarities that they were used and thought of in identical ways. Rather, the known ethnographic case should be used to develop a testable framework within which the archaeological case can be viewed.

Information gleaned from ethnographic contexts can be used to bolster the gap between the fragmentary material evidence of past human behavior that archaeologists observe and the cultural systems that produced these behaviors that are the ultimate object of our study. The links between behavior and archaeological remains must also be bridged by the understanding of these general relations and of processes affecting site formation and preservation. Binford has termed the identification of these links as *middle-range theory* (1976, 1981).

Ethnographic data can be used in ceramic analysis in a number of ways. A large number of ethnographic cases demonstrating a particular phenomenon may be used to consider regularities that crosscut cultural boundaries. For example, as will be discussed later, we know of no living societies where female potters regularly use the potter's wheel. This pattern may not have been true in all past societies with wheel-made pottery, but given its broad consistency in modern contexts, we can begin to consider the impact of technological features on the sexual division of labor in different types of potting industries. Contemporary patterns like this can thus be used as a framework for viewing and evaluating specific archaeological cases.

Another approach to ethnographic analogy is the "direct historical approach" (Steward 1942). This approach assumes historic continuity within a region between prehistoric and contemporary populations, and assumes, therefore, behavioral continuity in the way things were done and in material forms. Although in some contexts such assumptions may be justified, assumptions of spatial and temporal proximity alone do not confirm archaeological interpretations. These interpretations should be bolstered by independent supporting evidence, and the modern case should be used as an hypothesis to be evaluated and not assumed as a given.

Along with these warnings about the logic and form of analogical arguments in archaeology, it should be stressed that ethnographic data are critically important to archaeological analysis (Wylie 1985). Although not all prehistoric events, goods, or behaviors can be expected to have modern counterparts, a wide knowledge of the ethnographic literature on a particular topic can help us to identify regularities that transcend cultural boundaries and can expose us to alternative perspectives and interpretations that can be evaluated with archaeological data. The use of an ethnographic framework allows us to consider the similarities of a specific case with other known societies and to consider the differences and uniqueness of the particular culture under study.

CERAMIC ETHNOARCHAEOLOGY

Studies of traditional ceramics have been common in the ethnographic literature since the late nineteenth century and are still being written today (see Kramer 1985 for a comprehensive bibliography). Most of these works have been oriented toward documenting traditional manufacturing techniques and were often produced as a secondary focus of a larger research project. The studies vary considerably in the degree to which they place ceramic manufacture in a broader sociocultural context; by, for example, considering the social position or status of potters, the scale of pottery production and distribution, or learning contexts. As such, they are of variable value to archaeologists interested in these and other questions concerning ceramic production, distribution, and use in their cultural context.

More recently, a number of studies of pottery manufacture, use, and discard have been undertaken by researchers with an interest in problems of particular concern to archaeologists. These studies have focused on traditional pottery production in a broad range of areas and cultural contexts in the New and Old World. Researchers have examined a wide range of issues concerning contemporary ceramic manufacture and use, including raw material acquisition, artifact life span and discard rates, relations between vessel shape and vessel use, and technological constraints on vessel efficiency. The technology of pottery manufacturing techniques has also been detailed.

Social and cultural aspects of ceramic production have also been examined by ceramic ethnoarchaeologists. Studies of the social context of pottery production and the status of potters, of the transmission of knowledge on production and decorative techniques, and of indigenous systems of ceramic classification have been carried out. Still other studies have focused on the organization of ceramic distribution and the relations between production and distribution systems. Rather than summarize the many studies of ceramic ethnography here, I will consider the results of some relevant studies throughout the remaining chapters of this book in the discussion of particular aspects of ceramic research and particular questions about the past.

Ethnographic studies of pottery have provided general frameworks from which to view archaeological ceramics and particular research problems. Although their conclusions must be evaluated and tested in each archaeological case, the issues they describe are of broad relevance to archaeological studies. A knowledge of both the regularities and the range of variation that exist among traditional ceramic-producing societies provides a framework in which to situate our studies of the past. This is not to say that modern societies encompass the full range of choices and strategies that prehistoric potters may have employed. However, understanding the nature and use of ceramics in modern contexts, as well as the chemical and physical nature and constraints on ceramic production, provides a crucial baseline for understanding the place of ceramics in particular prehistoric societies.

RECONSTRUCTING CHRONOLOGIES

The use of ceramics in the construction of chronologies has a long history in archaeological studies, extending back to the work of Sir Flanders Petrie in Egypt in the late nineteenth century (Trigger 1989). The association of certain classes of vessels in stratigraphic levels within an archaeological site provides one means for constructing ceramic chronologies using the principle of stratigraphy. When such sequences are repeated in whole or in part across a number of sites within a region, it is possible to build up broad regional sequences through the technique of cross-dating. Recently, the availability of absolute dating techniques, especially radiocarbon or carbon-14 dating and dendrochronology, has allowed the dating of archaeological materials, including ceramics, that are found in association with organic remains with increasingly fine precision.

In many archaeological situations, however, archaeologists deal with single-phase sites or sites with disturbed stratigraphy and a paucity of materials that can be dated using absolute dating techniques. In such cases, alternative techniques must be employed to develop chronological sequences. One such method is *seriation*. Using seriation, archaeologists can examine changes in ceramic form over time using only the vessels themselves, largely independent of their context of recovery. Seriation has been defined "as the procedure of working out a chronology by arranging local remains of the same cultural tradition in the order that produces the most consistent patterning of their cultural traits" (Rouse 1967:157).

The critical assumption underlying seriation concerns the nature of artifact change. It is assumed that a class of objects is slowly introduced into a social system, gradually increases in popularity, and eventually declines in use and disappears. This is a pattern we frequently see in clothing styles in our own society, as new styles are introduced by a small group of fashionable individuals and then become widespread throughout larger segments of society as others adopt these symbols of fashion. Eventually these fashions go out of style as new fashions take their place. Witness the rise and decline of bell-bottomed pants during the 1960s and 1970s as a classic case of the rise, spread, and decline of a class of material culture.

The same kinds of patterns that we see in clothing styles can also occur in pottery fashions. A new pottery class, for example, may first be adopted by only one or two members of a community. As it becomes better known, and more accepted and more desirable, increasing numbers of people may begin to make and use similar pots, often modifying the ceramic form slightly along the way. Eventually the initially rare class of pottery will become very common and widespread. After a while, as new classes are introduced or come into vogue, the first class will decline in popularity, and it may ultimately disappear from use. When plotted on a graph whose vertical axis is time and horizontal axis is the percentage of particular ceramic classes in an archaeological context, the graph will take the form of a "battleship" or lenticular curve (see Figure 4.1). I will consider some of the cultural reasons underlying this pattern of material cultural change in a discussion of Miller's work in Chapter 6. For now, I will focus only on how these patterns of stylistic change can be used in the construction of archaeological chronologies.

Constructing a seriation involves calculating the relative frequencies of the different ceramic classes from a set of sites or loci and ordering the sets on the basis of the assumption of a pattern of lenticular change. Most simply, this can be done graphically by representing ceramic frequencies by site on strips of paper and then lining up those strips to best approximate the ideal "battleship curves" required by the assumptions on the nature of change in artifact popularity. An example of a seriation chart is presented in Figure 4.1; the raw data employed in its construction is presented in Table 4.1.

In the example, the frequencies of four ceramic classes from 14 sites are considered. At the bottom of the graph in Figure 4.1, Type 1 is at its peak of popularity and accounts for 62% of the ceramics from a particular site. At that site, 6% of the ceramics are of Type 2, none are of Type 3, and 32% are of Type 4. Site 1, in the center of the graph, has a very different distribution of ceramic classes, with 15% Type 1, 25% Type 2, 2% Type 3, and 58% Type 4.

As presented, Figure 4.1 gives us no way of knowing which way is up, or which end of the time axis is oldest. If the graph were turned upside down, it would just as accurately represent temporal changes in the distribution in the set of 14 sites. Other evidence must be called upon to determine the proper chronological ordering of the ceramic classes;

Site

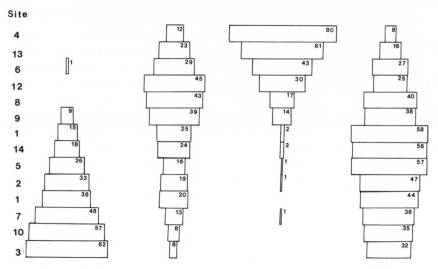

Figure 4.1.   An example of the seriation technique for ceramic chronology.

whether Type 1 faded out as Type 3 rose in popularity or vice versa. This evidence can include stratigraphic context, absolute dates, or dates of associated artifact classes.

Recently, a number of more sophisticated quantitative methods for constructing relative chronologies have come into use. These techniques require the use of computer analysis in order to date archaeological units or ceramic types. They permit the analysis of much larger sets of data in more complex ways—with techniques that would be impossible or extremely time-consuming without the use of a computer. The Brainerd–Robinson similarity matrix is one such method, which groups samples according to their overall similarity in frequencies of ceramic types (Cowgill 1972; Doran and Hodson 1975:272–274). As with traditional seriation techniques, units or sites with the greatest similarities in ceramic class frequencies are grouped closest together and assumed to be closest in time.

A second quantitative approach to ceramic chronology is nonmetric multidimensional scaling. In this approach, individual types are ordered, rather than archaeological units, and only the co-occurrence of types is considered, rather than their overall frequencies. Multidimensional scaling has proven particularly effective in dating individual graves from large pre- and protohistoric cemeteries, where small samples of artifacts from well-controlled archaeological contexts are recovered (see Steponaitis 1983 and later discussion).

TABLE 4.1. An Example of Ceramic Seriation:
Type Counts and Frequencies from 14 Sites

Site	Type 1 # (%)	Type 2 # (%)	Type 3 # (%)	Type 4 # (%)	Total
1	41 (18)	54 (24)	4 (2)	126 (56)	225
2	42 (36)	24 (20)	0 (0)	52 (44)	118
3	121 (62)	12 (6)	0 (0)	63 (32)	196
4	0 (0)	31 (12)	206 (80)	20 (8)	257
5	110 (26)	68 (16)	4 (1)	241 (57)	423
6	3 (1)	97 (29)	143 (43)	90 (27)	333
7	79 (48)	21 (13)	0 (0)	64 (39)	164
8	0 (0)	77 (43)	31 (17)	72 (40)	180
9	26 (9)	111 (39)	40 (14)	109 (38)	286
10	114 (57)	16 (8)	0 (0)	70 (35)	200
11	153 (48)	42 (13)	3 (1)	121 (38)	319
12	0 (0)	113 (45)	75 (30)	62 (25)	250
13	0 (0)	45 (23)	121 (61)	32 (16)	198
14	20 (18)	26 (24)	2 (2)	61 (56)	109

Reconstructing Chronologies: Case Study

A study of ceramic chronology that makes extensive use of data from fine-scaled stratigraphic excavations and sophisticated methods of computer analysis was conducted by Steponaitis (1983) in his work on Moundville ceramics from the southeastern United States. Moundville, located in western Alabama, has been the focus of archaeological research since the midnineteenth century (Peebles 1987). The site, which extends over an area of some 100 hectares, is one of the largest and most complex sites in North America. The site contained 20 artificial pyramidal mounds situated around a large rectangular plaza (see Figure 4.2). The largest of these mounds is 17 m high and 100 sq m in area at its base.

Archaeological research at Moundville has included the excavation of approximately 2,800 burials and 75 structures, as well as traces of a wooden palisade that enclosed the settlement. Prior to 1980, however, chronological control at the site was extremely limited. The major excavations at Moundville were conducted before 1940, when absolute dating techniques were unavailable. The entire site was defined as belonging to a single time period—the Moundville phase, ca. A.D. 1050–1550. In the late 1970s a new phase of research began at Moundville and in its general region (Peebles 1978; Scarry 1981; Welch 1986). This work included fine-scaled excavations at Moundville, with attention to microstratigraphy, and a program of regional survey and test excavations. Much of this work was oriented

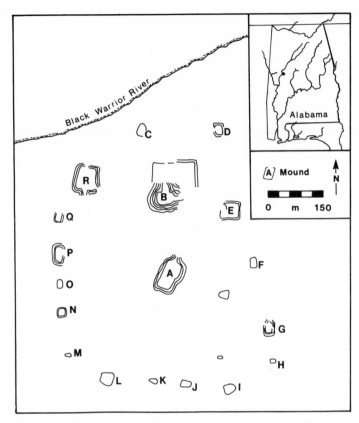

FIGURE 4.2. The Moundville site (after Welch 1986:24,27). Reprinted by permission.

toward refining the ceramic chronology in order that questions concerning the temporal development of the Moundville chiefdom and its central settlement could be considered.

In his analysis of the Moundville ceramics, Steponaitis employed two sets of data. The first was a collection of whole vessels recovered in burial excavations during the 1930s and presently housed in museum collections (see Figure 4.3). A total of 1,117 whole vessels was examined, including 833 for which precise provenience information was available. His second set of data was a collection of sherds from the recent excavations, with a sample of 8,212 sherds from well-controlled stratigraphic contexts (Steponaitis 1983: 9–14).

The first step of Steponaitis's analysis was the development of a sophisticated ceramic classification. The vessels were classed along six

FIGURE 4.3. Moundville ceramics: winged serpent motif (collections of the Museum of Anthropology, University of Michigan).

dimensions of variability. These were (1) type and variety classification, based on paste composition, surface finish, and tooled decoration (discussed in Chapter 3); (2) representational motifs; (3) painted decoration, including slipping, smudging, or painted motifs; (4) basic shape classes, including bottles, jars, and bowls and variants thereof; (5) secondary shape classes, such as the presence of appliqué or molded designs, rim form, and so on; and (6) effigy figures; vessels shaped like birds, frogs, human heads; and other naturalistic forms (Steponaitis 1983:48–78). Categorical classes were defined for each of these dimensions, and each whole vessel and all possible sherds were classed according to each dimension.

In constructing the ceramic chronology, Steponaitis first looked for categories within each dimension that appeared to be chronologically bounded. These were categories that did not occur in all ceramic or provenience samples or that were associated with particular strata or features. Twenty-four attributes that appeared to be chronologically sensitive were selected. Steponaitis then used information on the presence/absence of these attributes on vessels from grave lots in his seriation.

The technique used in the seriation was nonmetric multidimensional scaling. This technique is based on developing a distance or similarity measure for each pair of attributes by considering their frequency of co-occurrence in the total sample. The distance coefficients are then used to develop a scale or ranking of attributes (points). The attributes are ordered in such a way that distances between points (interpreted as distances between the midpoint of an attribute's range) correspond to the rank order of distance coefficients between points. In other words, if attribute a frequently co-occurs with attribute b, and rarely co-occurs with attribute c, points a and b will be placed closer together on a relative scale than will points a and c. Multidimensional scaling, unlike traditional seriation that considers only the dimension of time, permits the consideration of other dimensions that may also affect the ranking of the attributes. However, if an analysis using more than one dimension produces a linear ranking, one can reasonably assume that only one dimension (i.e., time) is significant to the scaling. Such was the case in this analysis, and Steponaitis was able to produce a relative scaling of the 24 attributes along a temporal scale.

He next computed a scaling of individual grave lots on the basis of the attributes that they contained and then divided the gravelots into three major chronological phases on the basis of patterns of change in attribute occurrence (Moundville I–III, with Phases II and III divisible into early and late components). The characteristics of ceramics from each phase were explicitly defined by the occurrence of particular ceramic attributes, and vessels from other grave lots and excavations could be easily put into this chronological framework.

Stratigraphic information from Moundville soundings was used to evaluate the adequacy of the seriation, and C14 dates from excavations and related sites were used to determine absolute range of dates for each phase. Thus, Moundville I was dated to A.D. 1050–1250, Moundville II to A.D. 1250–1400, and Moundville III to A.D. 1400–1550. Additional data on changes in a single attribute—handle shape—were also used to verify the seriation (Steponaitis 1983:90–132). With this analysis, the broad 500-year Moundville phase was subdivided into finer periods, making it possible to consider the chronological development of the Moundville site and polity, from a small single-mound nucleated settlement to a major chiefly center.

Steponaitis's work presents an example of the use of a sophisticated ceramic classification, based on categorical data, and a number of complementary analytical techniques in the development of a relatively fine-scaled chronology. The 150-year periods his analysis defined may be refined through future work into even finer units, as has been possible in certain parts of the world, where precise absolute dating techniques, such as dendrochronology (tree-ring dating), have permitted the definition of archaeological periods less than 50 years in duration (Kohler and Blinman 1987).

Reconstructing Chronologies: Discussion

The use of archaeological ceramics to establish chronological markers and sequences has without doubt been the primary focus of ceramic studies throughout the past century of archaeological research. Humans regularly improve or alter our material products, including ceramics, both to adapt to changing physical environments or circumstances and in response to changing cultural rules or contexts. Such changes in material culture forms may occur rapidly or gradually, as a result of minor and cumulative alterations. Large-scale changes in ceramic styles are commonly used by archaeologists to define broad chronological and cultural periods. Smaller-scale changes in ceramic form or design, within sites or regions, also provide an important means for refining chronological sequences and dating sites. It is only once chronologies are defined that we can begin to look at the processes underlying the changes cultures and regions undergo over time.

SUGGESTED READINGS

Comprehensive reviews of ceramic ethnography and ethnoarchaeology include Arnold (1985) and Kramer (1985). Specific studies of various topics in ceramic ethnography include work on raw-material acquisition (DeBoer 1984), artifact life span and discard rates (David 1972; DeBoer 1974, 1985; DeBoer and Lathrap 1979; Foster 1960; Longacre 1985), relations between vessel shape and vessel use (Braun 1980a, 1983; Henrickson and McDonald 1983; Smith 1985), and technological constraints on vessel efficiency (Braun 1983; Rye 1976; Steponaitis 1983, 1984).

The technology of pottery manufacturing techniques has been detailed (Arnold 1985; Guthe 1925; Rye and Evans 1976; Saraswati and Behura 1966; van der Leeuw 1976). Studies of the social context of pottery production and the status of potters (Arnold 1975, 1976, 1978, 1989; Balfet 1966, 1981; Birmingham 1975; Reina and Hill 1978; Rice 1981; Saraswati 1978; Scheans 1977), of the transmission of knowledge on production and decorative techniques (Friedrich 1970; Hardin 1979, 1984; Stanislawski 1973, 1978), and of indigenous systems of ceramic classification (Haaland 1978; Miller 1985; Saraswati and Behura 1966) have been carried out. Still other studies have focused on the organization of ceramic distribution and the relations between production and distribution systems (Balfet 1981; Allen 1984; Hodder 1981; Miller 1981).

Approaches to seriation and chronological reconstruction have been discussed by Brainerd (1951); Cowgill (1972); Doran and Hodson (1975:213–216); Kruskal (1971); LeBlanc (1975); Michaels (1973); and Rouse (1967). An additional application of the multidimensional scaling technique for ceramic chronologies is Pollock (1983b).

5

Using Ceramics to Answer Questions

II. Ceramic Use and Ceramic Production and Distribution

Along with focusing on when things happened in the past through the construction of ceramic chronologies, ceramic analysis can also provide a useful approach for examining how people lived—the nature of their daily activities, and broader questions concerning past economies, political systems, social organization, and beliefs. In this chapter, I will examine aspects of the first two of these topics: how we can use ceramics to study activities and the study of ceramic production and distribution systems.

CERAMIC USE AND ACTIVITY DISTRIBUTION

Ceramic vessels are tools—objects used in specific activities to serve specific ends (Braun 1983:107). The intended use of a vessel affects the final form the vessel will take in a number of ways. For example, the material constituents of the vessel may be selected on the basis of its intended use. Certain tempering materials or clays may be favored for cooking pots, whereas others are favored for water storage vessels, and luxury or ritual vessels may be made of other materials. From an archaeological perspective, there are several ways to approach the topic of ceramic use. The first involves the direct examination of the vessel materials and their constituents and evidence for uses, including wear traces and chemical residues

83

embedded in porous ceramic bodies. Another approach to interpretations of ceramic use is the examination of vessel shape. In addition, the study of spatial distributions of different classes of ceramics within and between sites is also important in assessing ceramic use and the spatial distribution of activities.

Several ethnographic and ethnoarchaeological studies of pottery raw materials have shown that the constituents of cooking pots often differ from those of noncooking pots (Mills 1984). Many of the differences seem to be due to the desire to increase the ability of cooking pots to resist thermal stresses associated with repeated heating and cooling. As discussed in Chapter 2, potters may take a number of approaches to increasing resistance to thermal stress. These include increasing the size and quantity of pores through the addition of organic materials or angular irregularly shaped temper particles; or adding tempering materials that have similar expansion rates to the clay body of the vessel, such as fine-grained clays or minerals such as calcite, plagioclase, and feldspars.

Differences in ceramic pastes and tempers can be observed through microscopic analyses. Where distinct patterns in raw materials are evident in locally produced and contemporaneous ceramics from a site or region, these may be related to differences in the uses to which the vessels were put. The functional significance of raw-material differences between vessels can be further assessed by examining vessel shape, context of recovery, and traces of use.

Potters make vessels in certain shapes for certain uses. Narrow-necked vessels are likely to be used for transporting water because less will spill from their openings than from wide-mouthed vessels. Round bases are advantageous on cooking vessels because they transmit heat easily and are less susceptible to breakage from thermal stress than flat-based vessels. Cross-cultural studies of relations between vessel form and vessel use have revealed pronounced regularities over time and space (Henrickson and McDonald 1983; Smith 1985). Factors such as the size of the opening, ease of access to a vessel's contents, volume (and weight when full), location of the center of gravity, and vessel stability, all seem to be partially determined by the intended function of a vessel.

This does not mean, however, that all vessels are ideally suited to their intended use. Vessel shape is also determined by normative ideas, fashions, and the technology of ceramic production. Nor is it the case that vessels are always used for the purposes for which they were originally intended. A cooking pot may sometimes be taken to the well to fetch water or may be used to store leftover food, or as a planter for houseplants. The use of a pot may also change throughout its lifespan as, for example, it is first used for cooking, then for a pet's drinking bowl, and finally as chinking in wall construction. However, in general, we expect that ceramic form is linked to ceramic use and that some general relations should pertain between a vessel's form and its primary function.

Additional evidence of ceramic use may be attained through the examination of wear traces found on vessels. Cooking vessels may be charred on the exterior, mixing bowls scratched on the base interior, and vessels traditionally covered with lids may be abraded along the top of their rim. Residues of materials held in vessels may remain on their surface or be absorbed into porous ceramic bodies and can be identified through chemical analyses. Given these differing lines of evidence—raw materials, morphology, use wear and residue analysis—it is frequently possible to make some inferences about the range of activities in which particular vessels recovered in excavations or surface collections were "most likely" used.

Under certain circumstances it may be possible to consider the precise spatial location of activities across a site using ceramic data. Such circumstances occur when vessels enter into archaeological deposits in the same area in which they were used. Such events are, however, not common in the archaeological record, and materials are often discarded away from their primary area of use. Given the great interest that many archaeologists have in the use of space and distribution of past human behaviors, much attention has been devoted, particularly in prehistoric studies, to the identification of activity areas.

An activity area is, simply, an area where specific past activities occurred that can be identified in the archaeological record. Behaviors such as sweeping or clearing the refuse of activities and depositing it in trash middens or dumps destroys most traces of past activity areas. Other natural and cultural processes affecting site formation and artifact dispersal can also lead to the displacement of materials once they have entered into the archaeological record. It is relatively rare, therefore, for ceramics to be deposited in their location of primary use. However, in certain use contexts or site destruction or abandonment events, just such a pattern could occur. The analysis of materials deposited in such contexts can provide a tremendous amount of information on the distribution of activities across a site. Vessels might be deposited where they were used in water-collecting locations, such as near wells or tanks, where a certain number of vessels are inevitably dropped and broken.

A more important context in which activity loci might be preserved archaeologically arises when a site or part of a site is suddenly abandoned or destroyed through natural or cultural disaster. These sudden events can include fires, floods, warfare-induced destruction or abandonment, or volcanic eruptions. In such contexts, and assuming limited postdepositional disturbance, materials may often be found in the areas in which they were last used. Ritual or votive deposits or caches represent another sort of activity-specific deposit in the archaeological record.

Actual studies of ceramic "activity areas" from well-controlled archaeological contexts are rare. Even when we cannot use ceramic distribution in the identification of specific activity areas, in many contexts, the spatial distribution of ceramics across archaeological sites can reveal much information about past behaviors. It is often the case that middens or trash deposits are located relatively close to occupation areas, for example, in abandoned rooms or buildings, against the back wall of a house or house compounds, in a neighborhood dump, and so on (Boone 1987). In the case of ceramics, sherds may often be incorporated into walls or roofs of a house or other structures in later construction phases. The assumption that materials tend to be deposited relatively near to where they were used underlies many of the attempts to use ceramics to examine intrasite social, economic, or political organization.

The assumption that ceramic distributions in archaeological contexts are closely correlated with locations of ceramic use is not without problems, however. In a study of the spatial distribution of ceramics recovered in surface collections in a 500-hectare region in South-Central New Mexico, Mills and colleagues noted that sherds that could be attributed to a single pot were often separated by distances of up to 150 meters (1990). They attribute these broad patterns of dispersion to the use of portions of broken vessels in later activities, resulting in considerable movement from the location of breakage and initial discard.

An archaeologist attempting to relate the content of ceramic assemblages from a site to the nature of past activities at that site must consider a number of factors contributing to the formation of ceramic assemblages (Mills 1989). Discard behavior and deposition processes must be taken into account, along with the nature and frequency of activities in which ceramics were used and the length of time that a site was occupied. If, for example, we find a site where cooking vessels are 10 times more common than large storage vessels, are we justified in claiming that food storage was unimportant in this society and that we are dealing with the remains of a group that was oriented toward the immediate consumption of its food resources? The answer to this question is, most probably, no. Other factors, like vessel volume and the ratio of cooking to storage vessels in use at any time, as well as differential rates of vessel breakage, must be considered in addition to overall vessel counts. The frequencies of vessel types in an archaeological assemblage is not necessarily a direct reflection of their frequency of use at any one point in time. This may be especially true for sites that are occupied for only brief periods of time, and at which all activities that occurred do not necessarily make their way into archaeological deposits.

In order to consider the relative importance of different activities involving ceramics at a site we must consider a variety of factors concerning how ceramics are used, broken, and deposited in specific cultural contexts. A number of ethnographic studies of contemporary ceramic use have focused on some of these questions, considering the length of time different classes of vessels remain in use in their primary function (their use life; see Table 5.1); the rate at which different classes of vessels are broken (breakage rate); the number of vessels of different classes that are in use in a household at any one time (see Table 5.2); and the rates at which different classes of vessels are reused and repaired following breakage.

Although different studies have come up with different results, at a very general level we can say that vessels that are moved frequently break more rapidly than vessels that are stationary. Exposure to thermal stress also leads to increased breakage rates. Cooking and serving vessels, therefore, can be expected to break at a higher rather than large, nonmovable storage vessels. Large storage vessels would in many domestic contexts therefore be expected to be recovered in much lower frequencies than small serving or cooking vessels. The frequency of different classes of vessels in particular archaeological assemblages is a function of the numbers of vessels that were in use during the site's occupation and their rate of breakage.

Highly valued vessels, such as pots used in rituals or given as gifts, can be expected to be relatively rare in most domestic archaeological deposits, especially if they were treated specially and kept in a secure place, away from household children and animals. The length of time that a site is occupied will also have an impact on the range of ceramic classes found there (Mills 1989). As a result of these and other factors that affect the structure and content of ceramic assemblages, care must be taken in making overly facile assumptions about activities on the basis of the distribution of functional classes in trash middens or on the surface of sites.

An additional factor to keep in mind when estimating the frequencies of different vessel classes in an assemblage is the relation between the sherds that archaeologists recover and the number of actual vessels that they represent. A single large vessel can break into dozens or hundreds of fragments, whereas a small vessel may only break into half a dozen. Breakage may also vary with context of deposition. A pot broken and discarded along a road or pathway will likely continue to be fragmented into smaller pieces as a result of human activities, whereas a vessel discarded in an abandoned room may remain in fewer and larger pieces. Differences in quantities of ceramics recovered in such cases do not relate to

TABLE 5.1. Ethnographic Studies of Vessel Use Life

	Vessel function			
Group	Cooking	Serving	Storage	Reference
Fulani	2.6	2.7	12.5	David (1972), David and Hennig (1972)
Kalinga				Longacre (1985)
Dangtalan	4.4	—	8.2	
Dalupa	4.5	—	7.2	
Tarahumara	1-2	1-2	—	Pastron (1974)
Tzintzuntzan	1-2.5	—	5.4	Foster (1960)
Maya				
Aguacatenango	1.1	.8	1.2	Deal (1983)
Chanal	1.9	2.0	2.3	Deal (1983)

(After Mills 1989:137). Reprinted by permission of *World Archaeology*, London.

differences in the importance or frequency of these different vessel classes in an assemblage. It is important therefore to attempt to monitor the number of vessels represented in an archaeological assemblage. Attention to refitting sherds to reconstruct vessels is one approach to this question.

Another approach to estimating the numbers of vessels represented in a sample involves calculating the percentage of a vessel that a particular sherd represents and then computing overall vessel-class frequencies proportionately. This is often done using rim sherds. Because vessel rims are typically circular and we can measure rim size easily with a rim diameter chart or other technique, we can also estimate what percentage of that

TABLE 5.2. Ethnographic Studies of Vessel Class Frequencies
(Mean Number of Vessels per Household)

	Vessel function				Sample
Group	Cooking	Serving	Storage	Other	(# houses)
Fulani	12.0	2.2	5.4	1.3	15
Shipibo-Coibo	3.7	4.7	2.8	2.0	18
Maya					
Chanal	35.6	5.1	6.5	15.8	53
Aguacatenango	48.7	10.1	7.8	18.7	50
Kalinga					
Dangtalan	5.1/6.2	—	1.8/1.1	2.8/6	49[a]
Dalupa	3.1/5.8	—	2.0/2.0	.5/1.1	44[b]

(After Mills 1989:138). Reprinted by permission of *World Archaelogy*, London.
[a]1975–1976/1979–1980 (Longacre 1985).
[b]1975–1976/1981 (Longacre 1985).

circle is present, that is, what percentage of a total rim is represented by a particular sherd. By recording rims in this manner we can more accurately compare frequencies of different vessel classes, so that a single large-diameter vessel that broke into many rim fragments is not weighted heavily in the sample merely by virtue of the large number of sherds recovered from it.

Ceramic Use and Activity Distribution: Case Studies

In this section I will consider two case studies that focus on ceramic use and the nature and distributions of activities at archaeological sites. The first case study involves research conducted by Barbara Mills and colleagues on ceramics from the southwestern United States. Mills examined the relations between ceramic raw material, form, and surface treatment to evaluate interpretations of ceramic use. In the second case study, I present the results of my research at the historic South Indian city of Vijayanagara, where warfare, abandonment, and fire created the possibility for identifying activity areas from ceramic distributions.

Ceramic Use at the Anderson Site, New Mexico

Studies of prehistoric ceramics from the southwestern United States have focused in large part on the beautiful and elaborately painted pottery of the late prehistoric periods. Much less attention has been paid to the unpainted plain and corrugated wares that comprise the majority of ceramic vessels from most prehistoric sites. In an analysis of ceramics from the Anderson site in southwestern New Mexico, Mills explored approaches to the analysis of ceramic use based on the analysis of a range of attributes from the total inventory of ceramics.

The Anderson site, located along the Palomas Creek drainage system in southwestern New Mexico (see Figure 5.1), is a multicomponent site dating from 600 to 1150 A.D. The Palomas region is characterized by an arid to semiarid environment, bordered on the east by the Río Grande drainage and on the west by the Black Range. The region was the focus of archaeological survey and test excavations in the early 1980s (see Nelson 1984). The Palomas area was sparsely occupied during prehistoric times, in marked contrast to the more densely populated and better known Mimbres culture area to the west and Jornado area to the south. Little archaeological research had been conducted in the region prior to the work by Nelson and her colleagues.

In a systematic survey of the Palomas drainage area, a total of 155 sites was identified (Lekson 1984). Of these, 46 contained architecture. Archi-

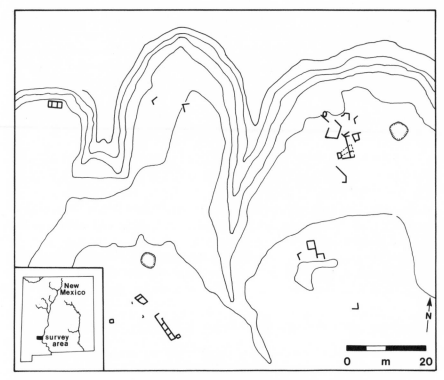

FIGURE 5.1. The Anderson site (after Nelson 1984:34). Reprinted by permission of the Maxwell Museum of Anthropology, University of New Mexico.

tectural sites included single-room field houses, small residential sites of 8 to 12 rooms, and larger residential sites with up to 50 rooms. Test excavations were carried out at one of these large sites—the Anderson site.

Occupation of the Anderson site occurred during the Late Pithouse period (A.D. 600–1000) and the Classic Mimbres period (A.D. 1000–1150). Occupational remains from these two phases were found in spatially distinct areas of the site, with Pithouse period remains in the western part and Classic Mimbres ceramics and architecture in the east. The settlement plan for the Late Pithouse period is not clearly identifiable from surface or excavated remains. During the Classic Mimbres period, the site consisted of at least 2 room blocks, with a total of approximately 50 rooms. Sample excavations at the site focused on interior and exterior spaces from both periods of occupation.

The analysis of ceramics recovered in excavations focused on a number of questions. First, ceramics were classed into traditional types according to the classifications developed in the Mimbres region (Gilman and Mills 1984). The distributions of temporally bounded types were examined and supported the division of the site into temporally distinct eastern and western zones. Variations in ceramic densities were also examined over time and space in order to consider depositional factors and variations in ceramic use. Although the patterns were not unambiguous, Gilman and Mills concluded that areas of high sherd density did not correspond to activity areas in general but rather were associated with discard practices after activity areas were swept clean.

Some interesting overall differences were identified in the relative frequencies of different functional classes over time. In particular, during the Late Pithouse period, bowls are more common than jar forms, whereas the pattern is reversed in the Classic Mimbres period. These chronological changes in the frequencies of functional types may result from a number of factors: actual changes in activity patterns and site function with concomitant change in the use of or need for ceramic containers, or changes in the materials used for storage, if, for example, baskets were replaced by ceramic storage jars, or differences in the length of occupation of the site, or other factors not directly related to ceramic use.

The distinctions between bowl and jar forms and painted versus unpainted forms in southwestern ceramics are traditionally interpreted as distinguishing serving vessels from cooking vessels. In analyzing the Anderson site ceramics Mills has attempted to evaluate these traditional interpretations of ceramic use, in particular, the distinction between cooking and noncooking vessels, by considering several variables. These include temper size, ubiquity, and shape, related to thermal shock resistance of cooking vessels, and vessel form and surface treatment. Her analysis demonstrated that these variables are linked and that cooking vessels could be distinguished from noncooking vessels on the basis of having coarse temper texture, and lacking painted decoration or slip. Vessel form was highly, though not perfectly, correlated with vessel use as well. Although bowls were not commonly used as cooking vessels, some bowls from the Late Pithouse period did fit into the cooking-vessel category in terms of their temper and surface treatment. In this period, vessel form alone did not serve to distinguish functional categories. Bowls and jars were functionally distinct in the Classic Mimbres period, perhaps indicative of increasing functional specificity in ceramic manufacture and use over time (Mills 1984:80).

Ceramic Use and Activity Distribution in Vijayanagara, South India

The city of Vijayanagara, located in South-Central India, was the capital of a large empire that controlled much of South India from 1350 to

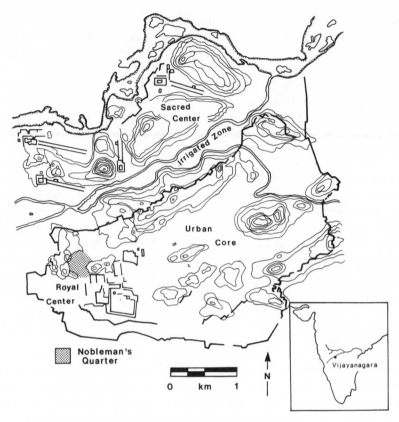

FIGURE 5.2.   Vijayanagara, India.

1565 A.D. (see Figure 5.2). Throughout its history, this Hindu empire was engaged in large-scale conflict with Muslim states to the north, and with other small polities throughout South India. In 1565 the armies of Vijayanagara were defeated in a major battle with a confederacy of five northern sultanates, and the empire largely collapsed. The victorious armies entered the hastily abandoned capital and remained there for 6 months, looting, burning, and defacing the thousands of houses, temples, and administrative buildings of this vast city.

The violent conflagrations that largely destroyed the city of Vijayanagara created the context for the archaeological deposition of certain material remains in or near the areas in which they were last used. Although we can assume that the residents of the city took many of their valuables with them as they fled their homes and that the arriving looters removed the remaining valuable goods, we can reasonably assume that nonvalued goods, such as ceramic vessels, would have been largely untouched by such actions. It is likely that many, if not most, of the locally produced earthenware pots would have been left where they were last used as the frightened occupants of the city abandoned their homes.

Since 1983, archaeological excavations at the city of Vijayanagara, conducted by the state department of archaeology (Nagaraja Rao 1983, 1985) have been uncovering the remains of a number of large elite residences that appear to have been burnt in the massive destruction of the city that followed the defeat of Vijayanagara forces. They have been focusing on an area of the city known as the "Noblemen's Quarter," and a dozen large architectural or "palace" complexes have been excavated in this area (see Figures 5.3 and 5.4). Seven of these structures exhibit evidence of burning, with a thick stratum of burnt wood and ash overlying floor-level deposits. I have analyzed ceramics from these burnt structures in order to examine the distribution of activities involving ceramics within and between the seven burnt palace compounds.

This kind of analysis requires several levels of linking arguments and some key assumptions. The primary assumption is that ceramics found on floor levels of the burnt palaces were deposited in or near their primary area of use; that is, that there was no significant movement of vessels during or after the abandonment and destruction of the city. Because analysis focused on materials found stratigraphically below burnt strata and historical evidence indicates that the city was abandoned and burnt in a very brief period of time, this assumption is supported by the available data. If this assumption holds, the distribution of particular ceramic classes within the palaces should be linked to the distribution of their use within each compound.

The first step in this analysis of activity distributions using ceramics must therefore consider the range of activities in which different ceramic classes may have been used. I divided the Vijayanagara ceramics into nine classes on the basis of size, shape, and presumed function. Functional interpretations were made on the basis of use–wear traces, such as vessel charring (though this, of course, is potentially affected by the burning of the structures) and abrasion, along with vessel shape, historical documentation, and analogies with modern vessel forms produced in the area (Junker 1985; Sinopoli and Blurton 1986). The functional, or vessel-use, classes that I defined include oil lamps, lids, bowls, small cups or jars, small and large cooking vessels, water storage vessels, and small and large water transport and storage vessels (see Figure 5.5).

In the analysis of the spatial distribution of these vessels, I first considered each class individually and then examined the co-occurrence of

FIGURE 5.3.   The Noblemen's Quarter of Vijayanagara.

the different vessel classes. A variety of areas containing different ceramic assemblages and interpreted as having been used in different ways were identified. These include dump areas, kitchens, shrines, and serving and storage areas (see Figure 5.6). Dump areas were characterized by very high frequencies of ceramics overall and by a wide diversity of vessel forms. Kitchens contained large numbers of small and large cooking vessels, as well as large storage vessels. Stone mortars, used for grinding spices and other foodstuffs, were also found in areas identified as kitchens, supporting interpretations made on the basis of ceramic distributions.

   Two shrines were identified on the basis of ceramic class frequencies.

FIGURE 5.4.   Compound 1, Vijayanagara Noblemen's Quarter.

These shrines, which appear to be located in the main room of the palace structures, contained large numbers of small oil lamps and small jars that appear to have a votive significance. There is no other archaeological indicator of household shrines; only ceramic frequencies can demonstrate their existence. Serving areas contained relatively high frequencies of small jars and water-serving vessels, whereas storage areas contained high frequencies of very large, nonportable storage vessels that could have held food or drinking water.

Differences between palace compounds could also be identified on the basis of the frequency of occurrence of the various vessel-use classes. Some of the compounds appeared to have been used as residential structures and contained a wide range of ceramic forms, including cooking, serving, and storage vessels. Others of the compounds appear to have been much more restricted in use and contain many serving and storage vessels, with very few food-preparation vessels. These structures may have been used as reception buildings or offices for various segments of the Vijayanagara elite or for other nondomestic purposes.

The analysis of ceramic distributions in the Vijayanagara palaces provides a means for examining the use of these elite structures and differences between them in a way that can contribute to and expand upon interpretations based on architectural form alone. In most cases, the an-

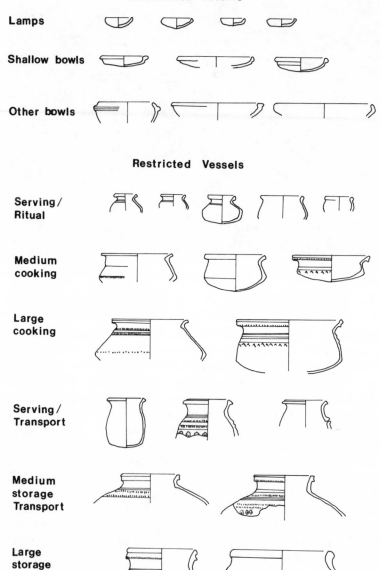

FIGURE 5.5.   Vessel-use classes: Vijayanagara ceramics.

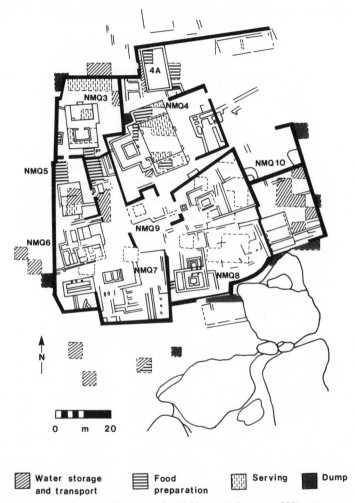

FIGURE 5.6.   The use of space in the Noblemen's Quarter of Vijayanagara.

alyses lent support to interpretations based on architecture. In other cases, the distribution of ceramics enabled us to identify spatial divisions that had no architectural indicators, such as the presence of internal shrines within two of the palaces. Ceramic interpretations coupled with other kinds of analyses can allow us to develop a fuller picture of the nature of the high-status residences in the imperial capital of Vijayanagara and evaluate models on the use of space and social organization within a complex urban site.

Ceramic Use and Activity Distribution: Discussion

Ceramics, like other classes of material culture, can be studied at a variety of levels: as formal abstractions, as artistic statements and stylistic messages, as chronological markers, and as tools or objects with particular uses. A concern with the use of goods is essential to understanding what humans did in the past, their behaviors and activities. An understanding of the use of goods is also key to examining the broader role of objects in human societies, in expressing social relations, in productive systems, and in political or religious contexts. In this section, I have examined two studies that explicitly examine ceramic use, with an interest in documenting the range of activities that occurred in past communities involving ceramics and the distribution of those activities within settlements. General aspects of ceramic use will also be considered throughout this book, as we examine other kinds of anthropological questions that archaeologists may approach through the study of ceramics.

CERAMIC PRODUCTION AND DISTRIBUTION

A primary concern of many archaeological studies is with the nature and organization of various economic systems—how societies meet their subsistence and other material needs. The production of utilitarian goods, such as ceramics, figures importantly in these concerns. Changes in the scale and organization of ceramic production have, in turn, been used to evaluate changes in political and social organization in prehistoric societies.

Along with studies of production systems, a second important focus in the study of ancient economies concerns how finished goods are distributed by their producers and acquired by their users. Are goods made and used by the same individuals, or are they made by some people and then used by others? As with ceramic production, the scale and organization of ceramic distribution systems vary considerably between societies and over time and provide a fruitful avenue of research for considering the nature and changes in economic systems, as well as political, and social structures.

Ceramic Production

Ceramic production systems exhibit considerable variation ranging from simple small-scale household-level production to much more complex large-scale production systems. Van der Leeuw (1977) has presented a

TABLE 5.3. The Organization of Ceramic Production

Productive system	Description
Household production	Small-scale production for use within individual households
Household industry	Production at household level for use beyond household consumption
Workshop industry	Increased scale and efficiency of production by specialist producers, often in relatively small-scale family workshops
Large-scale industry	Production on massive scale, employing large numbers of workers, highly specialized

useful typology outlining various levels in the organization of ceramic production as known from ethnographic and archaeological documentation (see Table 5.3). At the simplest level in his framework is *household production*, in which members of each household produce vessels for their own use. Such patterns are believed to have existed throughout much of prehistory in the southwestern United States, where pottery was produced by the women of the household, and may have held for many small-scale, nonhierarchical pottery-making societies throughout the world.

In household production, pottery is typically handmade and fired in the open, a relatively simple technology with little investment in raw materials, tools, or permanent facilities. In addition, pottery manufacture is periodic. A household's yearly needs for ceramic vessels can be satisfied in a relatively short period of time. Even in such a system, it is likely that pottery did move beyond the boundaries of the household, as containers for other materials, or as gifts, parts of dowries, or in exchange for other goods.

The second level of production described by van der Leeuw is the *household industry*. In this system, ceramics are still produced at the level of the household, though much of the production is oriented toward trade or sale beyond the household. The potters are not full-time specialists, and pottery making generally supplements agricultural activities or other sources of income. However, pottery is produced in larger quantities than in the first level, and pottery production takes place more frequently. The technology of ceramic production remains relatively simple and time-consuming. Household industries may emerge under a number of conditions. Widows or nonmarried women may become part-time specialists in order to generate necessary income (Balfet 1981), or members of households that lack access to sufficient good agricultural land may specialize in pottery production in order to supplement limited agricultural returns (Arnold 1985:226).

The third level of ceramic production defined by van der Leeuw is marked by the emergence of specialists who work virtually full-time at pottery production. This is a *workshop industry*, characterized by an increased scale and efficiency of production, typically involving major changes in ceramic technology. Vessels may be wheel- or mold-made. Both technologies permit the production of large quantities of vessels in a short period of time. Firing technology is also improved with the introduction of permanent ovens or kilns. Pottery is produced more or less year-round, with the exception of rainy seasons, and is distributed through markets, middlemen, or directly from the workshop. Because pottery making is a regular activity and there is incentive to produce many vessels, vessels can be expected to become increasingly standardized, as potters attempt to minimize time and energy invested per vessel.

Workshops are typically family enterprises; potters include both male and female members of a nuclear or extended family. Changes in the sexual division of pottery-making activities occur with the emergence of workshop industries. Ethnographic studies indicate that females are typically the major ceramic producers in the household production and household industries, whereas in workshop industries, males typically are the primary laborers. This is particularly true of work on the potter's wheel, which is often a male domain in workshop industries, whereas women work at other tasks such as hand building, firing, or gathering raw materials.

The last level in van der Leeuw's framework is the *large-scale industry*. This system of ceramic production is characterized by workshops or factories that employ large numbers of people and produce vessels on a massive scale. Production is full-time and large-scale investment in drying chambers and kilns minimizes the effects of rainfall and climate on the scheduling of production activities. Ceramics are extremely standardized, and productive technology is highly refined and highly specialized.

The broad classification of scales of organization of ceramic production is a useful framework in which to view ceramic manufacture. Other productive systems may exist, and van der Leeuw has discussed itinerant potters as one such example. This classification is not an explanatory framework for considering transitions from one production system to another. Such transitions must be viewed from the perspective of the political, social, and economic organization of the society under study. Nonetheless, the classification of ceramic production does seem to describe the most common modes of organization of ceramic production systems as known from worldwide ethnographic studies (see also Kramer 1985) and provides a general framework for viewing prehistoric, protohistoric, and historic systems of ceramic production.

The organization and scale of ceramic production has some very important implications for the nature of the finished products that we recover archaeologically. When pottery production is at the level of the household, vessels are typically simple in form, produced by coiling or other hand-building methods, and fired in open fires at relatively low temperatures. Because pottery manufacture in such industries is periodic, with vessels produced at certain times of the year or when needed by the household, there is a fair amount of variation in vessel shape and other attributes from year to year. The clay and tempering materials used by household potters are likely to be those locally available at little or no cost to the potters.

As the scale and frequency of ceramic production increases, so will the impetus for more sophisticated techniques for vessel production and firing. The introduction of the potter's wheel or, especially, of molds will lead to increased standardization of the final products. Increased frequency of manufacture may also encourage standardization, as it is more efficient to produce many identical or nearly identical vessels than to make each vessel unique. In addition, the range and variability of these standardized types may increase, as ceramics come to play increasingly important roles in daily life and as market or other demands become important to workshop survival and success. In order to fire larger numbers of vessels more efficiently, permanent firing facilities, such as kilns or ovens, may be introduced. Such facilities, in turn, generate higher firing temperatures and more efficient transmission of heat, resulting in well-fired vessels.

Innovations in production and firing techniques place constraints on the raw materials that can be used in vessel manufacture. The introduction of the potter's wheel, in particular, imposes limitations on the quality of clays and tempers that can be used. The potter's wheel is a very efficient tool, with which a proficient potter can form vessels in just a few minutes. Not all clays are suited to wheel-throwing, however, and potters must become more selective in the clays they use. In addition, more attention must be devoted to clay and temper preparation, as the presence of large nonplastic inclusions in a vessel wall can result in the vessel being torn apart on the wheel, due to the friction of the force of the wheel against the potter's hands.

Successful kiln firing requires the use of good quality, hot-burning fuels, that is, wood or coal, that must also be acquired by the potters. In contrast, low-burning fuels such as dung or brush are quite effective in open or pit firing. The effects of higher firing temperatures on finished vessels are readily observable in vessel hardness, chemical transformations of clay and tempering minerals, and degree of vessel oxidation.

Even in the absence of direct archaeological traces of pottery manufacture, such as firing or workshop facilities and implements, it may therefore be possible to argue back from the vessels themselves to the techniques that produced them, and in turn, to develop some reasonable expectations concerning the organization of ceramic production. The organization of ceramic or other craft production is not independent of the sociopolitical and economic contexts of the society in which the vessels are produced. The emergence of craft specialization, for example, has been linked to the ability of a society to produce an agricultural surplus to support non-agriculturalist segments of the population (Arnold 1976; Rice 1981).

It has been argued by Foster (1965), Arnold (1985), and others that specialized ceramic production often emerges in agricultural societies under conditions of population pressure. In such cases, they have proposed that specialists would arise from groups that occupied marginal agricultural lands and relied on supplementary income derived from ceramic manufacture and sale to meet their subsistence needs. Other factors such as the size and density of the consuming population, the nature and regulation of distribution and transportation channels, the valuation of ceramics and alternative vessel materials as well as social, ideological, and political factors may also condition or determine the nature and organization of ceramic production systems.

Ceramic production, as we have seen, can be organized in many ways and at a variety of scales. It should be noted that different scales and systems of production can coexist within a single society (see Santley *et al.* 1989). Balfet (1981), in a study of ceramic manufacture in contemporary North Africa, has documented the coexistence of three very different ceramic production systems. These are (1) household-level production, conducted by women to meet household needs; (2) household industries, with vessels produced by women with a view to regular trade within a village; and (3) workshop industries, with vessels produced by male specialists for wide distribution. The forms of vessels and the technology of their production vary for each production system. The household-level pots are handmade and differ in form from village to village; the household industry pots are made of higher quality clays and are more standardized in form; and the workshop industry vessels are wheel-made, are fired at higher temperatures and tend to be restricted to jugs and dishes. A household in the area will typically contain vessels produced in all three contexts, as well as vessels from major artisan centers (large-scale industries). The existence of multiple ceramic production systems has also been documented archaeologically in this region (Myers 1984).

The coexistence of multiple production systems can endure at more or less constant levels for long periods of time. In addition, the relative importance of one or another system of production can change over time. If, for example, trade routes or traditional market systems are disrupted and products of specialists can no longer be distributed, household production and household industries may become increasingly important. The existence of multiple modes of ceramic production, then, provides a highly flexible ceramic production system that can be studied through archaeological remains.

Archaeological studies of ceramic production can call on several lines of evidence. Included among these are direct traces of pottery manufacture (Stark 1985). Such traces include the remains of kilns or ovens. Materials frequently associated with firing areas include large numbers of misfired or overfired vessels, or "wasters," often blistered or warped, and kiln furniture—pieces of highly fired clay forms (saggars) placed between vessels to prevent them from sticking together during firing and to permit the flow of air between vessels in the firing chamber. Large deposits of ash from firings may also be present. The discovery of firing areas is most likely to occur when pottery production was at a fairly large scale, such as in workshop industries or large-scale industries. In household production, firing usually takes place in the open without permanent facilities and leaves little easily identifiable trace in the archaeological record.

Probable areas of vessel forming are more difficult to identify than large-scale firing areas. Recovery of molds, large deposits of raw materials, or pottery-making tools, such as stone anvils, wheel sockets or axles, and decorative stamps may be used to identify production areas. As noted earlier, additional indirect evidence on the organization of ceramic production may be inferred from the vessels themselves, including evidence for production techniques, firing temperature, and standardization.

Ceramic Distribution

Along with variation in the organization of ceramic production, considerable variation can exist in the ways in which ceramics are distributed and the distances that they are transported. The study of distribution systems is of great interest to archaeologists concerned with the nature of interaction between different cultural groups, including the study of diffusion and exchange systems. Distribution systems internal to a single cultural system may also be examined, with a focus on such topics as the presence or absence of centralized control of ceramic distribution in early states or the development of market systems (see Chapter 7). The study of ceramic distribution involves, first, identifying the source of the vessel, either the workshop or the region in which it was produced, and second, examining mechanisms by which it may have reached its ultimate destination.

Sourcing ceramics may be accomplished on stylistic grounds or by studying technological attributes, including clay and temper mineralogy. Methods such as neutron activation or x-ray spectroscopy can be used to characterize clays from various regions and to identify the probable sources of vessels, provided that sufficient regional variation in clays and tempers exists. Petrographic analysis can be used to identify regionally distinctive tempering materials. Macroscopic variation in ware color and paste consistency may also be used in some cases to identify probable locations of ceramic production.

The identification of distinctive regional, intraregional, or even individual ceramic styles may also provide evidence on the general location of pottery production. Both decorative treatment and vessel form may be distinctive to occupants of a particular region, and their presence outside of their core area indicates some sort of contact between regions. This contact may take the form of trade or gift-giving, or local imitation of nonlocal or exotic wares. Local imitations of exotic wares may be identified through chemical techniques, as well as microscopic or macroscopic studies of raw materials and construction techniques.

Within their region of production, ceramic vessels may be (1) used where they were produced; (2) sold or traded directly from production sites for use within or between communities in which they were produced; and (3) transported to and sold at weekly markets by the potters themselves, by middlemen, or by merchant groups. Because the ceramics are both bulky and breakable, transportation of large numbers of vessels over long distances is not very common. Foster has suggested that 150 miles is the maximum distance that pots will be transported in traditional economies (1965:56). Typically the distance is far less than the 150 miles range, though there are archaeologically documented cases for much greater movement as well. The mode of transportation also affects the distances ceramics may travel. For example, where water transportation is possible, pots may be transported greater distances than when they must be moved overland on the backs of draft animals or humans (Nicklin 1971; Ellen and Glover 1974).

Ceramic vessels sometimes are moved considerably beyond the bounds of their immediate area of production and primary use. It is probably fairly uncommon that vessels in and of themselves are objects of long-distance trade, except in contexts where the vessels are valuable objects, as indicators of status or ritual objects. Ceramic vessels may, however, serve as containers for materials that are traded long distances, such as oils, spices, wine, and so on. In such cases, vessels containing these materials may travel considerable distances; witness, for example, the Roman amphorae that are found throughout the extent of the Roman empire and beyond its bounds (Williams 1981 and later discussion).

Ceramic Production and Distribution: Case Studies

Many archaeological studies of the organization of ceramic production or distribution have been concerned with placing ceramic systems into a broader social or political framework. Some examples of these will be considered in subsequent sections. In this section, I wish to consider four studies that focus exclusively on aspects of ceramic production or exchange. These are (1) a study by van der Leeuw of ceramic production in Neolithic Europe; (2) research by Bondioli, Kenoyer, Pracchia, Shar, Tosi, and Vidale on ceramic production in the Harappan civilization of the Indus Valley region of South Asia; (3) work by Fulford, Riley, Williams, and Young on long-distance trade of Roman ceramics; and (4) research by Davidson, McKerrel, Watson, and LeBlanc on production and exchange of Halaf ceramics in northern Mesopotamia during the sixth millennium B.C. These studies represent just a few examples of work on ceramic production and exchange in archaeological contexts.

Neolithic Beaker Manufacture

Van der Leeuw's reconstruction (1976) of the production of Neolithic beakers from The Netherlands focused not on remains of production sites but on the vessels themselves and the traces they reveal of techniques involved in their production. Beakers are characteristic vessel forms of the Western European Neolithic. They are tall slender vessels with an "hour-glasslike" profile (see Figure 5.7). Beakers have received considerable attention in the European archaeological literature (see Clarke 1970, 1979) because of their ubiquity and widespread uniformity.

Several different beaker types have been defined on the basis of decorative treatment and vessel morphology in the Netherlands. These types are believed to be chronologically significant. Van der Leeuw was interested in documenting whether these chronological changes in Beaker form represent changes in the tradition of pottery making or if there was long-term continuity in pottery-making techniques and in vessel form over time. He defines a ceramic tradition as a consistent approach to vessel manufacture that endures over a relatively long time period with only minor modifications and improvements.

In his study, van der Leeuw first attempted to identify pottery-making techniques for 140 individual vessels that included representatives of the various beaker classes defined by traditional typologies (including Bell Beakers [BB], Protruding Foot Beakers [PFB], All-Over Ornamented Beakers [AOO], Maritime Bell Beakers [MBB], and Funnel-Necked Beakers [FNB]). He found that the traditional typologies, although encoding legiti-

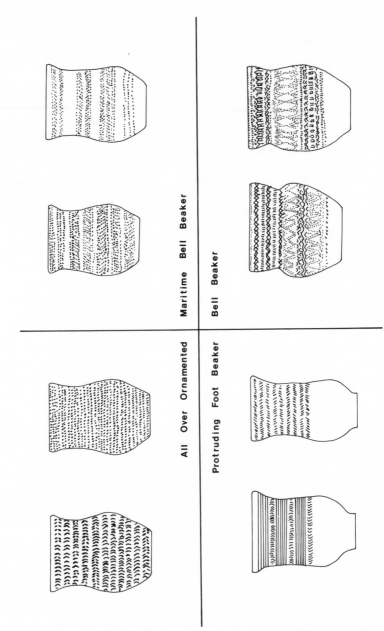

FIGURE 5.7. Neolithic beakers: the Netherlands (after Harrison 1980:16).

mate variation in vessel morphology or decoration, did not record patterns of pottery manufacture and were not adequate for his technological approach.

All of the beakers that van der Leeuw examined were formed using two major construction techniques: The pinching technique, used for forming the vessel bases, and the coiling technique, used in building the upper parts of the vessels. The use of these techniques poses problems for potters seeking to construct tall and narrow vessels. The main difficulty is the potential for sagging of vessel walls and distortion of the base during the coiling stages. Difficulties can also arise when coils are joined; these include distortions caused when the segments are pressed together, as well as differential shrinkage rates of base and coil segments. Van der Leeuw identified a number of strategies that potters could take to respond to these problems and then looked to see how they were resolved in the beaker groups.

He identified two primary techniques that were used by the Neolithic potters to prevent vessel sagging. The first involved wrapping the vessels with string during construction to provide support while building up vessel walls. The second technique involved building thick-walled vessels that did not sag and then scraping them with flint scrapers after they had partially dried. Both techniques left distinctive and easily identifiable traces on finished vessels, either the impressions of the string wrapping, or the marks of the flint scrapers. Although variations in each technique were observed, these did not correspond with traditional typological categories. Wrapping and scraping were not mutually exclusive approaches but instead occurred on all six common beaker forms.

Van der Leeuw therefore concluded that only one regional tradition of beaker making had existed in the Netherlands, with two co-occurring manufacturing techniques. The traditional typological categories developed by archaeologists do not result from different manufacturing techniques and cultural traditions but do in fact record chronological development within a single regional tradition. Van der Leeuw's study of Dutch Neolithic beakers thus provides information both on how these vessels were produced and permits the identification of a regional tradition of ceramic manufacture that endured for perhaps as long as a millennium and persisted through a sequence of stylistic changes in vessel form and decoration.

Harappan Pottery Production

The Harappan or Indus Valley civilization dates to the second half of third millennium B.C. and was the first state-level society of South Asia.

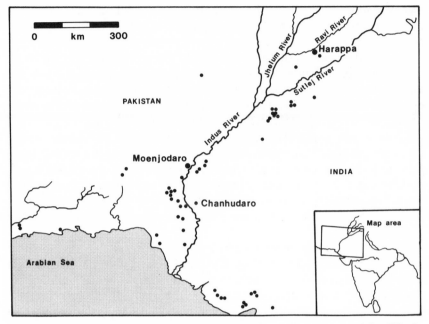

FIGURE 5.8.   The Indus River Valley and distribution of some Harappan sites (after Wheeler 1947:58).

Large numbers of sites are known from this period, and Harappan sites are found throughout Pakistan and northern India (see Figure 5.8). Most Harappan sites are relatively small, villages and towns, though a number of large urban centers are also known. Much archaeological research has focused on the best known of the urban centers, the sites of Harappa and Moenjodaro, as well as at a number of smaller town sites, including the site of Chanhudaro. It is from these three sites that some of the clearest evidence of Harappan craft production has been recovered.

Recent studies of pottery and other craft production at these Indus Valley urban centers have focused on the spatial distribution of production areas, rather than on the technology of production. These studies by Kenoyer, Pracchia, Shar, Tosi, Vidale, and others have examined surface remains of production activities from these third-millennium-B.C. urban centers. For ceramic production, indicators of production loci consist primarily of large quantities of misfired or overfired sherds, kiln furniture (including saggars placed between vessels and blistered or vitrified bricks that were part of the kilns themselves), vitrified pottery drops, and ash.

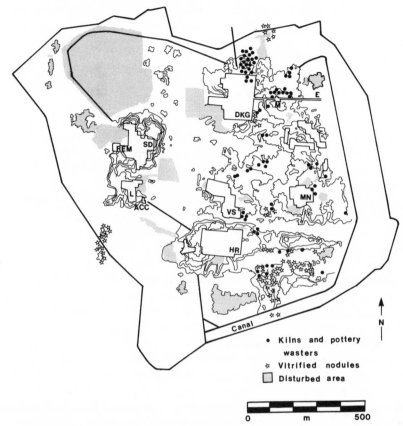

FIGURE 5.9.   Ceramic production areas at Moenjodaro (after Vidale 1989:173).

Recently, the remains of a number of superimposed pottery-making kilns have been identified at Harappa, adding considerably to our knowledge of the nature and continuity in ceramic production at that site.

At Moenjodaro, ceramic workshops were found across the surface of the site (see Figure 5.9). One region, however, located in area DK-G at the northern end of the site, showed a very dense cluster of ceramic production areas and may have been a "craft quarter" of some sort. Along with the construction of ceramic vessels, other fired clay objects including clay bangles were also produced by craftspeople working in this quarter. Other craft activities including shell working and steatite working were also found in this area. Given the large scale and diversity of production in this area of the site as contrasted to much smaller scale and more specialized craft-producing activities in other areas of Moenjodaro, the researchers have proposed that the DK-G area was an area where craft production occurred under the direct supervision and sanctioning of the Harappan ruling elite.

Twenty-nine distinct loci of craft production were identified from surface remains at the Harappan site of Chanhudaro. Extensive evidence of brick and pottery production was found on Mound I at the site. Traces of shell working, stone bead manufacture, steatite, and faience manufacture were also found at various locations. Ceramic manufacture was, however, much more common on Mound I than elsewhere, and ceramic manufacture appears to have been a major activity of the occupants of that area. Few finished products were found associated with the workshop areas, so it is difficult to say whether these workshops specialized in particular classes of ceramic vessels or produced a broad array of Harappan vessel forms (see Figure 5.10). The report of the 1935–1936 excavations by Mackay (1943) is silent on this important question.

Although extensive excavations were carried out at Moenjodaro and Chanhudaro, these were mostly conducted in the 1920s and 1930s when archaeological research in the region was primarily concerned with reconstructing chronological sequences and identifying links between the Indus and the early states of the Near East. Despite the identification of production areas, the excavators recorded little information on craft production or ceramic forms from these sites. Recent analyses of surface remains such as those described are providing important information to help in expanding our understanding of Harappan ceramic production. Although surface remains can provide much information on the spatial distribution of ceramic production activities and on the scale of production, they are less useful in examining chronological developments in productive organization.

Recent excavations of a number of stratified pottery kilns at the urban site of Harappa have provided important information on ceramic production throughout the occupation of the site. Multiple levels of superimposed kilns indicate that production locales remained in use throughout the occupation of the city, and at that site at least, "craft quarters" endured for generations, and perhaps, centuries (Kenoyer 1989a). The kilns are located in what is believed to be the nonelite residential zone known as Mound E (see Figure 5.11). Only a limited number of pottery types have been found in these production areas, indicating that the Harappan potters specialized in producing certain types of vessels. The kilns from Harappa are relatively small and do not seem to occur in large clusters or associated with central buildings or facilities. Kenoyer has therefore proposed that at Harappa ceramic production was most likely organized at a relatively small scale,

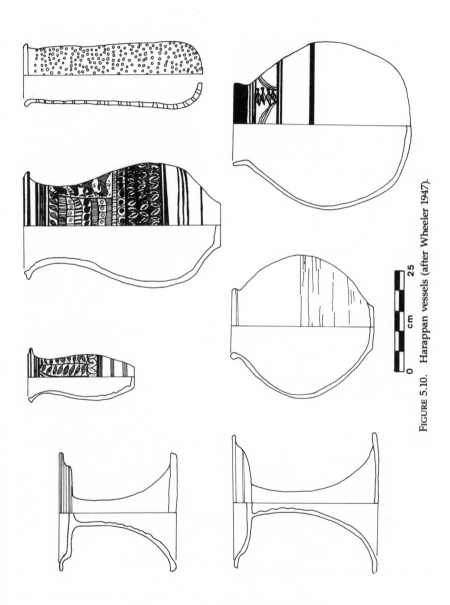

FIGURE 5.10. Harappan vessels (after Wheeler 1947).

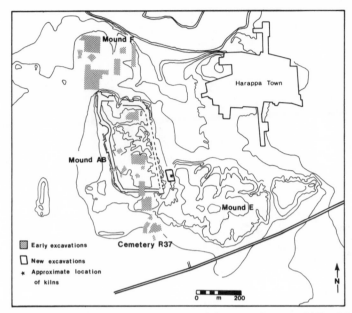

FIGURE 5.11.   Plan of Harappa showing approximate location of excavated kilns (after Dales and Kenoyer 1988). Reprinted by permission of G. Dales, University of California at Berkeley.

in van der Leeuw's terms as a household industry without large-scale supervision or control (also Wright 1989:153).

The identification of loci of craft production in Harappan period sites, their relation to architectural features and their location in urban settlements, provide useful indicators on a number of aspects of ceramic production. These include the scale of ceramic or other craft production, the links between craft production and administrative or religious structures and activities, and the degree to which craft producers and their activities were spatially separated from other societal segments. In addition, as recent regional surveys have demonstrated, along with production within major settlements, Harappan ceramics were also produced in isolated factory or production sites (see Mughal 1972, 1980, 1982). Such sites, in their very existence, imply the existence of some sort of effective transportation and distribution network to distribute their products.

Roman Ceramic Distribution

Studies of archaeological ceramics from the Roman empire, from the second century B.C. to the third century A.D., have revealed the existence of long-distance trade in a variety of ceramic classes. A number of lines of

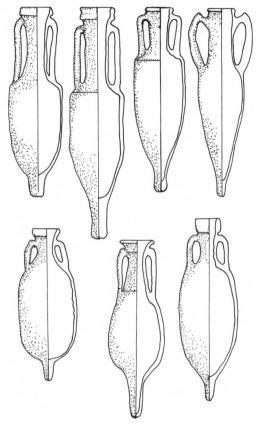

FIGURE 5.12.   Roman amphorae (after Williams 1981:124). Reprinted by permission.

evidence have been called upon to identify production areas, including the identification of workshop-specific stamps, vessel morphology, studies of ceramic petrology, and elemental analyses of clay and temper mineralogy.

One of the most common classes of Roman vessels that moved throughout the empire is the amphora. Amphorae are large narrow jars with conical or rounded bases and two vertical strap handles (see Figure 5.12). These were thick-walled sturdy vessels, used to transport olive oil, wine, fish oil, and fish products by ship throughout the empire (Williams 1981:123). Different types of amphorae that appear to have been produced in distinctive areas are identifiable on the basis of vessel morphology and paste composition. A number of amphorae kilns have been found in Italy; others are known from Spain, France, and Greece.

Within these broadly defined regional types, it has sometimes been possible to identify the products of individual workshops. For example, a number of vessels of a common first-century-B.C. amphora type are distinguished by the stamped inscription "SESTIUS," and can be traced to an estate owned by an individual of that name in Cosa, Italy. These amphorae are found throughout Europe and presumably were used to transport the products of Sestius's estate. The widespread distribution of these vessels is indicative of large-scale surplus production and distribution by individual estates during this period (Riley 1984:67). Neutron activation studies of clay sources from known kilns in Europe and amphorae recovered in North Africa (Tripolitana) also indicate estate production of vessels and estate-initiated long-distance trade (Riley 1984).

In a study of amphorae distribution throughout late Iron Age pre-Roman Britain, Williams (1981) has employed morphological and petrological data to examine changing production areas and trade routes. He uses this information to relate changes in trade routes to changing political situations in Rome, Britain, and Continental Europe. Prior to the first century A.D., virtually all amphorae found in England were produced in Italy or Greece. These types are also common in Northwest Europe, modern Germany, Belgium, and France, and the major transportation routes appear to have been along the Rhine River. Subsequently, Spanish vessels appear in greater quantities, particularly along the south–central coast of England, indicating an increased emphasis on maritime trade. Differences in the forms of amphorae found throughout Britain provide evidence for differences in the items traded to different areas of preconquest Britain; that is, Spanish fish paste and Italian wine amphorae cluster in eastern Britain in the early first century A.D., whereas to the west, wine amphorae produced in northern Spain are more common.

Other forms of vessels also traveled considerable distances throughout the Roman Empire, often as objects of trade in themselves, rather than as containers. For example, certain handmade cooking vessels found throughout the central Mediterranean have been sourced to the island of Pantelleria, south of Sicily, through petrological and neutron activation analyses of their distinctive ware (Peacock 1981:189; Riley 1984:61). Fine wares also traveled considerable distances during the Roman period and appear to have moved primarily along major supply routes for other commodities from a number of distinct production centers (Riley 1981:137). Studies of ceramic distributions during the Roman Empire, then, have proved useful in identifying trade routes, considering the organization of production and trade of ceramics and other materials, and examining changing political and social boundaries throughout the vast Roman Empire.

FIGURE 5.13. Halaf ceramics (after Mallowan 1936). Reprinted by permission.

Halaf Ceramic Distribution

The Halaf period in northern Mesopotamia (6000–4800 B.C.) is characterized by its finely made and elaborately decorated ceramics (see Figure 5.13; Frankel 1979). Halaf sites date to the early sixth millennium B.C. and are found from northern Iraq to eastern Turkey (see Figure 5.14). Halaf settlements were villages that ranged in size from 2 to 12 hectares and were characterized by a wheat–barley, sheep–goat–cattle subsistence base. Watson and LeBlanc have classified Halaf social organization as that of a simple chiefdom (1973). The widespread similarity found in Halaf ceramic forms and design motifs throughout the region has led to a concern with identifying the organization of ceramic production and the nature of ceramic distribution during the period.

The examination of ceramic decoration and the occurrences of individual motifs and design layouts from samples from seven major sites reveals a great deal of uniformity across the region (Watson and LeBlanc 1973). In their study, Watson and LeBlanc were unable to define any distinctive geographical boundaries across the Halaf area in the occurrence of different motifs, although they did identify variation in the quality and diversity of ceramics between sites. They proposed that trade in ceramics contributed to their widespread uniformity. Recently, attempts have been made to test this proposition. Davidson and McKerrel (1976) have conducted neu-

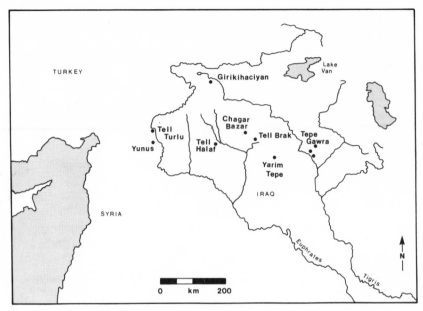

FIGURE 5.14.   Distribution of Halaf sites (after Frankel 1979:1). Reprinted by permission of British Museum Publications, Ltd.

tron activation analyses of Halaf ceramics from the sites of Tell Halaf, Tell Brak, and Tell Chagar Bazar, as well as from six unexcavated sites. The goal of their work was to determine the number of compositionally distinct Halaf wares found at each site. Samples of clays found near Tell Chagar Bazar and Tell Halaf were also analyzed.

Two broad compositional groups were identified through cluster analyses of values generated by the neutron activation analysis. The first group includes nearly all of the Chagar Bazar sherds and the local clay, as well as sherds from five of the six unexcavated sites. Sherds from Tell Halaf and its local clay source formed the second cluster that also included some sherds from other sites, including some from Chagar Bazar. The analysis of Halaf ceramics conducted by Davidson and McKerrel thus serves to identify two centers of pottery production, at Tell Halaf and Chagar Bazar, both relatively large Halaf sites, and also helps to define, to some extent, the scale of ceramic distribution.

Ceramic Production and Distribution: Discussion

Each of the four studies discussed in the section have examined various aspects of ceramic production and distribution in differing archaeological contexts. Van der Leeuw's work was concerned with the identification of a regional tradition of a pottery-making tradition; the Harappan work was concerned with location of production locales; the work on Roman pottery was concerned with the nature of Roman ceramic exchange, and work on the Halaf ceramics is concerned with both locations of production and the extent of ceramic distribution.

As documentary studies, each of the cases presented is a valuable example of an approach to the study of ceramic production and movement. More importantly, each study went further than the documentation of production techniques or distance from sources. Each attempted to relate the observed patterns to the broader sociological, economic, or political conditions that produced them.

SUGGESTED READINGS

Some additional references on archaeological approaches to ceramic use include Braun (1980a), Dunnell and Hunt (1990), Hall *et al.* 1990; Hally (1986), Mills (1989), Patrick *et al.* (1985), Rothschild-Boros (1981), Steponaitis (1983), and Vitelli (1989). For reference on activity areas, see Binford (1976); Binford *et al.* (1970); Yellen (1977). Discussions of site-formation processes include Schiffer (1976, 1985); Gifford (1981); Gifford-Gonzales *et al.* (1985). Assemblage formation and diversity is discussed in Kintigh (1984) and Leonard and Jones (eds.) (1989). Additional references on Vijayanagara ceramics include Sinopoli (1986, 1991, in press).

Some general references on ceramic production and distribution systems include Howard and Morris (1981), Plog (1980:Chapter 5), and van der Leeuw and Pritchard (1984). Additional sources on European Neolithic Beakers include Clarke (1970, 1976); Harrison (1980); and Mercer (1977). Studies of Harappan craft specialization include Bondioli, Tosi, and Vidale (1984), Pracchia, Tosi, and Vidale (1985), Halim and Vidale (1983), and Vidale (1989) at Moenjodaro (see also Kenoyer [1983] on bead making, and Vidale [1987] on steatite working), Kenoyer and Dales at Harappa (Kenoyer 1989a, 1989b), and Shar and Vidale (n.d.) at Chanhudaro. For information on Roman amphorae production and trade, see also Dyson (1976), Grace (1961), Peacock (1971, 1977), Riley (1981), Rothschild-Boros (1981). Additional sources on the Halaf include Akkermans (1987), Dabagh (1986), Mallowan (1936).

Using Ceramics to Answer Questions

III. Ceramics and Social Organization

Ceramics, like all material products of human activity, are used and produced in a social context. Individuals learn techniques of ceramic production from parents or other relatives, or from employers, and tend to replicate, to a greater or lesser extent, the production techniques and products of their teachers. Potters produce for consumers and make vessels in accordance with the demands of their users: demands for functionally effective and formally appropriate vessels. Culturally conditioned opinions on the appropriate form of ceramics or other objects ultimately determine whether new forms will be accepted or rejected and contribute to the historic continuity of particular forms over multiple generations. Goods, then, are produced in a system of meaning that governs definitions of appropriate forms, techniques, and use, as well as the assignment of value. Over the past two decades, a number of cultural anthropologists and archaeologists have considered goods in their social context and have produced both general theoretical frameworks for viewing material culture and specific tests of these frameworks in archaeological or ethnographic contexts.

CERAMICS IN THEIR SOCIAL CONTEXT

Early archaeological studies of ceramics and social organization, including works by Deetz (1965), Hill (1970), Longacre (1968, 1970), and

Whallon (1968, 1969), looked at vessels as the passive outcome of social
conditions. Each of these studies examined data from agricultural societies
in North America: the Arikara of the Central Plains, two pueblo societies of
the Southwest, and the Iroquois of the northeastern United States, respec-
tively. In each study, the researchers assumed, using ethnographic analogies to later potting communities, that pottery making was a household
industry and that the women of each household produced vessels for their
own use. Second, it was assumed that traditions and techniques of pottery
making were passed on from mother to daughter and that the latter became
habituated to and continually replicated particular productive techniques
and decorative styles.

Given this framework, the authors proposed that the products of
lineally related females would be more like each other than would pots
produced by nonrelated women or women related through marriage. The
greater the intensity and duration of interaction between potters, these
studies argue, the greater the similarity between the products (Whallon
1969:15). Spatial clusters of similar ceramics within sites or between sites
are thus assumed to result from clusters of coresident women who shared
the same learning contexts, implying matrilocal residence patterns.

The studies by Hill, Longacre, Deetz, and Whallon were extremely
important in fostering the recognition that ceramics could be used to
consider intra- and intersite social variation, that there could be more to
ceramic analysis than defining regional culture areas or chronological
sequences. In many respects, their work laid the groundwork for a large
number of later archaeological studies concerned with the relation between
material forms and social organization; they also stimulated a number of
important ethnographic studies of ceramic production and use. These
early studies have been criticized on a number of grounds (see Plog 1976,
1980), including, in some cases, the inappropriate use of certain analytical
techniques, lack of attention to archaeological contexts, and more importantly, for their overly simplistic assumptions concerning the transmission
of knowledge of ceramic manufacture.

Ethnographic studies of the transmission of the pottery craft in societies where pottery making is a household industry have demonstrated
that potters absorb influences from many sources and learn from many
individuals. Although certain aspects of pottery manufacture and decoration may be conditioned by learning contexts (as, for example, how one
holds a brush or other tools, or microcharacteristics of design application
and form), potters are typically very conscious of the forms their products
take and are very much in control of their products. Thus spatial clusters of
similar ceramics need not result from the presence of closely related potters. Potters can and do readily alter the form and style of their products for

a broad range of reasons, both economic and cultural. Potters, therefore, must be seen as active transmitters and transformers of their craft rather than as passive recipients of traditional knowledge.

Changes have occurred, too, in how goods themselves are perceived. In particular, goods have come to be viewed by a number of scholars as encoding and conveying meaning about the social, symbolic, and ideological order in which they are used. Thus goods are not neutral products of ingrained learned behavior but are produced by conscious actors working in specific social and symbolic contexts. The symbolic importance of goods is readily recognizable in contemporary contexts; clothing styles, house forms, jewelry, the foods one eats, and numerous other categories of goods convey information on the social or economic position of their user or on the image that the user wishes to convey.

"Goods," write Douglas and Isherwood, "are needed for making visible and stable the categories of culture" (1979:59). Even the simplest of cultures has, of course, a great many social categories, with a large number of multilayered sets of social relations. It is, therefore, not adequate to say simply that material culture participates in the definition and reinforcement of social relations. Different classes of goods and their specific contexts of production, distribution, use, and valuation must be considered independently in order to assess at what level they might be expected to convey and represent social relations, and what sort of relations they might convey or obscure.

Turning specifically to ceramics, consideration of the symbolic or significatory role of ceramics in specific contexts must entail the examination of (1) how they were used and the importance of such activities to individuals and society; (2) who would have seen them while they were in use; (3) contexts of production and distribution; and (4) the valuation of ceramic classes in themselves, and relative to nonceramic equivalents of metal, basketry, cloth, and the like.

In the discussion of ceramic production and distribution presented, I have considered distinctions between trade in Roman utilitarian and fineware vessels. These different classes of ceramic vessels were clearly used in very different contexts, and their forms, as well as their occurrence and distribution within and between settlements could be expected to convey very different sorts of social information. Access to highly standardized Roman fine wares, for example, could signify elite status, and its widespread uniformity across the empire may have served to express and reinforce the cohesiveness of the aristocracy throughout that vast polity. Amphorae, on the other hand, showed regional and estate-level variability and also varied in form in accordance with the materials that they transported. Although all amphorae were distinctively Roman, differences among them also expressed spatial and economic divisions within the empire.

Along with distinctions between elite and nonelite wares, vessel use and the context of use are very important to evaluating the degree and nature of social variation in ceramics and their possible potential symbolic content. While ceramic vessels may be put to a wide variety of uses, the major use of ceramics usually involves food—its storage, cooking, or serving. Ceramic forms are consequently associated with, and meaningfully linked to, the specific foods used by members of a society (and these may vary significantly between individuals and groups within that society), the means of food preparation, and the cultural significance of food consumption and sharing.

CERAMICS AND FOOD

Anthropologists from Radcliffe-Brown and Malinowski to Levi-Strauss have considered the centrality of food preparation and consumption and the cultural definition of foodstuffs in the construction of the social order. Cooking practices and rules of commensality are highly ritualized and internalized by individuals. And in food consumption, writes Goody,

> the identity and differentiation of the group is brought out in the practice of eating together or separately, as well as in the content of what is eaten by different collectivities; this is the arena of feasts and fasts, of prohibitions and preferences, of communal and domestic meals, of table manners, and modes of serving and service. (1982:38)

Douglas and Isherwood also see food as a medium for discrimination: of time, daily (breakfast, lunch, dinner), cyclical (feast day, birthday dinners), and life-cycle events (marriages, funerals); and of values, "the more numerous the discriminated ranks, the more varieties of foods needed" (1979:66, also 115; Douglas 1971).

The involvement of vessels in the highly ritualized and meaning-laden food systems of a culture contributes both to the conservatism of vessel forms and to the assignment of symbolic significance to vessels and their use. Thus royalty may eat off of plates of gold and commoners on wooden slabs or banana leaves; the "good china" may be used only on special feast days or to entertain the boss; and disposable plates are appropriate for outdoor picnics. The association of vessels with foods and contexts of use and with the user's status does not only apply to serving vessels but to food-preparation vessels as well. I do not wish to posit a direct correlation between societal complexity or the complexity of a cuisine and food-preparation techniques and complexity in ceramic vessels. Nor does all of the meaning embodied in vessels encode the same kinds or levels of information. In the examples presented, gold or wood plates express rank or status, the use of the "good china" denotes a specific time in the annual cycle, and disposable plates signify a particular kind of meal and dining context.

Yet, I would expect that at a broad scale, some general relations do hold between social complexity and the complexity of the material forms associated with food preparation and consumption, forms that serve to reinforce, define, and symbolize the underlying social order. Goody has noted that because the acquisition and consumption of foods are "linked to the mode of production of material goods, the analysis of cooking has to be related to the distribution of power and authority in the economic sphere, that is to the system of class stratification and its political ramifications" (Goody 1982:37).

It is in the symbolic importance of both food preparation and consumption that the symbolic significance of many classes of ceramic vessels must be situated and assessed. Both the differentiation of foods and of the access to specific foodstuffs and the varying social contexts of preparation and serving affect and determine the nature of the significance of variability in the vessels used. Ceramic vessels are not, however, the only vessels used in ceramic-using societies. Basketry, hide, stone, and various metal vessels may also be used, and the significance of ceramics must be considered relative to the significance and availability of these materials. Such questions are often difficult to approach archaeologically, where baskets and other organic materials are rarely preserved. Stone vessels should be regularly preserved, and metal vessels are also likely to be preserved, though they may often be corroded beyond recognition or, particularly in the case of precious metals, may often be looted and removed from their archaeological context. Even when the relative quantities and the availability of alternative vessels cannot be estimated, it is important to at least remember that they may have been present, that clay was only one of several media used for producing cooking, storage, and serving vessels.

As with rules concerning food sharing and food preparation, the relative ranks of different materials and different ceramic wares (e.g., porcelains vs. earthenwares) may vary contextualy. However, I would expect the valuation of such goods to be subject to some generally applicable rules involving the "cost" of their acquisition or production. Following Pollock (1983b:19–20), more "costly" goods may result from (1) the use of materials that are in limited supply locally or are nonlocal, (2) the care and elaboration involved in the production of the object, and (3) the abundance of the good or some dimension of it (e.g., size).

I have considered thus far only ceramics used in activities involving foodstuffs. Ceramics may be used in a number of other contexts as well, as ritual vessels, perfume holders, well linings, water pipes, dove cotes, and so on. Functional interpretations of such vessels may be approached through a consideration of their morphology and depositional contexts. A consideration of the relevance of varying vessel forms in symbolizing and defining social relations must take into account the nature and significances of the activities in which they were used. For example, the importance of ritual in formally and publicly expressing social positions of various types (male/female, rank, and so on; see Rappaport 1971) would be expected to extend to the material paraphernalia associated with ritual events. Other functional classes of vessels must be similarly considered with respect to their specific contexts of use.

ARCHAEOLOGICAL APPROACHES TO CERAMIC AND SOCIAL PATTERNING

I have attempted to demonstrate that ceramic and other material forms can be expected to encode social information concerning important social distinctions within a society. The context of use of ceramics has been discussed at a very general level, in order to consider the behavioral realms in which ceramics function and the impact that these realms have on ceramic variability. With this general framework in mind, we must now consider how to examine social variation in ceramics using archaeological data. This is a complicated process, involving the construction of numerous bridging arguments, the use of appropriate analytical techniques, and the evaluation of testable propositions.

The analysis of ceramic data in such studies involves, as do all archaeological studies, the recognition of patterns: consistent associations of ceramic classes, spatial clustering within sites, and so on. The assignment of specific meanings to these patterns operates on two levels. The first is an analytical meaning: ceramic cluster A is found in Area C, whereas ceramic cluster B is found only in area D. Differences between ceramic clusters A and B do not appear to be functional (i.e., the same array of general vessel-use forms are found in each cluster, indicating a similar array of activities in each area) or chronological. They can therefore be interpreted as representing meaningful social variation between the occupants of areas C and D.

The second level of meaning is much more difficult, and often impossible, for archaeologists to identify; that is, the meaning that the pottery makers and users assigned to specific symbols, colors, or forms. We can look at the archaeological contexts of material deposition and use and temporal changes in artifact occurrence and distribution in order to develop some abstract framework of "value" and access to and categorization of goods. Such information can then be used to infer much about the social system in which the goods were produced. We cannot, however, precisely define why some symbols were chosen over others, or what they signified to their prehistoric makers and users. The problem of the assignment of meaning is often easier to overcome in historic contexts where written records are available to help resolve these questions, though even here writing is not an unbiased reflection of systems of meaning but is a deliberate and sometimes manipulative recording of particular meanings.

Most studies of ceramics and social organization have focused on painted vessels and design form and structure. The reasons for this are readily apparent. Ceramic decoration is typically highly structured and easily recognized and potentially decodable. Unlike other dimensions of ceramic variability, such as vessel form, decoration belongs solely to the realm of expressive treatment. As noted earlier, within the technological constraints imposed by raw materials and pottery-making techniques, ceramic form is highly flexible. It is reasonable to expect, therefore, that microvariation in rim form, vessel shape, and other morphological characteristics within broad functional groups of vessels might also exhibit meaningful variation.

Because the assignment of meaning to particular attributes is an historical and, to some extent, arbitrary and nonstatic process (or at least one that we do not have direct access to), there can be no exact formula for determining which attributes to study and how to define them in an analysis of social variation in ceramics. While we can develop some general expectations based on criteria of contexts of use and visibility, value, and so on, we must also engage in an analytical process that involves intensive feedback between pattern recognition and interpretation. Analysis should involve a process of (1) developing a theoretical framework in which to view ceramic variability in general and in specific archaeological contexts; (2) identifying patterns or structure in a body of data; (3) evaluating the occurrence of these patterns over space and time and with respect to the underlying analytical framework; and (4) reevaluating and revising, when necessary, both interpretations of the data and the underlying theoretical perspective. The studies to be considered encompass varying theoretical and methodological approaches to ceramic variability and its relation to social variability.

Ceramics and Social Organization: Case Studies

In this section, I will consider four studies that use data on ceramics to consider questions of social organization. Three of them employ archaeological data: from Southwest Iran in the sixth and fifth millennium B.C.;

from the Eastern Woodlands of North America between A.D. 1 and A.D. 600; and from the Dutch Neolithic, 2700–2300 B.C. The fourth study, by Miller, employs ethnographic data on contemporary ceramics from Central India. The analytical methods and approaches to ceramic data employed in each of these studies vary considerably, as do the specific research interests of each scholar. Each, however, is concerned with the role of ceramics in expressing horizontal or vertical social relations within specific archaeological or ethnographic contexts and with what changes in ceramic form and decoration imply about changing social relations.

Susiana Ceramics and Sociopolitical Complexity

Pollock's study of Susiana ceramics from a number of sixth- and fifth-millennium sites on the Susiana Plain in Iran (see Figure 6.1) viewed stylistic variability in ceramic decoration as playing a role in signaling group identification and social group boundaries (1983a). This "information-exchange" approach to style, first explicitly defined by Wobst (1977), sees stylistic variability, like language, as a communications medium. The class of information that Pollock is concerned with is information on sociopolitical organization in emerging chiefly societies.

Pollock first develops a general model for the sorts of changes in stylistic complexity that would occur under two conditions of sociocultural change: (1) increased vertical differentiation of society, that is, differentiation into hierarchically ranked status groups; and (2) increased horizontal differentiation, that is, increased numbers of equivalently ranked, though behaviorally differentiated units. Both of these sorts of changes are characteristic of emergent political complexity—the development of chiefdoms and early states. Pollock proposes that these two forms of differentiation will result in two very different patterns of change in material goods.

With increased vertical complexity, classes of prestige or sumptuary goods are expected to emerge. These goods are characterized by an array of traits indicative of high energy or labor investment in their production and procurement. These include the use of distinctive, often rare or exotic, raw materials of high quality, and elaborate decorative treatment. Prestige goods are qualitatively different than nonprestige goods with equivalent utilitarian functions used by other segments of the society. Changes in horizontal differentiation should, on the other hand, result in stylistic variation that serves to distinguish between functionally equivalent goods, without marked changes in energy investment. Such changes might include introduction of new decorative motifs, new ways of ordering existing motifs, or differences in vessel form.

The Susiana sequence, identified at a number of sites in southwestern

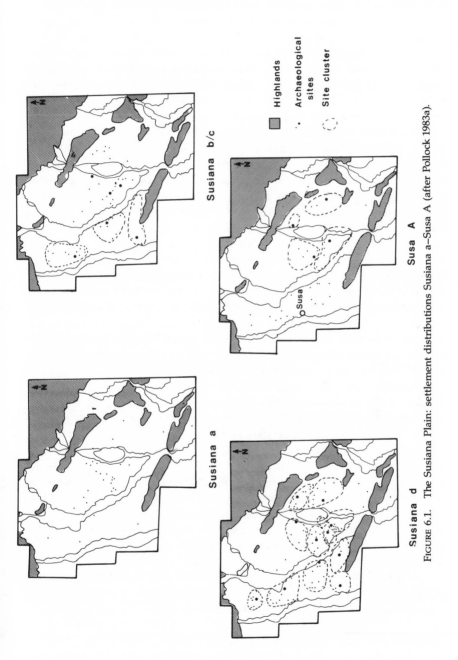

FIGURE 6.1.   The Susiana Plain: settlement distributions Susiana a–Susa A (after Pollock 1983a).

Iran, extends from the late sixth millennium until approximately 4000 B.C. This period, which has been initially divided into five chronological phases, Susiana a–e (Susiana e is also known as Susa A), was a time of fundamental changes in sociopolitical organization and craft and subsistence production. Variations in settlement size, architecture, and burial treatment provide evidence for ranked social differences during this period. Some specialization existed in ceramic production, probably only of elite ceramics, and irrigation agriculture came into use.

Using information on site size and location and analytical techniques drawn from cultural geography (central place analysis and rank size studies; see Johnson 1975, 1977, and Parsons 1972 for discussions of settlement pattern studies), Pollock has proposed the following developmental sequence for the Susiana Plain. During Susiana a, a small simply-organized chiefdom emerged in the center of the plain. During Susiana b–c, the eastern portion of the plain was integrated into a more centralized system, with the site of Chogha Mish emerging as the paramount settlement, whereas to the west were found a number of small clusters of settlements. In Susiana d, a large population increase occurred on the plain, and the polity centering at Chogha Mish fragmented. This period is dominated by the proliferation of many relatively small sites. During the subsequent Susa A period, the site of Susa emerged as a central place, and a large area of the Susiana Plain was integrated into a single polity. The Susiana sequence taken as a whole thus appears to be a time of pronounced changes in vertical and horizontal social integration.

Pollock examined changes in ceramic decoration from a number of Susiana sites. In choosing what class of ceramics to consider, she used information from ethnographic studies of chiefly societies. These studies frequently discuss the importance of food serving on the part of high-ranking figures: in public ceremonies, to laborers, and to high-ranking visitors. Feasting is an important part of chiefly activities that serves to reify and express status relations and the position of the chief as beneficent provider. Ceramic serving vessels may figure importantly in these activities, as well as in hospitality between lower level social groups and individuals. Pollock therefore chose to focus on a class of small serving vessels, decorated bowls that because of their context of use, might be expected to convey social information on status and group membership.

Serving vessels occur in relatively constant frequencies throughout the Susiana sequence, indicating that food-serving activities were important throughout. Using only bowls painted on their exterior, Pollock identified and coded decorative motifs, defined as an element or combination of elements that occur on a spatial division of a vessel. The number of motifs per period ranged from 37 during the Susiana-c phase to 70 during the

Susiana d. The Information Statistic (*H*) and measures of redundancy were used to evaluate design form and complexity in each of the five Susiana phases.

The Information Statistic provides a measure of the variety of distinguishable items or states of an item. Information in this sense is divorced from the concept of meaning and considers only the presence and frequency of alternative physical or expressive states. For example, where all pots are decorated with vertical black lines, no alternative states exist, and the presence of pots with vertical black lines conveys no information. But where some pots are decorated with vertical black lines, others with horizontal black lines, and others with horizontal or vertical red lines, then the alternate occurrence of one or another form does convey information. Whether these alternates are linked to variation in kin groups, religious groups, or so on must be interpreted independently. The Information Statistic is used to compute a measure of the range of distinctions between attributes or attribute states in a body of data, in the context of their frequency of occurrence in that assemblage. The presence of a large number of alternative states of an element form or configuration, and resultant high values of the Information Statistic, is expected to occur under conditions of horizontal differentiation. (The Information Statistic, or *H*, is computed as follows: $H = E\,(p_i \times \log p_i)$, where p_i equals the percentage of items in category i.)

The second measure employed by Pollock is a measure of redundancy. Redundancy refers to the co-occurrence of attributes in specific contexts, such that, for example, attribute a always occurs with attribute c. The presence of attribute a provides no additional stylistic or social information but serves to reinforce the message conveyed by the presence of attribute c. Redundancy thus helps to eliminate doubt about message content and decreases the possibility of misinterpretation. Redundancy is, however, costly, as more labor is invested in adding different attributes without a direct gain in message content. Increased redundancy is therefore expected to be associated with vertical differentiation and increased investments in energy and labor in the production of elite goods.

In her analysis, Pollock computed information and redundancy statistics for ceramic design data from the Susiana subphases (Phases b and c were joined together because of small sample size). Values for redundancy were low in the Susiana-a period, a time of relatively low social integration. They increased during Susiana b–c, a period defined on the basis of settlement pattern data as a time of increasing centralization, and decline again in Period d. During the Susa A period, a new vessel form appears, decorated goblets that appear to be elite vessels. Redundancy values for the goblets and the decorated bowls are very high in this period. The redundancy values, therefore, conform very well with Pollock's interpretation of changing sociopolitical organization derived from settlement pattern studies.

The Information Statistic increases linearly from Susiana a through d, supporting Pollock's interpretation of increased horizontal differentiation and population increases during these periods. The value of the Information Statistic for painted bowls declines slightly in the Susa A period, indicating a decrease in horizontal differentiation in this period of large-scale political centralization and consolidation.

Pollock's study of Susiana ceramics presents a very explicit and sophisticated framework for studying change in the complexity and organization of ceramic design and for relating changes in decorative treatment to broader social and political changes. She approaches ceramic design from an "information exchange" framework. This framework certainly does not encode the way the makers and users of the Susiana vessels classified their pots. It does, however, provide measures of patterns that were of relevance to, and would have been perceived by, Susiana people as they used ceramic vessels in daily and occasional activities. By using only one class of ceramic vessels, Pollock effectively factors out the effects that differing contexts of use and visibility could have on ceramic design and stylistic communication. Settlement pattern data was used to provide an independent measure of changing sociopolitical organization, against which ceramic variability could be assessed.

Middle–Late Woodland Ceramics and Regional Networks

The work of David Braun (1977, 1980b, 1985) on changes in ceramic decoration in the midwestern United States during the period A.D. 1 to A.D. 600 provides another example of the "information exchange" approach to ceramic decoration. This period encompasses the transition from the Middle Woodland ("Hopewell") to the Late Woodland cultural phase. The Hopewell period is characterized by extensive long-distance trade networks; the construction of large earthen burial mounds and earthworks, with evidence for differential treatment of the dead (social ranking); and a distinctive assemblage of material culture, including elaborately decorated ceramics (see Figure 6.2). The Hopewell period was a time of increasing sedentism, increased reliance on an agricultural economy, and population growth.

Some of these trends continued during subsequent Late Woodland phases, following the disappearance of the Hopewell archaeological complex. In particular, population continued to increase, as did sedentism and reliance on agriculture. The material culture of this period differed consid

FIGURE 6.2.   Hopewell vessels (collections of the Museum of Anthropology, University of Michigan).

erably from that of Hopewell, however. A marked decline occurred in ceramic decoration and in the long-distance exchange of nonutilitarian items. Elaborate burials also disappeared in the Late Woodland period. Most scholars of the Middle–Late Woodland transition have argued that the Late Woodland period was a time of social disintegration and fragmentation, as a previously unified social system fragmented into isolated units.

Braun argues against this traditional explanation. He proposes that in a period of increased population densities and reliance on agriculture in an environment characterized by pronounced local fluctuations and patchy distributions of resources, such as occurred in the Late Woodland, it would be critically important to develop and maintain ties with residents of other areas. Such ties, including marriage relations, trading partners, or clan or totemic ties, would provide increased access to distant resources should local ones fail. Braun expects, therefore, that following the Hopewell period, as both population and economic uncertainty increased, so also did the intensity of regional contact and integration.

Braun tests these two models of Late Woodland integration using data on ceramic decoration. Like Pollock, and following Wobst (1977), he takes an information-exchange approach to stylistic variation, viewing ceramic decoration as a visual mode of communication through which social identities were expressed. He proposes a direct relationship between the degree of ceramic design variation over space and time and the degree of social differentiation. The implications of this relationship are, for Braun, that increased local social isolation should produce a reduction in decorative variability within each locality, and an increase in variability between localities, as contact between localities diminishes and behavioral differentiation between them increases.

On the other hand, Braun believes that increasing cooperation between localities should produce a reduction in ceramic variability within and between localities. Braun's assumptions and expectations for ceramic variation and the levels at which it might be expected to communicate social groups identity are not explicitly stated. He does not consider either the range of social groups that might be present or how ceramics might come to represent or signify such groups. Braun restricts his concern to the level of "locality" and uses ceramic data to examine locality boundaries.

Information was recorded on the decoration of ceramic vessels from nine habitation sites, representing five localities. Rim sherds of jars, probably general-purpose cooking vessels, were examined. Information was recorded on the number and form of decorative bands that encircled the rim. Decoration was restricted to impressed designs, and 32 design elements were defined. These were grouped into 38 design configurations. The Information Statistic was used to assess the diversity of decorative elements, of element and configuration combinations, and of configurations per element, by chronological period. Chronology was controlled by the recognition that rim sherd thickness decreased over the period of study. Groups of sherds of similar thickness were assumed to be roughly contemporary and were grouped together in the analysis. For all measures of the Information Statistic, the value is highest during the Late Middle Woodland period and drops in the subsequent periods. This is the pattern that Braun predicted under circumstances of increased regional cooperation, and, in Pollock's terms, would be characteristic of periods of decreased horizontal differentiation.

Braun's study identified some marked changes in decorative treatment in the Middle–Late Woodland transition. These changes took the form of increased uniformity of design over time and space and decreased complexity in design composition. Braun also interpreted declines in the exchange of exotic goods during this period as evidence of decreased social differentiation, though he lacks specific settlement data to further support his interpretation.

Although the decorative patterns tend to support Braun's model, the use of domestic cooking vessels poses a problem in this analysis. If, as was stressed earlier, we view potters as conscious actors and their products as reflectors and communicators of some set of group identities and social relations, then we must ask at what level domestic vessels could be expected to communicate in specific cultural contexts. Would we expect cooking vessels to encode information on regional or local-group identity, and if so, why? The solution to this question involves consideration of production contexts, contexts of use, and valuation relative to other materials. The fact that Braun did find support for his argument in his analysis does help to indicate that ceramics may well be appropriate for the study of social variation at this level in this particular context. Similar studies of other classes of material culture during the Mid–Late Woodland transition in this region would also serve to strengthen his case.

Dutch Neolithic Ceramics and Social Change

In Chapter 5, I examined the technology of beaker production during the Dutch Neolithic. I will now consider a study, by Hodder, of chronological changes in ceramic decoration throughout the Neolithic in relation to changes in Neolithic society (Hodder 1982b). Intensive Neolithic settlement of The Netherlands began around 2700 B.C., an extension of the TRB culture of Western Europe. The TRB occupation was followed by the PFB culture at 2400 B.C. and then by the BB (Bell Beaker) culture at *ca.* 2300 B.C. The last two phases showed some overlap. Hodder used information on ceramic decoration and pottery form, as well as stone-axe decoration and burial treatment, to consider changes in social organization during these periods.

Hodder first summarized and assessed the nature of the changes in these classes of artifacts, before placing them in a broader cultural context. Unlike Pollock and Braun's perspective, Hodder's work is explicitly particularistic and case specific. Although very much agreeing that goods are meaningfully constructed, Hodder would argue that it is not possible to develop a general framework for considering their role independent of particular historical contexts. He argues that "material items come to have symbolic meaning as a result both of their use in structured sets and of the associations and implications of the objects themselves, but that the meanings vary with contexts" (1982a:10). "There is," he states, "no direct link between social and ceramic variability" (Hodder 1982a:10), and goods can be used to symbolize and legitimate a variety of social or ideological relations or to deny or disrupt them.

Thus, Hodder first looks for structure and patterns in material remains within classes of goods and between different classes of goods and then attempts to interpret those patterns in the context of other archaeological information, rather than develop models or expectations for structure and change in particular artifact classes and then evaluate them using archaeological data. Despite these basic philosophical and methodological differences, we shall see that Hodder's conclusions about changing material and social forms in the Dutch Neolithic have some strong similarities to those drawn by Pollock and Braun in very different archaeological contexts.

Hodder examined changes in design structure on various vessel forms that occurred throughout the TRB sequence, which could be divided into seven chronological phases (TRBa–g; see Figure 6.3). Between Phases a and c, the impressed designs were organized in thin horizontal bands around the vessel rim and in vertical bands on the body of the vessel. During Phase a, these bands were not separated by explicit boundaries, which were introduced in the form of zigzag lines in Phase b. During Phase b, the designs in each zone became more complex and came to include both vertical and horizontal elements within the dominant horizontal (rim) or vertical (body) decorative structure. During Phase c, decoration came to cover less of the vessel's surface but became structurally more complex. Boundaries between upper and lower decorative bands continued to be stressed, and the complexity and the opposition of vertical and horizontal decorations and empty spaces within bands became important. Throughout Phases a through c, designs in the upper and lower bands of the vessels were independent of each other.

The same basic design structure continued in Phases d and e, though with a number of changes. In particular, the lower and upper design bands became more closely related, such that spaces in one band corresponded to areas of decoration in the other band. Boundary lines separating the bands disappeared, and the bands became more equal in size. Overall, during these phases, ceramic decoration became more complex and more highly structured. During Phases f and g, fewer pots were decorated, and the variety of vessel forms decreases. Designs became simpler. TRB Phases f and g are contemporary with early PFB phases.

The PFB vessels were decorated quite differently than earlier TRB vessels (see Figure 6.4). The vessel surface was divided into a series of horizontal bands, and decorations took the form of horizontal lines and oblique impressions, created by cord wrapping the during vessel forming (van der Leeuw 1976 and previous discussion). These multiple bands of decorations are repeated around the vessel sometimes with alternating orientation. Many fewer decorative contrasts occur in PFB vessels than were found on early TRB pots. Unlike the TRB decoration, each band was related to the one above and below it. The variety of vessel forms and of decorative treatment is quite low during this period.

Hodder next examined stone-axe morphology and ornamentation and burial treatment to see if they paralleled the changes observed in ceramic

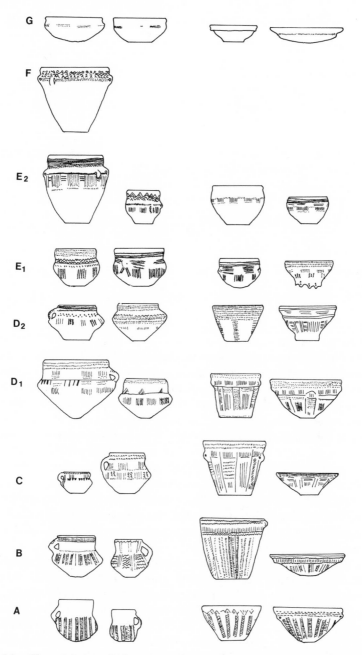

FIGURE 6.3. Changes in ceramic decoration: TRBa–g (after Hodder 1982b:164). Reprinted by permission of Cambridge University Press.

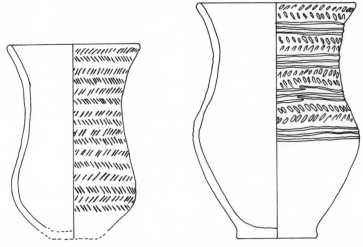

FIGURE 6.4. PFB ceramic decoration (after Hodder 1982b:168). Reprinted by permission of Cambridge University Press.

decoration. The decoration of stone axes with incised motifs, like ceramic decoration, decreased in elaboration during the late TRB period. Changes in burial treatment also occurred throughout the sequence. During TRB Phases a–e, as ceramic decoration became increasingly complex, with more oppositions and contrasts, burial treatment also became complex. Evidence for communal internments in large megalithic burial structures that were used over relatively long periods of time, and evidence for elaborate burial rituals are used by Hodder to support interpretations of strong corporate-group identity. Hodder proposes that these corporate groups were linked to specific territories and were able to muster sufficient labor to construct such facilities. Megaliths ceased to be constructed in Phases f and g. During the PFB period, burial practices were simple, restricted to individual internment under earthen barrows, without any evidence for extensive ritual activity.

Using these three parallel lines of evidence—changes in ceramic decoration, stone-axe form and decoration, and burial treatment—Hodder then considered broader structural changes in Neolithic social organization. The presence of complex burials involving corporate groups and the development of elaborate, highly structured ceramic decoration during the TRB period are interpreted to indicate increasing social (horizontal) differentiation and the recognition and expression of increasingly well-defined concepts of group identity. During the late TRB and PFB periods, decorative contrasts and ritual complexity decline markedly. These periods were marked by changes in settlement patterns as populations expanded to less fertile areas. Communities began to specialize in particular subsistence pursuits such as fishing or herding, leading to greater regional interdependence. The decreases in design complexity and mortuary treatment is interpreted by Hodder as relating to decreases in the importance that individuals and groups ascribed to local social boundaries.

Although phrased in very different terms, Hodder's study has some strong similarities to interpretations drawn by Pollock and Braun. Like Braun, Hodder sees a decline in decorative complexity and group boundary expression during a period of decreased economic independence at the single community level. The archaeological evidence of the preceding early TRB phases, including the construction of large megalithic tombs, provides support for interpretations of increasing social differentiation of localized groups. Such differentiation corresponds to Pollock's definition of horizontal differentiation, which she predicted would be characterized by increased variation in ceramic decoration, including design form, placement, and structure. Such changes are identified by Hodder as occurring throughout TRBa–e.

Hodder, however, would argue against using his case study to support the interpretation that there are general patterns between material culture change and social change. From his perspective, it may be that in some cases, such as in the Dutch Neolithic, where pronounced social tensions exist between groups claiming access to territorial rights, variability in some classes of material culture might be used to express and legitimate those claims. In other systems with similar tensions, such claims might not be expressed through the same classes of material culture, or expressed at all materially. Rather, material culture might be used to deny existing tensions and could be highly uniform over broad areas. Thus, Hodder argues, one must work on a case-by-case basis and consider a wide range of data on settlement, economy, and various classes of material culture to consider the relations between material and social forms in particular contexts.

Ceramic Forms and Cast Identity in Malwa, India

The fourth and final study to be considered in this section differs from the previous three in two important ways. First, it uses ethnographic data. This has an obvious advantage over archaeological studies, in that one has complete pots to work with, rather than fragments, and one can ask the vessels' makers and users why they use specific vessels and what the vessels "mean." Second, this study does not focus exclusively on ceramic

decoration but primarily considers vessel shape. Like the previously discussed studies, Miller (1982, 1985) is concerned with social change and its
relations to changes in material culture.

Miller's research was conducted in the village of Dangwara in the
Malwa region of Central India. Previous studies of sociopolitical organization and religious beliefs and practices in the area (Mayer 1960; Mathur
1964) provided Miller with a well-established framework in which to situate his research. Like all communities organized along caste principles,
Dangwara is a hierarchical society, with members of each subcaste differentiated according to ritual status, traditional occupation, diet and rules of
commensality, access to material prerogatives, and, to some extent, economic status (though the latter may crosscut caste boundaries).

In his work in Dangwara, Miller studied the techniques of ceramic
manufacture and the variety of forms produced in the six active pottery
workshops in the village. He also studied the range of variation within and
between specific vessel forms and between products of different workshops. He found that although there was some interworkshop variation in
the shape and proportions of common vessel forms (using measures of rim
diameter, mouth diameter, neck diameter, maximum diameter, height of
maximum diameter, and vessel height), the products of different workshops tended to overlap a great deal. Miller used similar techniques to
consider the range of variability between differently named vessel forms
identified by Dangwara villagers. For the most part, the different forms did
show significant morphological variation and could easily be sorted into
classes or types using traditional archaeological techniques to assess vessel
shape. These "archaeological classes" corresponded closely to indigenous
categories.

Along with considering ceramic production, Miller also examined
ceramic use in Dangwara. He conducted a "pottery census" in 63 households in the village. The sample included at least one household from each
of the 30 castes represented in the village and 3 Muslim households. He
looked at the number and range of ceramic forms present in each household and the uses to which they were put. Miller also recorded information
on the presence, forms, and use of metal vessels. Using this census data, he
then considered the distribution of ceramic forms in relation to caste
ranking (high/medium/low), wealth (wealthy/average/poor), and family
size and found a generally high correlation between the quantity, diversity,
and forms of pottery and other material items and these dimensions of
social variability.

Miller next focused more closely on processes relating specific vessel
forms or painted decorations to specific domestic or ritual activities and
caste hierarchy in Dangwara. In the study of domestic vessels, attention
was focused on the specific contexts in which most vessels were used—the

storage, preparation, transport, and serving of food or water. Dietary rules, encompassing proscriptions on what foods one can eat, how foods are prepared and served, and commensality or food sharing, are of critical importance in caste differentiation and group identity.

Metal and earthenware vessels, associated with food preparation are closely linked to their contexts of use and may come to be symbolically associated with particular foodstuffs, preparation techniques, and status relations (see Figure 6.5). Miller described a particular cooking vessel, the *jhawaliya*, that has become exclusively associated with cooking meat. The jhawaliya is never used by non-meat-eating groups, even though it could just as effectively be used for preparing vegetarian meals. Thus, along with rankings of people and foodstuffs, vessels in Dangwara are also ranked along generally accepted criteria. In addition, the ranking of castes, foodstuffs, and vessels are not independent. Rather, the material goods, foods and pots, are associated with and reinforce systems of social ranking. Certain vessel forms used in Dangwara are associated with, and found in, low-caste households, whereas other forms were associated with higher castes.

Miller next considered how these associations between material forms and social status are used by individuals or groups seeking to raise their own position in the social hierarchy. Miller terms this process *emulation*. This general process has often been observed in South Asia and has, in that context, been referred to as "Sanskritization" (Srinivas 1967). Sanskritiza

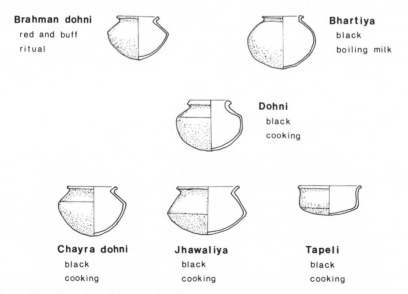

Brahman dohni
red and buff
ritual

Bhartiya
black
boiling milk

Dohni
black
cooking

Chayra dohni
black
cooking

Jhawaliya
black
cooking

Tapeli
black
cooking

FIGURE 6.5.   Ceramic cooking vessels in Dangwara, India (after Miller 1985:xi–xii). Reprinted by permission of Cambridge University Press.

tion is defined as the process by which a low Hindu caste or tribal group attempts to raise its status by adopting, or emulating, the rituals, customs, or ideology of higher ranking groups. Miller extends the study of emulation to domestic goods, with a particular focus on ceramic cooking vessels.

The cooking vessels, generally referred to as *dohni*, are divisible into four vessel form classes. The dohni was originally associated with cooking milk products and thus was ranked fairly highly. Over time, the dohni came to be used by low-caste people for cooking meat and other polluting activities and was also used for cooking pulses and vegetables. In adopting this form, low-caste groups were adopting an object symbolically associated with high-status activities.

From the perspective of high-status groups, the ranking of the dohni was lowered through its association in some households with impure activities. They therefore adopted new vessel forms, free from this perceived taint. These were the *bhartiya* and the vessel called the *brahman dohni* and differed only slightly in form from the original dohni. When introduced, the bhartiya and brahman dohni were used only by high-caste individuals and only for milk preparation.

As the emulation process continues, we may expect that these new forms will also be adopted by lower status groups and used in a broader range of activities. If this occurs, it will again be necessary for higher ranking individuals, if they are to maintain traditional social distances, to adopt new forms that will continue to reflect and convey hierarchical social positions. If the frequencies of the various vessel forms in use at specific points in time were plotted on a graph, distributions would resemble the battleship curves, discussed earlier in the discussion of seriation. Emulation and changes introduced in high-status groups that then filter down to the rest of the society are probably major mechanisms for material culture change in ranked and stratified societies.

Ceramics and Social Organization: Discussion

The four studies discussed examine relations between ceramics and social organization in four very different social contexts. Each, taken on their own merits, appears to have been fairly successful in this goal. Other researchers, specialists in each of the four areas discussed, might argue with their archaeological interpretations of the broader environmental, social, and economic contexts, or with the chronological sequences proposed. I have, for the most part, taken the contextual information provided by each author as given and presented their analysis and interpretations.

Each author took a somewhat different perspective on their data and on broader theoretical issues and used different techniques in their analysis. In particular, they differed in the degree to which they felt that the cases they studied could be taken as exemplars of general processes of material culture change and its relations to social organization. Hodder, for example, argued that each case and each class of material culture must be treated independently and there was no basis for assuming cross-cultural regularities in these processes, whereas Pollock argued that there are general patterns in the nature of material cultural change in contexts of increasing vertical or horizontal differentiation.

The sorts of changes that Pollock proposes are abstract and formal changes in design complexity or elaboration. They do not imply anything about the content of the changes—what classes of material culture they will occur on, what form designs, and the like will take, and what these designs will symbolize to their makers/users. These questions, particularly the last two, are indeed case-specific and historically conditioned, and the last question especially can rarely be answered by prehistoric archaeologists. The general processes of artifact change and factors affecting the relations between material and social forms, are, however, more accessible and provide a framework in which we can view specific historical cases.

Each of the four studies looked at temporal changes in ceramic decoration or vessel form in the context of broader archaeological or ethnographic knowledge. The nature of ceramic variability was examined in a contrasting framework, time a compared to times b, c, d, e; time b, compared to times a, c, d, e, and so on. This is an important and necessary feature of studies of material culture and social organization. Temporal contrasts are not the only ones that can be examined; spatial differences in material culture may be examined within or between sites (area a, compared to areas b, c, d, e; site A compared to sites B, C, D, E). All such studies require careful control of data recovery and analysis, so that one is dealing with comparable contexts; pots from kitchen areas could be different than pots from residential areas because of activity differences rather than social differences. Because, as has been noted earlier, it is difficult to impossible to discover precise "meanings" from archaeological data, we must look at the structure of data and compare it to other relevant data sets, in order to get a more abstract sense of their meaning and occurrences. While we can characterize a single site or phase by the presence of particular material forms, it is only by placing the occurrence of those forms in a broader spatial and/or temporal context that we can develop some understanding of their relation to the broader cultural system in which the objects were used.

SUGGESTED READINGS

For general discussions on the social meanings of material culture, see Douglas (1982), Douglas and Isherwood (1979); Appadurai (1986); Hodder

(1978, 1981, 1982a, 1986). For studies of the social contexts of transmission and learning in ceramic production, see Arnold (1989); Friedrich (1970); Hardin (1979, 1984); Stanislawski (1969, 1973). For discussions of style and archaeology, see Conkey (1978, 1982, 1989); Dunnell (1978); Sackett (1982); Washburn (1977, 1989); Wiessner (1983, 1984); Wobst (1977). For additional approaches to ceramic design, see David *et al.* (1988); DeBoer and Moore (1982); Hegmon (1990); Kintigh (1985); Plog (1976, 1980, 1983); Watson (1977).

Using Ceramics to Answer Questions

IV. Ceramics and Political Organization

As many of the discussions presented in earlier chapters make clear, the social, political, economic, and ideological systems of past societies are often closely interwoven. Political leaders are often religious and economic leaders as well, and studies of both social organization and economic organization are closely connected to each other and to questions of political and ideological organization. While some of the topics presented have considered the relations between ceramics and political structure in a general sense, in this section I wish to focus on a particular aspect of those relations and consider the centralized administration of ceramic production in complex societies.

In all politically complex and hierarchical societies (including chiefdoms, states, and empires), the political elite is involved, to a greater or lesser extent, in the polity's economy, including the production and distribution of subsistence and other goods. This involvement may be indirect, such as taxation levied on the production and distribution of subsistence resources, domestic goods, and luxury goods. Or, administrative involvement in production and distribution may be direct, taking the form of workshops and markets controlled and administered by royal representatives (see Sinopoli 1988).

Economic systems in complex societies are diverse and in most cases are probably administered in a variety of ways. Agricultural production may be organized differently than the production of domestic ceramics, which may be organized differently than the production of jewelry, or the production of armor, and so on. In addition, as Balfet's (1981 and previous discussion) discussion of varying modes of ceramic production in North Africa demonstrates, within any class of goods, different forms or variants may be produced in very different contexts. In cases where a class of "elite ceramics" exists, it may be that its production will be more carefully regulated than will the production of nonelite vessels.

The nature and degree of administered regulation of production of specific products is probably the result of a large number of economic, social, political, and ideological factors. These include the importance of product to the well-being of the polity and the risks involved with its procurement or production; the "value" of the product to the social/ religious/political elite (often one and the same in early states and empires); and the presence and size of a bureaucratic apparatus that could administer production. These and other relevant factors will vary from case to case.

Feinman, Kowaleski, and Blanton (1984) have proposed that administrative control of economic institutions, including craft production, can be expected to occur in contexts of high population density, high investment of labor in agricultural production, and high political consolidation. The authors note that the control of ceramic or other craft production will result in two phenomena that have important archaeological implications. The first is the increased scale of production, and the second is a decrease in competition between producers.

Increases in the scale of production result in increased standardization of products, as pottery workshops adopt new time-saving techniques and implements, such as the fast wheel or molds, and pottery making becomes more routinized. Decreased competition results in a decrease in the variety of vessels produced. Declines in the amount of time invested per vessel on secondary features such as decoration should also occur, as these are often features that competing producers use to appeal to consumers. It should be noted, though, that elaboration and energy investment may vary with the intended users of the vessels, and it is expected that elite ceramics will always be characterized by high-energy investment. Changes in the degree of standardization and elaboration/energy investment can thus be used to consider changes in the organization and regulation of production independent of direct traces of production sites. The location and scale of production sites and studies of exchange patterns can also be considered in these analyses.

These two dimensions of ceramic variability, standardization and elaboration require a fairly fine-grained ceramic typology for their effective evaluation, as well as some measure of the degree of accepted variation within types. With most production techniques and firing conditions, a certain amount of variation will inevitably occur between individual vessels. If products are highly standardized, this variation will be limited, probably on the order of a few millimeters in wall thickness and a few centimeters in diameter or vessel height. It is useful, therefore, to consider the distributions of quantitative measures in these studies, rather than to rely on traditional typologies and intuitive impressions of ceramic uniformity. In addition, information on the contexts of use and valuation are important to order to distinguish among classes of ceramics and possible coexisting modes of ceramic production.

CASE STUDIES

Three studies of the relation between administrative systems and ceramic production will be considered in this section. The first, by Feinman and his colleagues, focuses on ceramic production in prehispanic Oaxaca, Mexico. The second, by Johnson, considers changes in production and exchange networks during early state emergence in southwestern Iran. The last study, by Costin, Earle, D'Altroy, and others examines ceramic production in the context of Inka imperial expansion in the Yanamarca Valley of Peru.

Ceramic Production in Oaxaca

Over the past three decades, a complete archaeological survey and intensive excavations have taken place in the Valley of Oaxaca in South-Central Mexico (see Figure 7.1; Blanton 1978; Blanton et al. 1982; Kowaleski et al. 1983; Kowaleski et al. 1989). Approximately 2,700 sites have been identified, and an 11-phase chronological sequence has been developed for the period 1500 B.C. to 1500 A.D. (see Table 7.1). By 1500 B.C., small agricultural villages existed in each of the three arms of the valley. By ca. 1150 B.C., one of these, San José Mogote, had emerged as a major center some 80 ha in size. Household-level craft specialization is evident during this period, and cemetery data indicate the emergence of hierarchical social ranking. The subsequent 500 to 600 years saw the emergence of competing chiefly centers in each of the three arms of the valley and fluctuations in dominance between them. The site of San José Mogote was destroyed and abandoned in ca. 500 B.C.

At that time, a new site was occupied on the mountain top in the valley's center. This site, Monte Albán, eventually became the capital of a polity that controlled the entire Valley of Oaxaca and areas between its bounds. The developmental sequence of the Monte Albán state belongs to

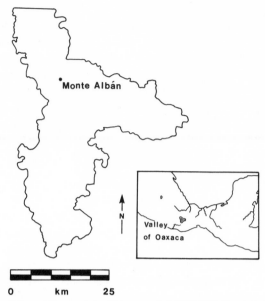

FIGURE 7.1. The Valley of Oaxaca (after Feinman *et al.* 1989:332). Reprinted by permission of the *Journal of Field Archaeology*, Boston University.

the chronological phases Monte Albán (MA I–V, divided into subphases. During its initial settlement in Early MA I, Monte Albán reached a population of approximately 5,000 and was the largest site in the valley. Despite the spatial extent and political importance of Monte Albán, considerable regional autonomy continued to exist; the valley was not yet integrated into

TABLE 7.1. Valley of Oaxaca: Chronological Sequence

Phase	Date	Cultural period
Tierras Larges	1450–1150 B.C.	Early Formative
San José	1150–850 B.C.	Early Formative
Guadalupe	850–700(?) B.C.	Middle Formative
Rosario	700–500 B.C.	Middle Formative
Monte Albán Early I	500–250 B.C.	Middle Formative
Monte Albán Late I	250 B.C.–B.C./A.D.	Late Formative
Monte Albán II	B.C./A.D.–200 A.D.	Terminal Formative
Monte Albán IIIa	200–450 A.D.	Early Classic
Monte Albán IIIb	450–650 A.D.	Late Classic
Monte Albán IV	650/700–1200 A.D.	Early Postclassic
Monte Albán V	1200–1520 A.D.	Late Postclassic

a single political system. By Late MA I, Monte Albán had increased in size to urban proportions, with an estimated population of more than 17,000. Subsidiary centers emerged in the three arms of the valley. The number of small village or hamlet settlements also increased, and a five-level settlement hierarchy existed during this time of high political and economic integration.

During the subsequent MA II phase, the hierarchical settlement pattern continued. Monte Albán declined in size somewhat, as did the scale and intensity of monumental construction at the site. Population in the Valley of Oaxaca also declined slightly, but the Monte Albán state expanded its control beyond the boundaries of the valley. Thus the internal authority of the Monte Albán state seems to have diminished while Monte Albán influence expanded. Inscribed stelae at Monte Albán and other sites record information about military conquests. Long-distance trade of obsidian and a variety of other materials was widespread in this period.

Monte Albán IIIa was a time of major population increase and high organizational complexity within the Valley of Oaxaca. The city of Monte Albán grew in size, and considerable construction occurred at the site. The size and number of urban settlements and the percentage of the population residing in cities increased as the rulers of the Monte Albán state reconsolidated their authority within the Valley of Oaxaca.

MA IIIb was a time of political collapse in the Valley of Oaxaca. The population of the valley declined drastically, with most of the residents of the valley clustered at Monte Albán or within 15 km of the city. Monte Albán grew to its largest size during this phase, and a lot of monumental construction occurred in the city. Lower order administrative sites decreased in number and scale, and state control appears to have been quite restricted, as considerable regional autonomy emerged.

During the subsequent MA IV period, Monte Albán was no longer an important settlement, and no single administrative center had emerged to replace it. The valley was no longer consolidated into a single polity. This pattern continued into the MA V period when the valley of Oaxaca was organized into a number of small territorial units, which the researchers refer to as "petty kingdoms" (Kowaleski et al. 1989:307). These kingdoms had an average population of about 8,000 people, though they varied in size and presumably in their overall importance in the valley. During the MA V period, there is evidence for a high degree of craft specialization and broad distribution networks.

In his study of ceramic production in the Valley of Oaxaca during the Monte Albán sequence, Feinman examined several lines of evidence (Feinman 1980, 1985; Feinman et al. 1984; Feinman et al. 1989). He used data on (1) the spatial context of ceramic production and the association of production centers with administrative sites (identified by pyramidal platform mounds); (2) the spatial concentration of ceramic production and distribution zones; (3) the standardization of the ceramics; (4) the variety of ceramic types and raw-material sources used at each site and overall; (5) estimates of the amount of energy invested per vessel by vessel class (production step measure). He used the traditional ceramic typology developed by previous researchers in the area (Caso, Bernal, and Acosta 1967).

Feinman proposed that during periods of increased administration of production activities, there would be increased standardization of ceramic types found across the valley and a decrease in energy investment per vessel. Production centers would tend to be concentrated near or at administrative centers, and the number of clay sources exploited would decrease. Decreased administration of production would yield the opposite patterns.

During Early MA I, Feinman found that ceramic production was relatively decentralized; most common vessel types and wares varied in different parts of the valley. Some vessel types were widespread during this time. These were the fancy decorated gray-ware serving vessels. Feinman interprets these as having been associated with ritual events and display activities that may have linked kin groups from different parts of the valley. During Late MA I, a time of increased political consolidation, five of the six identified production sites were located at sites with administrative architecture. These workshops were large in scale, and pottery was mass-produced. Standardization of vessels increased, and energy invested per vessel decreased in certain common vessel forms. These common types were distributed homogeneously throughout the valley, providing evidence for centralized production and widespread distribution networks. Although the state may not have directly managed this highly centralized system of ceramic production, the security and scale of integration of the Oaxacan state certainly played an integral role in the development of centralized productive systems. Administrative sites typically contained larger numbers of ceramic types than nonadministrative sites. Their greater access to ceramics, and presumably to other resources, is linked to their political and economic importance in the Monte Albán state.

During MA II, as the polity expanded beyond the valley and internal population declined, Feinman observed increases in ceramic diversity at nonadministrative sites. However, pottery production areas were typically located at administrative centers. Energy invested per vessel increased, and several new, highly decorated forms were introduced. These forms were widespread, but the occurrences of each form were restricted to more or less discrete sections of the valley. More common vessel forms continued to be widely distributed throughout the valley. The MA II data indicate that the production of common wares may have remained centralized, whereas the production of fine wares became localized. Access to these fine wares was restricted to local elites. This pattern of elite wares provides evidence for regional competition within the Valley of Oaxaca and of the growth of regional commercial institutions and trade systems that were largely independent of the rulers at Monte Albán.

During MA IIIa, population and the intensity of administrative activity increased dramatically within the valley as external influence declined. Pottery production increased in scale and was directly under state control. Thirteen of 16 identified production loci were located in settlements with administrative architecture. Pots became highly standardized. Energy investment per vessel declined, as did the overall number of ceramic types produced. Both plain and decorated forms were distributed homogeneously throughout the valley. Administrative sites typically contained many more ceramic types than nonadministrative sites, though the impact of sample size on ceramic diversity is not considered. Imported ceramics from the Central Mexican capital of Teotihuacán were found at Monte Albán, providing evidence for elite control of long-distance exchange networks and exotic goods.

During MA IIIb when much of the valley was depopulated and population centered in or around Monte Albán, there is evidence for large-scale ceramic production at the capital itself. Certain vessel forms were highly standardized and mass-produced. Energy investment per vessel was low. Many types were found throughout the valley; other forms were more restricted in distribution, found in limited areas of Monte Albán or certain parts of the valley. The highest variety of ceramic types was found at Monte Albán. One ceramic form, funeral urns, seems to have been important in elite mortuary treatment. These urns are found in large numbers at Monte Albán and other administrative sites and are seldom found in villages.

During the subsequent MA IV period, pottery production areas were identified at a number of sites with administrative architecture, indicating that production may have been under administrative control of local regions. Energy input per vessel increased and standardization decreased, indicating increased localization and decreased centralization of ceramic production in the Valley of Oaxaca.

Sixteen pottery-production locales were identified from the MA V period. Only one of these is located in a major center. Workshops were typically located in peripheral areas with access to more than one petty kingdom. Many of the workshops specialized in making a limited range of pottery types or wares, though there is no evidence for direct political control over ceramic production. Several ceramic forms were widely distributed across the valley, and ceramic boundaries do not correspond to political boundaries. Workshop and ceramic distributions support an interpretation of distribution of ceramics through a number of regional market centers, largely independent of political or administrative control.

Feinman's analysis demonstrates a high correspondence between the degree of centralization of the Monte Albán polity and the degree of centralization of ceramic production. Whether or not the Monte Albán state directly administered ceramic production in state-sponsored factories, it seems clear that throughout the Oaxaca sequence political centralization and productive organization were closely linked. The scale of ceramic production increased during periods of high centralization. The scale of ceramic distribution also increased, probably concomitant with increases in the scale and security of transportation networks. Competition between producers decreased as production became more centralized. Declines in competition between potters led to declines in energy investment and elaboration of vessels, as potters no longer competed to attract a limited market. By the end of the Oaxacan sequence though, a somewhat different pattern had emerged as large-scale production centers governed by market systems developed. By MA V, pottery production seems to have become partly disembedded from political organization, though political factors affecting access to markets and possibly taxation still must have had some impact on ceramic manufacture and distribution.

Uruk Ceramic Production and State Emergence

Johnson's (1973, 1987) study of early state emergence on the Susiana Plain in southwestern Iran was concerned with the emergence of administrative hierarchies and changes in local exchange networks (see Figure 7.2). He primarily used settlement pattern data (site size and location), though he also examined administrative architecture and artifacts and ceramic and lithic production. In his analysis, Johnson used data from 67 Uruk-period sites that had been identified through systematic surveys of the plain. Ceramics were analyzed to consider temporal variation between sites. The ceramic chronology was based largely on stratigraphic excavations that had been conducted at the sites of Susa, Tepe Farukhabad, Uruk, Nippur, and others, and on a seriation of surface finds. Three main chronological phases were defined: Early Uruk (3750–3500 B.C.), Middle Uruk (3500–3300 B.C.), and Late Uruk (3300–3150 B.C.). The Uruk sequence was preceded by the Terminal Susa A period (4100–3750 B.C.) and followed by the Jemdet Nasr period (3150–2950 B.C.; see Table 7.2).

Johnson used settlement pattern data to consider changing organizational systems during these periods. During the Terminal Susa A period, only 18 sites were found on the Susiana Plain. A two-level site hierarchy was identified. Most of the sites were small villages, less than 2 ha in

TABLE 7.2. Susiana Plain: Chronological Sequence

Period	Approximate dates
Terminal Susa A	4100–3750 B.C.
Early Uruk	3750–3500 B.C.
Middle Uruk	3500–3300 B.C.
Late Uruk	3300–3150 B.C.
Jemdet Nasr	3150–2950 B.C.

extent. Two sites were significantly larger, both about 5 ha. The sites occurred in three linear clusters, presumably along watercourses. The number and diversity of settlements increased during the Early Uruk period. Forty-nine sites have been identified from this period. A third level of site hierarchy emerged, with Susa reaching a size of 12 ha. Sites were more integrated, with small sites distributed equidistantly around larger settlements. Two settlement and administrative foci existed, at Susa and Abu Fanduweh, both on the western side of the plain (Johnson 1987:110).

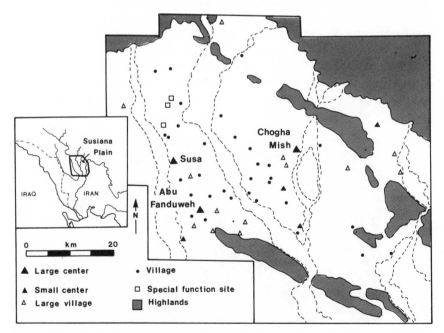

FIGURE 7.2.   Middle Uruk settlement patterns in the Susiana Plain (after Johnson 1973:122). Reprinted by permission of the Museum of Anthropology, University of Michigan.

Stamp seals occurred with increased frequency during this period and became more complex, indicating increased administrative activity.

Fifty-two sites and a four-level settlement hierarchy are known from the Middle Uruk period. Sites include small villages, large villages, small centers, and a large center at Susa. Johnson identifies this period as a period of developed state societies on the Susiana Plain (see also Wright and Johnson 1975). Public architecture increased in scale and elaboration at the larger sites. Administrative artifacts, such as stamp and cylinder seals, counters (bullae), and bevel-rim bowls (see Figure 7.3; possibly rationing vessels) are found throughout the plain, indicating a high degree of administrative integration. During the subsequent Late Uruk period, sites on the northwestern and easternmost portions of the plain were abandoned. Susa declined markedly in size as did most other sites. A three-level settlement hierarchy existed with centers at Susa and Abu Fanduweh in the west and Chogha Mish on the eastern portion of the plain. Cylinder seals were common at the three centers. Military motifs became popular during this period, perhaps indicative of increased conflict within the plain. The Late Uruk period appears to have witnessed a breakdown and fissioning of the highly centralized Middle Uruk system.

Little is known about ceramic production during the Terminal Susa A period, though production appears to have been fairly dispersed. During the Early Uruk period, craft production became spatially centralized. Ceramics were wheel-made or wheel-finished in large quantities, and work shops were located in major centers. Johnson used metric data to distinguish the products of two production centers, one at Susa, the other at Abu

FIGURE 7.3.   Bevel-rim bowls (collections of the Museum of Anthropology, University of Michigan).

Fanduweh. Ceramics from these two centers could be distinguished on the basis of statistical differences in rim shape and rim orientation among vessels of the same broad morphological class, though sample sizes were small. During the Early Uruk period, the frequencies of ceramics from each production center are correlated with distances from the center of the plain and the Abu Fanduweh area. Residents of villages and town sites appear to have been acquiring their ceramics from nearby production and administrative centers, indicating a relatively low level of regional integration.

Ceramic production is known from three sites of the Middle Uruk period and occurred at a fairly large scale (see Figure 7.4). Eight firing facilities were identified at one of the sites. Production was mainly restricted to the larger centers of the period—Susa, Abu Fanduweh, and Chogha Mish. Ceramics from each production center occur in nearby sites and along exchange routes that integrated the entire plain, indicating a larger scale of regional integration than in the Early Uruk period. Ceramic data are limited from the Late Uruk period. The same three production centers were operating, and quantitative differences in diagnostic attributes of their products were identified. Sample sizes were too small, however, to consider distribution patterns.

In his work, Johnson used a number of classes of data to consider sociopolitical organization on the Susiana Plain throughout the Uruk sequence. Included among these were settlement pattern information, the form and distribution of administrative artifacts, and the identification of production loci and distribution networks. He used metric data on ceramics, including measures of thicknesses, angles, and handle dimensions. To identify workshop variants within common classes and then plotted their distribution across the plain. This provided evidence on the extent of exchange networks that proved to be related to the degree and extent of political integration on the plain at various periods. Like Feinman, Johnson observed clustering of production loci at administrative centers and expanded distribution networks during times of high regional integration. These patterns indicate that during the time of high centralization of the Susiana Plain in the Middle Uruk period, ceramic production was controlled by and limited to political centers. Distribution networks were at the very least facilitated by the relative security of a centralized state and may well have been directly controlled by the Susiana rulers.

Ceramics and Inka Imperial Expansion in Yanamarca, Peru

A study of the impact of political change on ceramic production and use in Inka-period Peru has been a focus of research by Costin, Earle, D'Altroy, and their colleagues in the Upper Mantaro Valley of Central–

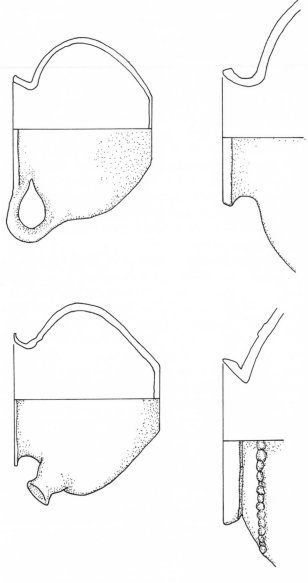

FIGURE 7.4. Some Uruk jar forms (after Wright 1981:1067–108). Reprinted by permission of the Museum of Anthropology, University of Michigan.

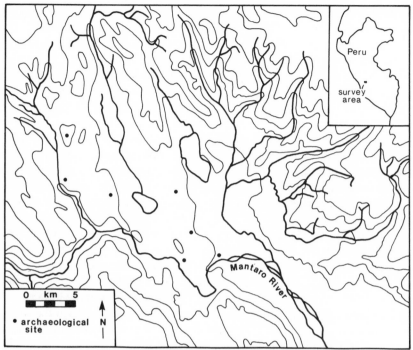

FIGURE 7.5. The Upper Mantaro Valley (after Costin *et al.* 1989:109).

Highland Peru (Costin 1988; Costin *et al.* 1989; Costin and Earle 1989; D'Altroy and Bishop 1990; Earle 1987; Earle *et al.* 1986; Earle and D'Altroy 1989; Owen *et al.* 1988). The Upper Mantaro Valley is an environmentally and topographically diverse valley occupied by the ethnic group known as the Wanka (see Figure 7.5). The valley floor, at an elevation of some 3,000 meters above sea level, is a fertile maize-producing region. Upland agriculture (3,400–3,700 m) focuses on potatoes and quinoa. The uplands also provide grazing lands for llamas and alpacas.

Archaeological research in the area has focused primarily on two periods. The first of these periods is known as the Wanka II period and dates from 1350–1460 A.D. This was the period immediately prior to Inka conquest. During the succeeding Wanka III period (1460–1533 A.D.), the Mantaro Valley was incorporated into the Inka empire. The Wanka III period ended in 1533 with the Spanish Conquest of the Inka.

During Wanka II, the Upper Mantaro region was occupied by a number of competing chiefdoms. Leaders of these chiefdoms were based at fortified hilltop centers, with populations of 8,000 to 10,000 inhabitants, surrounded by small villages and hamlets. Conflict was endemic, and defensive concerns restricted settlement and agricultural activities largely to the higher elevations and protected locales.

In 1460 A.D., the political environment of the region changed dramatically as the valley was conquered by the Inkas and incorporated into their expanding empire. The Inka rulers, based in their capital at Cuzco, instituted far-reaching changes in the Upper Mantaro region, as they did throughout their widespread realm. These changes included the construction of a complex road network to facilitate communication and the transport of staple products, as well as the construction of imperial storehouses and administrative centers. Inka control strategies also included large-scale movement of populations and their forced settlement into specialized communities.

In the Upper Mantaro region, a number of changes occurred with Inka conquest in the Wanka III period. Among the most dramatic changes was a shift in settlement away from protected hilltop locales and down into the fertile valley floor. Maize agriculture was intensified, and the rich agricultural fields of the area were of critical importance to the Inka rulers. An Inka administrative center, Hatun Xauxa, was constructed in the valley, and a major highway lined with more than 50 large storage complexes and other imperial facilities ran through the valley, linking it to the major cities of Cuzco and Quito.

Despite broad consistencies, Inka imperial strategy varied considerably across their realm, as in different contexts they chose to either exploit or undermine traditional social, political, and economic structures (Schreiber 1987:266). In 1982 and 1983, the Upper Mantaro Archaeological Research Project (UMARP) conducted excavations at a number of sites in the Upper Mantaro Valley in order to examine the impact of Inka imperial strategies on local economies and on local political and social hierarchies.

Twenty-nine house compounds, or patio groups, were excavated by the UMARP team, from six single-component sites. Research focused on high-status and low-status residences from both central towns and small villages. Ten commoner and seven elite houses from the Wanka II period were excavated, along with eight commoner and five elite houses from the Wanka III period of Inka domination. Research has focused on documenting the organization of and changes in agricultural and craft production, including the manufacture of ceramics, textiles, stone tools, and metal objects. The UMARP team has also examined changes in access to specific classes of goods with the transition to Inka domination.

Costin's analysis of ceramics from the Upper Mantaro has focused on the impact of Inka conquest and incorporation on the organization of ceramic production; ceramic use; and the variations in access to vessel types in elite and nonelite contexts. A neutron activation study of Inka ceramics by D'Altroy and Bishop (1990) also provides important information on these topics.

Three main ceramic forms were produced in the region during the Wanka II and Wanka III periods. These include globular cooking jars made on micaceous clays, large and small storage jars, and serving bowls or basins. The technology of ceramic production was stable throughout the sequence and, in fact, has changed little in the region to the present day. Vessels were handmade using the coiling technique and then scraped, smoothed, and decorated. Polishing and the application of painted designs were the major decorative techniques employed by the Wanka potters. During the Wanka III period, several new forms of pottery appear in the region. These are highly decorated imperial forms that are found, with some regional variations, throughout the empire, and appear to have played a role in symbolizing and legitimating Inka political bonds.

Local ceramic production changed slightly between Wanka II and III. During both periods, pots were produced by household specialists at a limited number of settlements and were distributed throughout the valley. During Wanka II, several clay sources were used, and pottery was produced in at least three different communities. During Wanka III times, the number of clay sources utilized declined. The number of production areas similarly declined, though the scale of production somewhat increased.

Changes in local ceramic production do not appear to have resulted from deliberate Inka policies affecting ceramics but were the indirect consequences of other Inka policies in the region. The first of these was the major population shift that occurred in the valley following Inka conquest. Upland settlements and clay sources were abandoned as both population and ceramic production shifted to the valley floor.

A second policy that affected local ceramic production was the intensification of maize agriculture in the lower elevations. The productive yields of the Mantaro Valley were of great importance to the Inka economy. Increased agricultural activity likely limited time available for other activities, such as ceramic production. Fewer ceramic producers existed, and those who did produce pottery for the inhabitants of the valley therefore appear to have increased their rate of production and number of vessels produced. These changes did not involve the creation of large-scale workshops or massive technological changes but instead were small-scale local responses to the new political environment.

Ceramic use also underwent some changes following Inka conquest. During the Wanka II period, elite households contained significantly greater quantities of decorated ceramics than commoner houses. These ceramics required greater labor to produce than undecorated wares, and their presence in high-status contexts provides evidence for differential access to certain goods and the labor involved in their production. The most elaborately decorated forms from Wanka II sites are storage jars and serving vessels. The high frequency of these forms in elite contexts is tied both to differential accumulation of stored foods among different social segments and to the importance of feasting and ceremonial activities in expressing and maintaining elite status. Imported ceramics, mostly long-necked storage jars, also occurred in significantly higher frequencies in elite contexts.

During the Wanka III period, differences between elite and commoner households in locally produced ceramics disappeared. In particular, storage vessels were no longer important in elite contexts, as the accumulation of surplus products came under the exclusive control of the Inka. The local elite did not entirely lose their status or positions as feast givers and providers with Inka conquest; however, their positions now depended on the economic and ideological support of the Inka rulers. In these changed contexts, new forms of Inka imperial ceramics replaced the earlier, more local styles of high-status vessels.

Inka imperial ceramics were produced at a regional or subregional level. They exhibit some local variation but were of a broadly recognizable style, painted with elaborate geometric designs in a limited range of vessel forms, including large jars and plates (see Figure 7.6). The production of these vessels occurred within special state facilities, independent of local

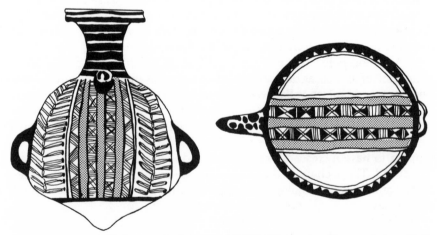

FIGURE 7.6.   Imperial Inka ceramics (after Kendall 1973:175). Reprinted by permission of B. T. Batsford, Ltd.

domestic ceramic manufacture (D'Altroy and Bishop 1990). The manufacture of and access to Inka imperial pottery was directly controlled by the rulers, who probably distributed these vessels to local elites as gifts or payments for services rendered (D'Altroy and Bishop 1990:134). Inka imperial pottery is comparatively widespread in the Upper Mantaro region and is found mostly in imperial facilities and in elite households. Its relative abundance compared to other nearby valleys is attributable to the strategic and economic importance of the Upper Mantaro region for agricultural production. Most imperial ceramics found within the valley came from the nearest regional production center; some vessels, though, traveled even greater distances. One plate found at the administrative center of Hatun Xauxa was produced in an imperial pottery workshop in Cuzco, the Inka capital.

The impact of Inka conquest on ceramic production and use in the Upper Mantaro Valley took several forms. The effect on local ceramic production and use was indirect; changes in the scale and location of production resulted from local responses to new patterns of settlement and agriculture. The Inka also introduced new kinds of status materials into the local system. These goods served as potent material symbols of Inka authority and position, and as such, were carefully controlled and distributed by the Inka rulers to achieve political ends.

CERAMICS AND POLITICAL ORGANIZATION

Discussion

The three studies presented in this chapter each illustrates the impact of increased political centralization on ceramic production. As is clear from each of these studies, the production and distribution of material culture, even such utilitarian goods as ceramics, are often dramatically affected by political changes. Early states and empires frequently act to control the production and distribution of goods to serve both political and economic ends. Deliberate control of production can include the existence of state-run workshops or governmental product controls for specific classes or subclasses of products.

Along with the deliberate manipulation of production or distribution, the emergence of centralized political systems can impact ceramic production in a number of less direct ways. The creation of political security within a state can allow market systems to develop in areas that were previously ridden with conflict. Taxation on products can encourage increased production and greater standardization as potters attempt to maximize output and minimize cost per vessel.

The interest and role of centralized polities in craft production probably varies tremendously with the scale and organization of the political system and the nature of the product. The Inka example provides evidence that even within a single class of goods, such as ceramics, the nature of state involvement in production and distribution may vary widely, from small-scale, localized, specialized production of utilitarian vessels, to centralized control of production and distribution of imperial ceramics.

As each of these studies demonstrates, the study of archaeological ceramics can provide a useful tool for examining political systems and economic centralization. The study of ceramics alone is, however, not sufficient to understanding overall systems of economy and political centralization. To do this, it is essential to look at a range of products from a range of contexts. Ceramics are one of the most easily accessible products for archaeologists to study, but this says little about their inherent significance in ancient societies and ancient economies.

SUGGESTED READINGS

Along with the case studies discussed in this chapter, other works on political organization and ceramic or other craft production can be found in Brumfiel and Earle (1987), Benco (1985, 1987), and Rice (1984a, 1984b, 1989). The Indus Valley research discussed in Chapter V also considers this issue.

8

Directions in Ceramic Research

Ceramics are among the most common classes of artifacts recovered in many archaeological contexts. Because of this, we rely on ceramics to answer many of the questions we wish to ask about the human past. The relations between ceramic variability and these questions—on political, social, economic, or ideological organization and change—are not always obvious or straightforward. In many cases, other classes of material culture might be more suited to approaching such questions. For example, clothing styles, tattoos, and other perishable media of expression would probably be more useful than ceramics in many contexts for considering questions of social organization and the definition and expression of social boundaries. Goods with high political and economic significance may be more subject to administrative control in early states than domestic ceramic vessels. Yet ceramics are often what archaeologists have to work with. Although they may not be suited to all questions, careful work within a logical theoretical framework can enable us to use ceramics to answer a broad range of questions that go beyond the construction of traditional typologies, chronologies, and the identification of broad culture areas.

Throughout this book, I have presented a number of studies that attempt to use ceramics along with other classes of data to ask a variety of questions. Other questions can certainly be proposed and examined using ceramic data, and other approaches to some of the questions discussed may be employed. The cases presented are not meant to provide a cookbook of ceramic analysis, illustrating recipes for the "correct" approach to particular research questions. Rather, I have chosen a number of examples that demonstrate some of the range and variation in contemporary studies of archaeological ceramics.

162   CHAPTER 8

Although ceramics have been important to archaeological studies
since the beginnings of the discipline more than two centuries ago, recent
decades have seen considerable expansion in the scope and sophistication
of ceramic analysis. This expansion is due to a number of factors: internal
and external to archaeology, theoretical and technical. The optimism of
"processual archaeology" in the 1960s and 1970s led to the recognition that
the careful study of archaeological remains, including pottery, could yield
information about a wide variety of aspects of past cultures (Binford 1962;
Binford and Binford 1972). Within this framework, archaeologists attempted to develop and answer questions concerning cultural processes—
the factors and mechanisms underlying cultural change—both in specific
contexts and more abstractly at comparative and general levels. These
ambitious goals helped to contribute to the expansion of the scope and
scale of archaeological research in many ways, including the development
of regional and quantitative approaches to archaeological data; the emergence of ethnoarchaeology and interests in contemporary material culture;
and interests in factors affecting the nature and formation of the archaeological record. The strengthening and diversification of theoretical approaches, to the past, to material culture, and to the archaeological record,
continues to be a topic of fervent and, often, fruitful debate within the
discipline (see, for example, Binford 1989; Dunnell 1989; Hodder 1986; 1989;
Shanks and Tilley 1987).

Ceramic analysis has benefited from and participated in these theoretical and methodological developments in archaeological and anthropological thought and will undoubtedly continue to do so. The explicit
situating of material culture in its cultural and/or social milieu has allowed
consideration of many of the topics presented in this book: the study of
ceramics and social organization, ceramics and political organization, and
the organization of ceramic production, among others. Artifacts are now
seen as products of conscious actors, acting in particular cultural contexts
that can be at least partly accessed through archaeological analysis.

In addition to developments that place ceramics in their social or
cultural context, a number of significant methodological and technological
developments are also contributing to changes in ceramic analysis. Many
of these derive from developments outside the field of archaeology, in
physics, chemistry, and computer sciences. As these techniques become
more accessible and affordable and archaeologists become more knowledgeable of their use, the sophistication of approaches to ceramic analysis
will continue to increase. Throughout this book, I have presented some of
the approaches that archaeologists have taken to the study of ceramics. In
the remainder of this chapter, I wish to consider some current directions in
approaches to archaeological ceramics.

CERAMIC CLASSIFICATION

Contemporary archaeologists often take a variety of approaches to ceramic classification even within a single research project. Traditional systems of ceramic classification remain important in identifying and presenting materials in a common archaeological language that is shared by, and accessible to, the broader cohort of archaeologists working in a particular region. The need to present our data to the archaeological community in a comparative and usable framework and the success of traditional classifications in defining broad temporal and regional patterns assure that these approaches to ceramic classification will continue to flourish (Kohler and Wandsnider 1990).

Beyond traditional typologies, quantitative approaches to ceramic classification will be increasingly important for answering more specific research questions. Such classifications may be based on technical analyses of ceramic raw materials or quantitative analyses of variability in vessel morphology or decoration. Approaches to these problem-oriented classifications are and should be varied and responsive to particular research interests. Even within these particularistic frameworks, archaeologists should continue to strive for improved standardization of variable definitions and measurement techniques in order to facilitate comparability in data analyzed by different researchers. Although anthropological and archaeological theory benefits considerably from the existence of a diversity of perspectives and research interests, archaeological analysis is often weakened by a similar diversity in the presentation of archaeological data. By presenting ceramic data in explicitly specified and/or standardized ways, we allow others to more fully evaluate our results and apply alternate perspectives to the analysis of our data.

CERAMICS AND CHRONOLOGIES

The role of ceramics in constructing ceramic chronologies has lain primarily in the recognition of temporal changes in ceramic form, materials, or decoration. These studies will certainly continue. More detailed analyses of these and other temporally varying dimensions of ceramic variability will contribute to the construction of finer-grained chronologies. Use of computer-assisted techniques, like multidimensional scaling (Chapter 4), also contribute to the improvement of chronologies and the incorporation of large ceramic samples in chronological construction.

Refinements in carbon-14 dating, dendrochronology, and other chronometric dating techniques can also contribute to the development of increasingly fine ceramic chronologies, which can be applied to sites not datable through absolute dating techniques. There are, at present, few techniques available to directly date ceramics, though kilns or other non-mobile firing facilities may be dated through paleomagnetic dating techniques. The technique of thermoluminescence dating can be used to directly date ceramic vessels or sherds in limited contexts, though it is not suited for widespread applications (Rice 1987).

CERAMIC ETHNOARCHAEOLOGY

Ceramic ethnographers and ethnoarchaeologists document ceramic manufacturing and firing techniques, pottery distribution systems, ceramic use, breakage, and deposition, as well as the social conditions of pottery production and distribution. The insights that have emerged from such studies are playing an important role in the development of general frameworks for the study of archaeological ceramics. In many regions of the world, the production of ceramics is declining as alternative vessel materials, such as plastics and metals, increase in availability and popularity. It is therefore extremely important to continue to gather evidence on pottery making in regions where the craft is still vibrant. Such work is ongoing in many areas of the world.

An extremely promising trend in ceramic ethnoarchaeology is the development of long-term research projects, oriented toward looking at ceramic production, use, and deposition over decades, rather than at a single instant in time. Longacre's work and revisits among the Kalinga in the Philippines is one example of such a project. Archaeology is obviously concerned with the long term; even our single-component sites typically encapsulate many years or decades of human occupation and activity. Ethnographic data on the long-term use of ceramics and processes of ceramic deposition will provide important frameworks for considering the nature and composition of archaeological assemblages. Revisits to research areas over years or decades will provide archaeologists with important data.

As archaeologists, we may lament the decline or loss of traditional ceramic industries in response to new raw materials and demands. These changes in materials and techniques are, however, not without their inherent interest. Material culture change, often in the context of a wide range of other changes, is a feature of human existence. While we may be tempted to harken back to a purer past, when pots were pots and potters were traditional, we should recognize that this is not the case. The pace of change has certainly varied throughout prehistoric and historic times, as has the value attributed to traditional forms and traditional ways of doing things; the existence of change cannot be denied.

The study of changes in contemporary pottery-making industries, and related materials, will help to provide useful models for viewing material culture changes in the more distant past. Miller's analysis (Chapter 6) of the changes in pottery forms in Dangwara, India, in response to the ideological conditions of Indian society, provides one approach to material culture change that has considerable relevance to archaeological data. Changes in pottery forms, production, distribution, use, and the values assigned to ceramic vessels may occur in response to a variety of factors: the availability of alternative vessel materials, regional or local market conditions, or, even, the demands of the tourist trade (as among contemporary Pueblo potters in the southwestern United States or Shipibo–Conibo potters in South America). The impact of these and other external or internal factors on ceramic technologies is an important avenue for future ethnographic research.

The occurrence of functionally analogous vessels of distinct materials is also not unique to the present day. Even where pottery industries continue to thrive, in many areas of the world individuals make choices in the vessel materials that they use, for example, between metal or ceramic cooking pots, or metal, plastic, or ceramic water-carrying or storage jars. As discussed in Chapter 6, the ceramics that we recover from archaeological sites were also not the only kind of vessel available to ancient peoples. The study of the use and forms of ceramics and alternative vessel materials in ethnographic contexts can help in developing models for considering the stability and/or change in material media in a range of cultural contexts. Factors of cost, availability, the "prestige value" of goods, taste (of foods or in styles), and tradition are all likely to play a role in the choices consumers make among alternate vessel materials.

The study of ceramic use and production in contemporary contexts also gives us the opportunity to look at variations within communities with far greater specificity than we can in many archaeological contexts. Ceramics, like other goods, are made and used by individuals or small groups of individuals. Within any society or community, conceptions about goods and uses of goods will vary at the level of the individual and various (and varying) social groups. As archaeologists, we seldom can link the materials we recover with specific individuals. Such links may occur with pottery when we can distinguish fingerprints left by potters on their vessels or individual decorative styles, but these are relatively rare. By considering individual and group variation in contemporary pottery-making and pottery-using communities, ceramic ethnoarchaeology can aid in developing more sophisticated models for considering such variation in the past.

Ceramic ethnoarchaeology provides us with more than "cautionary tales" on the complexities of human behavior. Through the study of pottery in contemporary contexts and through experimental techniques, we will be able to generate new models for understanding the past and provide a conceptual framework in which to place archaeological data. This is not to imply that current practices encompass all possible past practices, only that the archaeological remains that we recover do not speak for themselves. The concepts, models, and implicit or explicit knowledge we bring to our analyses have an important impact on our results. By being knowledgeable of the diversity and patterning in contemporary ceramic use, we heighten our ability to study ancient ceramics.

CERAMIC USE AND ACTIVITY DISTRIBUTION

The importance of ceramics as goods used for particular purposes has long been recognized by archaeologists, and a number of approaches have been taken to identifying ceramic use. The analysis of variations in vessel shapes, raw materials, responses to various stresses, and use wear all play a role in assessments of vessel function. Analyses of archaeological context are also important in assessing vessel use; for example, we may be able to distinguish mortuary vessels from other pots on the basis of their context of recovery, and so on.

The analysis of residues on the surfaces of vessels provides a promising means for examining the uses of ceramics in more detail. Such analyses are most effective for the study of fatty products, such as animal fats or milk or resins, though postdepositional factors and the multiple uses of many vessels must also be taken into account. Ethnoarchaeological censuses of vessels in use in a variety of contexts, their rates of breakage, and incorporation into archaeological deposits can aid our interpretations of the relative significance of different functional classes of ceramics in various kinds of archaeological assemblages. Data from ceramic censuses can also be used in computer simulations to model the formation of archaeological assemblages over varying time periods and in different contexts.

The interpretation of vessel use will also benefit from increasing attention to the range and nature of variation within broad vessel classes in morphology and other features. Multiple approaches to ceramic classification, already discussed play a key role in improving our ability to assess ceramic use. At a very broad level, separating bowls from jars, for example, may help to distinguish serving from cooking vessels. An examination of quantitative variation within such broad categories, along with consideration of their context of recovery, may help in the identification of meaningful subgroups of cooking or serving vessels. Although we might not necessarily be able to identify what was cooked or served in different classes, the recognition of the differences within a ceramic inventory is in itself important.

CERAMIC PRODUCTION AND DISTRIBUTION

The identification of techniques of ceramic production can be carried out on the basis of visible traces of production marks. X-ray techniques can be used to identify nonvisible traces, such as where coils or molded segments of a vessel were joined and the joints smoothed over. Again, ethnoarchaeological work among contemporary pottery workers is providing an important source of information on the social organization of ceramic production and techniques of ceramic production in contemporary contexts.

The study of ceramic raw-material sources, and of ceramic production and distribution, are probably benefiting more than any other area of ceramic analysis from developments in the physical and chemical sciences. The identification of ceramic raw materials from petrographic analysis, neutron activation analysis, and a range of other techniques is becoming part of the repertoire of many ceramic analyses. These techniques are providing increasingly fine precision for the identification of raw materials, thereby allowing the identification of sources exploited by ancient potters, the approximate locations of ceramic production, and the extent of ceramic distribution systems. Once sources are identified, it becomes possible to consider in more detail the nature and extent of production and exchange systems. Models derived from the fields of cultural geography and economics, as well as from anthropology, can be evaluated in order to assess prehistoric exchange.

CERAMICS AND SOCIAL ORGANIZATION

As discussed in Chapter 6, studies of ceramics and social organization have focused in large part on the analysis of ceramic design and the topic of style. The significance and recognition of stylistic patterning in archaeological materials is the subject of much recent debate in archaeology. Stylistic variation includes both individual variation, resulting from learning, skills, and self-expression; and variation at more inclusive levels that are tied to social group identification or boundaries and are referred to by Wiessner as *emblemic style* (1983:256–257). The way that humans use material culture, including ceramics, to define and structure and alter social interactions and relations is a topic of considerable interest to archaeologists, and debates on the meaning and content of style will no doubt continue.

Analyses of ceramic decoration and other aspects of ceramic variation will continue to contribute in a very significant way to this debate. The techniques of symmetry analysis (Washburn 1977, 1989) and the reconstruction of the rules for designs, or design grammars, will continue to be important for considering the structure of design and social expression. Along with decoration, variations in ceramic forms can also be studied. The study of the similarities or differences in ornamentation across multiple media is another potentially productive avenue for considering social organization. Parallels in decorative motifs in ceramics, textiles, basketry and petroglyphs, for example, in some areas of the southwestern United States could be studied to consider the multiple levels and contexts of stylistic representation and communication.

Studies of ceramics and social organization have generally focused on the identification of social boundaries or distinctions within sites or in broader regions. An additional social category that may be fruitfully approached through ceramic analysis is that of gender. Archaeologists have only recently become interested in the study of gender in the human past (Conkey and Spector 1984). The cultural construction of gender categories, the definitions of behaviors and attributes of females and males, is a feature of all extant human societies and was most probably a feature of past societies as well. Women and men are often seen as occupying separate domains, with different responsibilities and obligations, and in many contexts, having different social and jural rights and privileges.

Gender-based differences in activities and behavior have material implications that can be studied by archaeologists interested in gender as a social category or in changes in gender structure. Ceramics may be important to such studies in a number of ways. Ethnographic and historic studies of pottery-making industries demonstrate a link between the sex of potters and the organization of ceramic production. That is, it has been observed that when pottery making is organized at the level of household production or as a household industry (Chapter 5), women are most often the major potters. When pottery making is a full-time industry, potters include both males and females, often of a single family working in a single workshop. And in many areas of the world, the use of the potter's wheel is exclusively a male activity.

Generalizations derived from the present cannot, of course, be directly applied to the past. They do, however, provide frameworks for viewing past social systems that can be evaluated with archaeological data. In areas with considerable cultural continuity, archaeologists have assumed that the sexual organization of pottery production that we see in the present also held in the past. Many studies of ceramics and social organization in the southwestern United States, for example, have explicitly assumed that pottery makers were women. If this assumption can be supported, and in this region it seems that it can, then the production, and perhaps, ownership and distribution of pottery may well be a female domain (Conkey and Spector 1984). The identification of differential patterns in the distribution of gender-specific goods can provide a useful means for examining past gender systems (see Gibbs [1987]; Welbourn [1984] for some approaches to the study of gender and material culture).

The relations between ceramics and gender may be linked to ceramic use as well as to production. I have discussed earlier the integral relation between many classes of ceramics and food preparation and consumption. Ethnographic studies of the division of labor have shown that the preparation, cooking, and storage of foods (particularly plant foods) are most often "women's work." The reasons for this do not concern us here, but the universality of the association between women and food preparation in ethnographic contexts may point to its importance in the past. Again, if ceramics can be shown to have been differentially used by males and females, temporal and spatial patterning in ceramic distributions can be studied to consider gender systems and their change over time. The link between ceramic forms and cooking techniques and cooking techniques and female labor requirements is one such topic that might be studied.

CERAMICS AND POLITICAL ORGANIZATION

Specialization and systems of economic control are two characteristics that have received considerable attention in archaeological approaches to the rise and nature of political complexity and social hierarchy. The durability and abundance of ceramics and our ability to identify ceramic production systems and sites from archaeological materials have contributed to the importance of pottery in studies of the economies of early states and empires. Studies of the nature of political control of economic systems contribute to our understanding both of the emergence of these societies and of the way they operate in different historical contexts.

Because ancient economies, like modern ones, were diverse, no single class of materials will tell us all we wish to know about the administrative control of craft production. Ceramics may be produced differently than cloth, which may be produced differently than jewelry, and so on. Even within the category *ceramics*, differences can exist between elite and non-elite wares, and so on; such is the case for Inka pottery production discussed in Chapter 8. A focus on the nature and interaction of politics and economy in the past thus requires the study of a range of archaeological materials (and written records, where available), including, but not limited to, archaeological ceramics.

CONCLUSIONS

Throughout this book, I have tried to highlight the potential and successes of ceramic research for archaeological analysis. My concern has been with the relevance of ceramics analysis in answering questions about the human past, both at the level of particular historically unique case studies, and at more general and comparative levels. The study of archaeological ceramics has been an integral part of archaeological research since its inception and will no doubt continue to be so.

New analytical techniques, theoretical perspectives, and increased awareness of the formation and nature of the archaeological record will continue to play a role in the expansion and development of ceramic studies for archaeological analysis. These techniques bring with them a certain risk, that of overspecialization. The tremendous growth of knowledge and information in archaeology in general and the study of archaeological ceramics, in particular, makes it impossible to be a master of all specializations or types of analysis. Within ceramic analysis, we now distinguish between ceramic sociologists and style experts, materials analysts or ceramic technologists, ceramic ethnographers, and so on. Many archaeologists with interests in ceramics wear a number of different hats, including those with little direct connection to pots. Different aspects of ceramics, as well as other kinds of archaeological data, though studied by specialists, need to be carefully integrated in order to achieve most archaeological research goals. As I have tried to demonstrate, archaeological ceramics are of interest and worthy of study in and of themselves, as aesthetic objects and human creations, but they are even more interesting as one of many sources of information that archaeologists can use to learn about the human past.

Appendix
Statistical Techniques for Ceramic Analysis

Statistics may be defined as a method or set of methods for dealing with data in one of two ways. Descriptive statistics provide summary information on data in a standardized form. Inferential statistics provide a method for making inferences about populations, using principles of probability. Archaeologists typically work with samples, or parts of populations. A *population* is defined as the collection of *all* things that have certain characteristics, whereas a *sample* is *any part* of a population.

Information on ceramics may be recorded along qualitative or quantitative scales of measurement. These scales record very different sorts of information and, therefore, must be analyzed differently. Quantitative data measure precise quantities or parameters and require the use of parametric statistics. Qualitative measuring scales do not encode quantitative parameters, and nonparametric tests are used in their analysis.

In the following sections, I will first consider some descriptive and inferential approaches to the analysis of quantitative data before turning to the analysis of qualitative data. This appendix presents only a brief introduction to this topic; more complete information on these topics can be found in any introductory statistics text.

QUANTITATIVE DATA: DESCRIPTIVE STATISTICS

The goal of descriptive statistics is to summarize data in such a way that the researcher can assess their range and form. Such summaries may take graphic or numerical form. A common and useful graphic technique is the *histogram*. A histogram allows one to visually examine the frequency *distribution* of a variable. A frequency distribution measures the number of occurrences of a variable over a particular range or interval. It is produced by dividing the data into a number of discrete intervals of equal length and counting or graphing the number of cases that occur within each interval.

Figure A.1 contains histograms of a set of data, measurements of rim diameter for a sample of 90 vessels, with diameters from 5 to 30 cm. In constructing histograms, the most important factor to consider is interval width. An interval that is too small or narrow may be too influenced by measuring biases to reveal meaningful patterning. One that is too large may obscure patterns by grouping dissimilar cases together. In Figure A.1, the same data are plotted at four different intervals. Histogram a, with an interval width of 1 cm reveals very strong evidence of a measuring bias; even numbers are recorded much more frequently than odd rim diameters. Any patterning that may exist in the data is obscured by this too small interval. Histogram b reveals a neat *bimodal distribution* pattern with evidence for two rim-diameter classes, one from 4 to 14 cm and the other from 15 to 30 cm. Modality refers to the number of peaks in the distribution. Histogram c, with a 5-cm interval, also reveals a bimodal distribution, but the larger interval size tends to obscure the midpoint of each of the modes and the symmetry of their distribution. Histogram d, with an interval of 10 cm, reveals a unimodal distribution, with a peak at about 25 cm. Each of these histograms is accurately representing the recorded data; each is true. Yet they differ considerably in their usefulness in assessing the nature of the variability in the data. Histogram b, with an interval of 2 cm, is, in this case, most useful in summarizing the data. It is large enough not to be affected by measuring biases, yet small enough not to obscure existing patterns.

These four examples point out a very important feature of statistics—that is, although statistical descriptions may be used to identify patterns in one's data, it is also very easy to distort or misrepresent data and to "lie" with statistics (Thomas 1978). When evaluating data with histograms or any other techniques, it is important to produce multiple graphs at varying intervals to thoroughly examine data distributions.

Another technique for graphically presenting frequency distributions is the cumulative frequency graph. This approach has been very popular in summarizing lithic inventories of the Paleolithic and has been less frequently applied to ceramics (Bordes 1972). Cumulative frequency graphs are produced by calculating the frequency of cases in each interval (number of cases in interval divided by total sample). Frequency, which ranges from 0.0 to 1.0, or 0% to 100%, forms the vertical, or y, axis of the graph, and the measured values of the variable form the horizontal, or x, axis. The cumulative frequency is defined as the frequency of cases at or below a particular

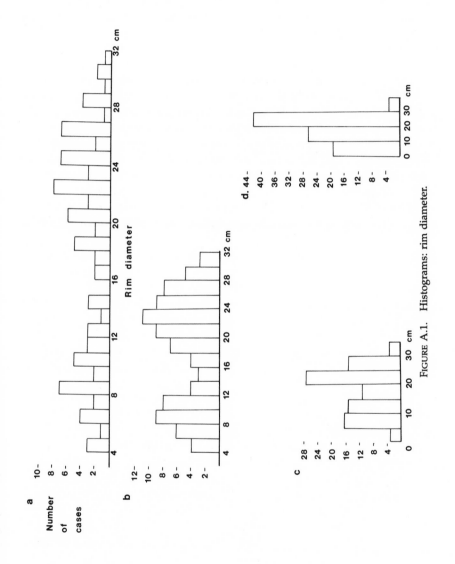

FIGURE A.1. Histograms: rim diameter.

value. The graph of cumulative frequency therefore takes the form of a
single line that necessarily increases from 0.0 to 1.0 as more cases fall below
the value on the *x* axis. The shape of the line (the *ogive*) provides information on the percentage of cases that fall within certain classes. Figure A.2
presents a cumulative frequency chart of the rim-diameter data from Figure A.1.

Cumulative frequency graphs are often used for graphing the frequency of different artifact types in a given assemblage. Each point along
the *x* axis in such graphs represents a different type, and its frequency of
occurrence is added to the frequency of types that lie to the left of it on the
graph. Although a common graphic technique, problems in this technique
result from the fact that the types that form the *x* axis are not necessarily
related to each other in any intrinsic way and can therefore be ordered in a
variety of ways. The ordering of the types can have a major impact on the
shape of the graph and must be consistent from site to site or between
levels within sites.

Numerical values may also be used to summarize information on
quantitative variables. These values include the mean, median, mode,

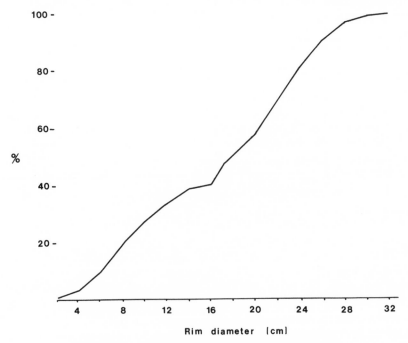

FIGURE A.2. Cumulative frequency chart: rim diameter.

standard deviation, and variance. To compute the sample mean, or average ($\bar{x}$), simply sum the values of all the cases and divide the total by the number of cases in the sample (n). The population mean is computed, where possible, in a similar manner. The *sample median* is the middle value of the sample, such that half of the cases fall below that value and half lie above it. The *sample mode* is the most commonly occurring individual or interval value. In the set of rim-diameter data presented in Figure A.1, the sample mean is equal to 17.6 cm and the median is equal to 20 cm.

The sample variance and *standard deviation* measure the distribution of the variable around the sample or population mean. Sample variance (s^2) is computed by calculating the distance of each case (x_i) from the sample mean. These values, $x_i - \bar{x}$, are squared to eliminate negative values and summed over all cases. This sum is divided by the sample size minus one ($n - 1$), to attain a sample average of distance from the mean. The formula for sample variance thus is:

$$s^2 = \frac{\sum (x_i - \bar{x})^2}{(n - 1)}$$

The sample *standard deviation* (s) equals the square root of the variance. In the sample of rim diameter, the sample variance is equal to 57.07, and the sample standard deviation equals 7.55. These measures do not provide information on the bimodality of the data that was observed in the graphic representations of the variable distribution. They do provide a way of summarizing the data useful in itself or in comparison these vessels with other samples. The population variance is represented by σ^2 and population standard deviation by σ.

Along with assessing the modality of variable distributions, other aspects of frequency distributions can also be considered. These include the shape and skewness of the sample, and by inference, the population distribution. The shape of the sample distribution can be compared with distribution patterns derived from probability theory. The most important of these is the *normal distribution* or bell-shaped curve (see Figure A.3). This is a symmetrical distribution, in which the highest frequency occurs at the mean, and frequencies fall off symmetrically around the mean.

The *standard normal distribution* is defined as having a mean of 0.0 and a standard deviation of 1.0. Because the normal distribution is symmetrical about the mean, the mean, median, and mode are equal. The standard normal distribution has some important characteristics. The total area under the curve is equal to 1.0. Of this, .68 or 68% of the area lies within 1 standard deviation above and below the mean; .95 or 95% of the area under the curve lies within 1.96 standard deviations above and below the mean

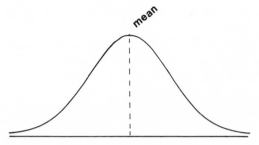

FIGURE A.3.   Normal distribution or bell-shaped curve.

(see Figure A.4). Given these properties, it is possible to calculate precisely the percentage of the area under the curve that lies above or below a particular value in a standard normal distribution.

Variables drawn from a population with a normal distribution can be assessed in a similar manner, by converting variable scores to standardized scores, or *z-scores*. A *z*-score is computed by transforming the variable scores so that the mean is set equal to 0 and the standard deviation equals 1.0. The formula for computing a *z*-score is:

$$z = \frac{x_i - \bar{x}}{s}$$

The *z*-score is, in effect, measuring how many standard deviations a particular value, x_i, is from the mean. The area under the curve between the mean and the *z*-score value can be used to calculate the percentage of cases that fall above or below that value. Suppose, for example, the variable rim thickness is normally distributed with a mean of 1.8 cm and a standard deviation of .36 cm, and we want to calculate what percentage of cases are

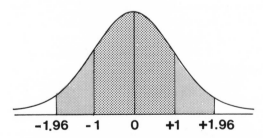

FIGURE A.4.   The standard normal distribution.

less than and greater than 2.4 cm. To do this, we first compute the z-score for the value 2.4:

$$z = \frac{2.4 - 1.8}{.36} = \frac{.6}{.36} = 1.67$$

We can then turn to a table of proportions of area under the standard normal curve and look up the values for a z of 1.67 (see Table A.1). We find that the area between the mean and z is equal to .4525 and that the area beyond z equals .0475. Because the normal distribution is symmetrical, the total area below the mean is equal to .50. The total area below a z value of 1.67, therefore, is equal to .50 + .4525 = .9525, or 95.25%. In our example, then, 95.25% of the values of the rim-thickness variable of a particular population are less than 2.4 cm. A value greater than 2.4 would occur in this population less than 5% of the time. Phrased another way, there is a 95% probability that members of this population will have rim thicknesses of 2.4 cm or less.

Although sample parameters will, if the sample is sufficiently large, approximate the population parameters, they will seldom be exactly equal. If, however, a large number of samples are drawn from the same population, we can expect that the deviations of the sample means will fluctuate closely around the population mean. The sample of sample means can be plotted and will be approximately normally distributed with a mean approximately equal to the population mean and a unique standard deviation or sample variance. The following theorem will hold: "If random samples of size n are repeatedly drawn from a normally distributed population with mean μ and variance σ, then the sampling distribution of sample means will also be normal, with mean $\mu_x - \mu$ and variance $\sigma_x^2 = \sigma^2/n$" (Thomas 1976:186). The expression σ_x is known as the *standard error* of the mean, and is, in effect, the standard deviation of the distribution of sample means. The standard error of the sample means will decrease as the number of samples taken increases. Because the sample mean is normally distributed, we now have a new way of finding the probability of selecting an entire sample. This requires a somewhat modified way of calculating z-scores:

$$z = \frac{\bar{x}_i - \mu}{\sigma_x}$$

We can use this formula to consider the probability of the occurrence of a certain sample mean in the same manner that we considered the probability of an individual value occurring in a given sample. Thus, although previously we considered the probability of a sherd greater than

TABLE A.1. Table of z-Scores

z	Area between mean and z	Area between z	z	Area between mean and z	Area between z	z	Area between mean and z	Area between z
0.00	.0000	.5000	0.43	.1664	.3336	0.86	.3051	.1949
0.01	.0040	.4960	0.44	.1700	.3300	0.87	.3078	.1922
0.02	.0080	.4920	0.45	.1736	.3264	0.88	.3106	.1894
0.03	.0120	.4880	0.46	.1772	.3228	0.89	.3133	.1867
0.04	.0160	.4840	0.47	.1808	.3192	0.90	.3159	.1841
0.05	.0199	.4801	0.48	.1844	.3156	0.91	.3186	.1814
0.06	.0239	.4761	0.49	.1879	.3121	0.92	.3212	.1788
0.07	.0279	.4721	0.50	.1915	.3085	0.93	.3238	.1762
0.08	.0319	.4681	0.51	.1950	.3050	0.94	.3264	.1736
0.09	.0359	.4641	0.52	.1985	.3015	0.95	.3289	.1711
0.10	.0398	.4602	0.53	.2019	.2981	0.96	.3315	.1685
0.11	.0438	.4562	0.54	.2054	.2946	0.97	.3340	.1660
0.12	.0478	.4522	0.55	.2088	.2912	0.98	.3365	.1635
0.13	.0517	.4483	0.56	.2123	.2877	0.99	.3389	.1611
0.14	.0557	.4443	0.57	.2157	.2843	1.00	.3413	.1587
0.15	.0596	.4404	0.58	.2190	.2810	1.01	.3438	.1562
0.16	.0636	.4364	0.59	.2224	.2776	1.02	.3461	.1539
0.17	.0675	.4325	0.60	.2257	.2743	1.03	.3485	.1515
0.18	.0714	.4486	0.61	.2291	.2709	1.04	.3508	.1492
0.19	.0753	.4247	0.62	.2324	.2676	1.05	.3531	.1469
0.20	.0793	.4207	0.63	.2357	.2643	1.06	.3554	.1446
0.21	.0832	.4168	0.64	.2389	.2611	1.07	.3577	.1423
0.22	.0871	.4129	0.65	.2422	.2578	1.08	.3599	.1401
0.23	.0910	.4090	0.66	.2454	.2546	1.09	.3621	.1379
0.24	.0948	.4052	0.67	.2486	.2514	1.10	.3643	.1357
0.25	.0987	.4013	0.68	.2517	.2483	1.11	.3665	.1335
0.26	.1026	.3974	0.69	.2549	.2451	1.12	.3686	.1314
0.27	.1064	.3936	0.70	.2580	.2420	1.13	.3708	.1292
0.28	.1103	.3897	0.71	.2611	.2389	1.14	.3729	.1271
0.29	.1141	.3859	0.72	.2642	.2358	1.15	.3749	.1251
0.30	.1179	.3821	0.73	.2673	.2327	1.16	.3770	.1230
0.31	.1217	.3783	0.74	.2704	.2296	1.17	.3790	.1210
0.32	.1255	.3745	0.75	.2734	.2266	1.18	.3810	.1190
0.33	.1293	.3707	0.76	.2764	.2236	1.19	.3830	.1170
0.34	.1331	.3669	0.77	.2794	.2206	1.20	.3849	.1151
0.35	.1368	.3632	0.78	.2823	.2177	1.21	.3869	.1131
0.36	.1406	.3594	0.79	.2852	.2148	1.22	.3888	.1112
0.37	.1443	.3557	0.80	.2881	.2119	1.23	.3907	.1093
0.38	.1480	.3520	0.81	.2910	.2090	1.24	.3925	.1075
0.39	.1517	.3483	0.82	.2939	.2061	1.25	.3944	.1056
0.40	.1554	.3446	0.83	.2967	.2033	1.26	.3962	.1038
0.41	.1591	.3409	0.84	.2995	.2005	1.27	.3980	.1020
0.42	.1628	.3372	0.85	.3023	.1977	1.28	.3997	.1003

TABLE A.1. (*Continued*)

z	Area between mean and z	Area between z	z	Area between mean and z	Area between z	z	Area between mean and z	Area between z
1.29	.4015	.0985	1.72	.4573	.0427	2.15	.4842	.0158
1.30	.4032	.0968	1.73	.4582	.0418	2.16	.4846	.0154
1.31	.4049	.0951	1.74	.4599	.0409	2.17	.4850	.0150
1.32	.4066	.0934	1.75	.4599	.0401	2.18	.4854	.0146
1.33	.4082	.0918	1.76	.4608	.0392	2.19	.4856	.0143
1.34	.4099	.0901	1.77	.4616	.0384	2.20	.4861	.0139
1.35	.4115	.0885	1.78	.4625	.0375	2.21	.4864	.0136
1.36	.4131	.0869	1.79	.4633	.0367	2.22	.4868	.0132
1.37	.4147	.0853	1.80	.4641	.0359	2.23	.4871	.0129
1.38	.4162	.0838	1.81	.4649	.0351	2.24	.4875	.0125
1.39	.4177	.0823	1.82	.4656	.0344	2.25	.4878	.0122
1.40	.4192	.0808	1.83	.4664	.0336	2.26	.4881	.0119
1.41	.4207	.0793	1.84	.4671	.0329	2.27	.4884	.0116
1.42	.4222	.0778	1.85	.4678	.0322	2.28	.4887	.0113
1.43	.4236	.0764	1.86	.4686	.0314	2.29	.4890	.0110
1.44	.4251	.0749	1.87	.4693	.0307	2.30	.4893	.0107
1.45	.4265	.0735	1.88	.4699	.0301	2.31	.4896	.0104
1.46	.4279	.0721	1.89	.4706	.0294	2.32	.4898	.0102
1.47	.4292	.0708	1.90	.4713	.0287	2.33	.4901	.0099
1.48	.4306	.0694	1.91	.4719	.0281	2.34	.4904	.0096
1.49	.4319	.0681	1.92	.4726	.0274	2.35	.4906	.0094
1.50	.4332	.0668	1.93	.4732	.0268	2.36	.4909	.0091
1.51	.4345	.0655	1.94	.4738	.0262	2.37	.4911	.0089
1.52	.4357	.0643	1.95	.4744	.0256	2.38	.4913	.0087
1.53	.4370	.0630	1.96	.4750	.0250	2.39	.4916	.0084
1.54	.4382	.0618	1.97	.4756	.0244	2.40	.4918	.0082
1.55	.4394	.0606	1.98	.4761	.0239	2.41	.4920	.0080
1.56	.4406	.0594	1.99	.4767	.0233	2.42	.4922	.0078
1.57	.4418	.0582	2.00	.4772	.0228	2.43	.4925	.0075
1.58	.4429	.0571	2.01	.4778	.0222	2.44	.4927	.0073
1.59	.4441	.0559	2.02	.4783	.0217	2.45	.4929	.0071
1.60	.4452	.0548	2.03	.4788	.0212	2.46	.4931	.0069
1.61	.4463	.0537	2.04	.4793	.0207	2.47	.4932	.0068
1.62	.4474	.0526	2.05	.4798	.0202	2.48	.4934	.0066
1.63	.4484	.0516	2.06	.4803	.0197	2.49	.4936	.0064
1.64	.4495	.0505	2.07	.4808	.0192	2.50	.4938	.0062
1.65	.4505	.0495	2.08	.4812	.0188	2.51	.4940	.0060
1.66	.4515	.0485	2.09	.4817	.0183	2.52	.4941	.0059
1.67	.4525	.0475	2.10	.4821	.0179	2.53	.4943	.0057
1.68	.4535	.0465	2.11	.4826	.0174	2.54	.4945	.0055
1.69	.4545	.0455	2.12	.4830	.0170	2.55	.4946	.0054
1.70	.4554	.0446	2.13	.4834	.0166	2.56	.4948	.0052
1.71	.4564	.0436	2.14	.4838	.0162	2.57	.4949	.0051

(*continued*)

TABLE A.1. (*Continued*)

z	Area between mean and z	Area between z	z	Area between mean and z	Area between z	z	Area between mean and z	Area between z
2.58	.4951	.0049	2.84	.4977	.0023	3.10	.4990	.0010
2.59	.4952	.0048	2.85	.4978	.0022	3.11	.4991	.0009
2.60	.4953	.0047	2.86	.4979	.0021	3.12	.4991	.0009
2.61	.4955	.0045	2.87	.4979	.0021	3.13	.4991	.0009
2.62	.4956	.0044	2.88	.4980	.0020	3.14	.4992	.0008
2.63	.4957	.0043	2.89	.4981	.0019	3.15	.4992	.0008
2.64	.4959	.0041	2.90	.4981	.0019	3.16	.4992	.0008
2.65	.4960	.0040	2.91	.4982	.0018	3.17	.4992	.0008
2.66	.4961	.0039	2.92	.4982	.0018	3.18	.4993	.0007
2.67	.4962	.0038	2.93	.4983	.0017	3.19	.4993	.0007
2.68	.4963	.0037	2.94	.4984	.0016	3.20	.4993	.0007
2.69	.4964	.0036	2.95	.4984	.0016	3.21	.4993	.0007
2.70	.4965	.0035	2.96	.4985	.0015	3.22	.4994	.0006
2.71	.4966	.0034	2.97	.4985	.0015	3.23	.4994	.0006
2.72	.4967	.0033	2.98	.4986	.0014	3.24	.4994	.0006
2.73	.4968	.0032	2.99	.4986	.0014	3.25	.4994	.0006
2.74	.4969	.0031	3.00	.4987	.0013	3.30	.4995	.0005
2.75	.4970	.0030	3.01	.4987	.0013	3.35	.4996	.0004
2.76	.4971	.0029	3.02	.4987	.0013	3.40	.4997	.0003
2.77	.4972	.0028	3.03	.4988	.0012	3.45	.4997	.0003
2.78	.4973	.0027	3.04	.4988	.0012	3.50	.4998	.0002
2.79	.4974	.0026	3.05	.4989	.0011	3.60	.4998	.0002
2.80	.4974	.0026	3.06	.4989	.0011	3.70	.4999	.0001
2.81	.4975	.0025	3.07	.4989	.0011	3.80	.4999	.0001
2.82	.4976	.0024	3.08	.4990	.0010	3.90	.49995	.00005
2.83	.4977	.0023	3.09	.4990	.0010	4.00	.49997	.00003

(After Runyon and Haber, *Fundamentals of Behavioral Statistics*, 1972: 290–291). Reprinted by permission of McGraw-Hill.

2.4 cm in thickness, we can now consider the probability of recovering a sample of sherds with a mean thickness of greater than 2.4 cm from a particular population.

A more developed expression of this theorem is the Central Limit Theorem. The Central Limit Theorem states: If random samples are repeatedly drawn from a population with a mean μ and a variance σ^2, the sampling distribution of the standardized sample means will be normally distributed with a $\mu_x = \mu$ and $\sigma_x^2 = \sigma/n$. This approximation becomes more accurate as n becomes larger. The shape of the population distribution is irrelevant to the distribution of the sample means that will always have a normal distribution if n is sufficiently large. The importance of the Central Limit Theorem to statistical analysis is twofold. First of all, many of the things we measure are the sum result of a number of factors. The Central Limit Theorem is applicable to all sums and thus is relevant to many of our measurements. They will appear, therefore, to have normal distributions. Second, many of the statistics we use to evaluate data are themselves sums or averages, and the principles of the Central Limit Theorem are therefore relevant.

As noted previously, many variables used in archaeological analysis exhibit approximately normal distribution patterns, when sample sizes are sufficient to accurately represent their distributions. This pattern results from the clustering of variables around a central value, with a falloff in value frequency as the distance from the center increases. One reason for this pattern is expressed in the Central Limit Theorem and relates to the complex and cumulative nature of many variables. A second, behavioral basis for such patterns lies in cultural concepts of appropriate artifact form. These concepts define, more or less precisely, what an artifact of a particular sort should look like. Artifacts will vary around this ideal or normative form as result of a variety of factors—including the skills of the individual producer in replicating the form, varying perceptions of the ideal, the materials used, and so on. A large sample of these artifacts will therefore exhibit a range of variation. Most artifacts will come near to the central "ideal" form, whereas others will vary around it, producing variable frequency distribution patterns that conform to a normal distribution.

Multimodal frequency distributions, then, can provide evidence that there was more than one ideal to which the pottery producers conformed. These norms might include ideas about size, differing conceptions held by different groups of producers, stylistic variations within a class of artifacts, and so on. Identification of modes in distribution patterns is therefore extremely important to studying and interpreting artifact variation. A number of tests exist to identify modes and evaluate the normalcy of a variable distribution. However, visual inspection of frequency distribution patterns, graphed at varying intervals, is often sufficient.

The *skewness* of distributions is another measure of their shape. Skewness is important when distribution patterns are unimodal but asymmetrical— where the mean, median, and mode are not equal. These graphs will appear to have a tail, leaning to the right or the left. Many archaeological distributions are skewed. The graph of body thicknesses presented in Figure A.5 presents an example of a skewed distribution. In this graph, the mean thickness is equal to .55 cm. Although no vessels can have body thicknesses of less than 0.0, a number of sherds in this sample have quite

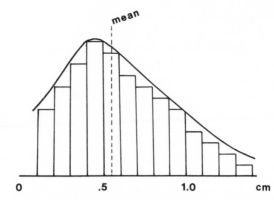

FIGURE A.5.   Skewed distribution: distribution of body thickness.

large thicknesses of up to 1.3 cm. The graph of the frequency distributions of this variable is therefore asymmetrical and skewed to the right.

The shape of variable distributions and the properties of the normal distribution will prove very important in later discussions of some inferential statistical tests. Before turning to those, two more descriptive techniques, one graphical and one numerical, will be considered. These techniques, the *scatter plot and correlation coefficient*, are methods for describing the relations between two sample variables. Variables may be related in a number of ways: (1) they may be independent, such that variation in one variable is not accompanied by variation in the other; (2) they may be linearly related, such that as one variable increases in value, the other also increases (positive linear relationship) or decreases (negative linear relationship); or (3) they exhibit more complex patterning, such as nonlinear relations or clustering.

A scatter plot or scattergram is a method for graphically representing the relations between two quantitative variables. The x and y coordinates of the plot each chart the range of one variable. The data points chart the score of each case on each of the two variables. As with histograms, the scale at which the variable values are graphed can dramatically affect the form of the scatter plot, and plots at several different scales should therefore be generated. Figure A.6 illustrates some of the relations between a pair of variables that can be identified through scatter plots. In Example a, no relation is evident between the two variables, rim diameter and vessel height. Example b illustrates a positive linear relationship between the variables, such that as rim diameter increases, vessel height also increases. In Example c, a negative linear relationship is evident, as rim diameter increases, vessel height decreases, indicating a gradient from narrow-

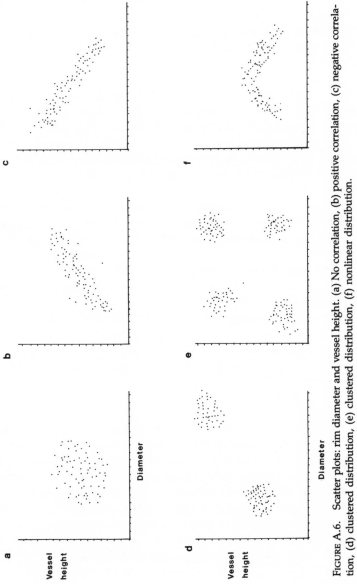

FIGURE A.6. Scatter plots: rim diameter and vessel height. (a) No correlation, (b) positive correlation, (c) negative correlation, (d) clustered distribution, (e) clustered distribution, (f) nonlinear distribution.

mouthed tall vessels to wide-mouthed shallow vessels. Examples d, e, and f exhibit more complex relations between the two variables with discrete classes or clusters of vessels evident in the first two cases, and a pronounced nonlinear relation evident in the last.

The correlation coefficient provides a quantitative measure of the relation between two variables. There are several types of correlation coefficients, though all share a number of characteristics. In all cases, the coefficients can range between 1.00 and −1.00. A high positive value indicates a strong positive linear relationship. A negative value, close to or equal to −1.00, indicates a strong, negative linear relationship. A value of 0.00 indicates no linear relationship between the two variables. In this section, we will consider one correlation coefficient, the *Pearson rho* (*r*) that can be used with interval or ratio-scaled variables. A second correlation coefficient appropriate to ordinal or ranked scale variables will be considered in a subsequent section.

The Pearson rho coefficient provides a measure of "the extent to which the same individuals or events occupy the same position on two variables" (Runyon and Haber 1972:96). One way of assessing this is by examining the relations of the z-scores for each pair of variables over each case in the sample. This provides an assessment of the relative distance (in terms of units of the standard deviation) of each case from the sample mean and of the total relations over the entire sample. A more common and easily computable formula employed in computing the Pearson rho coefficient is:

$$r = \frac{\sum (z_x z_y)}{n} \quad \text{or} \quad r = \frac{\dfrac{\sum xy}{n} - \overline{xy}}{s_x s_y}$$

The derivation of this formula need not concern us here. In effect, the Pearson rho correlation coefficient provides a measure of each xy coordinate in relation to its distance from the x and y sample means, in standardized units. In the examples presented in Figure A.5, Example a has a correlation coefficient close to 0.0, indicating no linear relation; Case b has a high positive correlation coefficient of $r = .85$, indicating a strong positive linear relationship; Case c has a high negative correlation coefficient of $r = -.85$, indicating a strong negative linear relationship. Case d would also have a high positive correlation, whereas Cases e and f would have low correlation coefficients, indicating no linear relationship. The correlation coefficients for Cases d–f clearly do not provide an effective assessment of the relation between the two variables in each case. A relation does exist in each of these cases between the x and y variables, though these relations are not simple linear ones, and simple linear relations are *all* that correlation coefficients can measure.

Although variable distributions need not be normal for the Pearson rho correlation coefficient to be appropriate, they should be unimodal and approximately symmetrical. These requirements do not hold for one or both variables in Examples d through f, and therefore the correlation coefficient is neither appropriate nor effective in describing the relations between the two variables. A careful examination of scatter plots in each of the cases permits the researcher to more accurately define these relations and to consider statistical tests or approaches, such as dividing the sample into subsamples, that can more accurately assess them. The computation of correlation coefficients should always follow the examination of variable distributions as evident through histograms and scatter plots.

QUANTITATIVE DATA: INFERENTIAL STATISTICS

Each of the techniques discussed presents a way of describing and summarizing data in an economical and meaningful form. Data analysis, however, must go beyond the description of data to make statements about the populations of interest. In defining ceramic types, for example, we want to be able to say that the similarities within vessels that we are defining as a single type, or the differences between our types, are so great that they could not be due to chance or random variation. Inferential statistics provide a means for assessing the reliability and significance of inferences based on sample data.

In order to make such assessments, the sample data must be sufficiently large and must be an unbiased representation of the underlying population. The sample data should be a *random sample* of the underlying population, selected in such a way that each member of the population has an equal chance of being selected. A random sample drawn from a population with a normal distribution will, if sufficiently large, be approximately normally distributed, and the mean and standard deviation of the sample should approximate the population mean and standard deviation. The known properties of the standard normal distribution, discussed earlier, provide the basis for statistical inferences about the population.

The computation and interpretation of inferential statistics are based in *probability theory*. Probability theory is concerned with the possible outcomes of experiments. These experiments should be repeatable multiple times under similar conditions with potentially diverse outcomes. Probability theory considers the likelihood of each potential outcome of the experiment or the relative frequency of each outcome. For example, suppose we are analyzing the variable color on a random sample of 1000 pots. In this sample, 500 are black, 200 are brown, and 300 are red. What is the probability that a sherd drawn from the population will be red? To answer this question, we must calculate the relative frequency of red sherds in our sample and assume that our relative frequencies in our sample of 1000 pots are approximately equivalent to the population from which it was drawn. This is equal to 300/1000 or .30. There is, therefore, a .30 or 30% probability that a sherd drawn from that population would be red, or, put another way, if one were to draw a sample of 100 sherds from that population, one would expect 30 of them to be red in color. Suppose though, in our sample of 100 randomly selected sherds, we have 55 black, 18 brown, and 27 red sherds. With probability theory and inferential statistics, we can evaluate the likelihood that this sample came from the same population as our sample of 1,000 sherds.

Inferential statistics involve *hypothesis testing*, evaluating the probability that an event or data configuration could occur by chance. Hypothesis testing requires an explicit definition of alternative hypotheses and the parameters for the acceptance or rejection of these hypotheses. These hypotheses are statements about the underlying population from which the sample being examined was drawn. In statistical tests, two mutually exclusive hypotheses are defined. The first, the *null hypothesis* (H_0), typically the hypothesis we wish to disprove, specifies hypothesized values for the population parameter. The second, or *alternative hypothesis* (H_1), asserts that the population parameter is some value other than the one proposed in the null hypothesis.

As an example, suppose we are examining size differences between two classes of bowls, measured by vessel volume (v). We want to test whether Class A bowls differ in size from Class B bowls. We define two hypotheses assessing this relation. The null hypothesis states that Class A bowls and Class B bowls do not differ in size. The alternative hypothesis would say that these two classes do differ in size. The null hypothesis would thus take the form:

$$H_0: V_A = V_B \quad \text{or} \quad V_A - V_B = 0$$

The alternative hypothesis would take the form:

$$H_1: V_A \neq V_B \quad \text{or} \quad V_A - V_B \neq 0$$

This alternative hypothesis is *nondirectional*; it is not concerned with whether V_A is less than or greater than V_B, only that it is different. Nondirectional alternate hypotheses are called *two-tailed* hypotheses because values of V_A that are either greater or less than V_B can disprove the null hypothesis. We can also test *directional* or *one-tailed* hypotheses. An example of this would be the hypothesis that Class A vessels are larger than Class B vessels. The opposite (null) hypothesis would state that Class A vessels are equal to or smaller in size than Class B vessels.

$$H_0: V_A < V_B$$
$$H_1: V_A \geq V_B$$

Once we have determined our hypotheses, we must next decide under what conditions we will accept or reject the null hypothesis. Typically, we reject the null hypothesis when the probability that it is true is less than 5% or that given our assumptions about the population distribution, there is a less than 5% chance that Class A and Class B could be drawn from the same population. This 5% level, though commonly used in archaeological analysis, is not etched in stone; we may select greater levels, such as 10% or more exclusive levels such as 1%.

Because our statistical tests are based on samples and we do not have access to the entire population, we cannot absolutely prove our hypotheses. What we can do is reject or fail to reject our null hypothesis. When employing the 5% or .05 level of significance, we reject the null hypothesis when a given result occurs by chance only 5% of the time or less, given our assumptions about the population parameters. One does this by assuming that the null hypothesis is true and by calculating the probability of a particular outcome on the basis of this assumption (Runyon and Haber 1972:167).

Two types of errors can occur in these analyses. The first, called a Type I Error, is that we may reject the null hypothesis when it is in fact true. If we set our significance level at .05, then the probability of making a Type I Error is 5%. That is, if Classes A and B are from the same population of vessel-size parameters, in 95% of our experiments, the size values V_A and V_B will be similar enough that we will not reject the null hypothesis. In 5% of the experiments, however, the values of V_A and V_B will differ so that we would reject our null hypothesis, even when the population parameters are in fact equal.

The second type of error, a Type II Error, is that we fail to reject the null hypothesis when it is in fact false. This is more common than a Type I Error. If we define a .05 level of significance, we will not, for example, reject the null hypothesis, if there is a 94% probability that V_A and V_B are not equal, even though this result may reflect actual and important differences in the population parameters. Our definition of the level of significance, therefore, affects the probability of making a Type I or Type II Error. Researchers generally lean toward the conservative side, feeling that it is better to improperly fail to reject the null hypothesis than it is to improperly reject it. Because the population is typically not known to the researcher, it is not possible to know when either type of error has occurred.

Thomas (1976:209–220) has described a six-step procedure for hypothesis testing. The first two steps, already described, are (1) to state the statistical hypotheses that will be evaluated and (2) to select a level of statistical significance (the probability of a Type I Error). The third step is to (3) select the appropriate statistical model with which to evaluate the hypotheses and compute the probability statement. As we will see later, each statistical test is characterized by a set of assumptions concerning the underlying population distribution. In selecting a statistical test, we are accepting that its assumptions hold for the conditions we are examining.

The fourth step is (4) the definition of the values above or below which we will reject the null hypothesis. To do this, we must transform the probability distribution of the test statistic into standardized units, such as z-scores. In one-tailed tests, with a .05 significance level, we will reject our null hypothesis when our observations fall within the 5% area under the normal curve that contains unacceptable deviations from the null hypothesis. This area, which can be defined from a chart of areas under the normal curve, corresponds to a z-score of −1.64 or 1.64, depending on the directionality of the null hypothesis. For two-tailed tests, the area of rejection will be that area either less than or greater than the 95% range that is symmetrical around the mean. Because the significance level and total area of rejection is fixed at .05, each tail can only contain half of that area, or .025, in its area of rejection, a z-score of 1.96 or −1.96.

The fifth step (5) is to perform the computations of the statistical test, to convert sample values into some measure that can be evaluated relative to a standardized distribution and to make a decision to reject or fail to reject the null hypothesis. Finally, Thomas's sixth step (6) is to state the decision in nonstatistical terms, that is, in a way that has direct relevance to the problem under study.

Consider as an example, a class of red-painted jars. Previous research has indicated that these jars have a mean maximum diameter of 30 cm, with a standard deviation of 5.4 cm. An archaeologist working near the region where these jars are found recovers a sample of 400 apparently similar jars that have a mean maximum diameter of 39 cm. She or he wants to test whether these jars could belong to the known population of red-painted jars. The null hypothesis (Step 1) of this analysis is that the sample mean maximum diameter is equal to the mean maximum diameter of the known population. The alternative hypothesis is that the means are not equal. The level of significance we will evaluate (Step 2) is .05, and we can assume that our sample is a random sample from a normally distributed population (Step 3). This is a two-tailed test. We will therefore reject the null hypothesis when the standardized value of mean maximum diameter is greater than 1.94 or less than −1.94. To convert this z-score to actual maximum diameter values, we can use the following formula, solving for x and assuming that H_0 is true (Step 4):

$$z = \frac{\mu_i - \mu}{\sigma}$$

$$= 1.94 = \frac{30 - \mu}{5.4}$$

$$= \mu = 30 \pm (5.4 \times 1.94) = 19.52 \text{ or } 40.47$$

Thus we will reject the null hypothesis if our sample mean maximum diameter is less than 19.52 cm or greater than 40.47. Because the sample our archaeologist is examining has a mean maximum diameter of 39 cm, that is less than the 40.47 cm that marks the boundary of the area of rejection, we cannot reject the null hypothesis in this instance (Step 5). We therefore (Step 6) cannot reject the hypothesis that the sample of 400 jars belongs to the known population of red-painted jars from the region and will, at least provisionally, group them with that population. This, in turn, implies that this new sample is linked to previous samples in a meaningful way: as a product of the same cultural group, through trade, or in other ways that must themselves be evaluated.

In the example presented, we assumed that something was known about the parameters of the population of red-painted jars. In many cases, we do not know the population parameters—the mean, variance, and standard deviation—and therefore cannot calculate the standard normal z-score against which we can evaluate our sample. We therefore must estimate the necessary parameters from the sample itself. Some of the properties of the distribution and standard error of a collection of sample means have been discussed earlier in the consideration of the Central Limit Theorem. The standard error, or standard deviation of the sample means, can be estimated by:

$$s_{\bar{x}} = \frac{\sum_{i=1}^{n} (\bar{x}_i - \bar{x})^2}{n}$$

We would like the value $s_{\bar{x}}$ to be a good approximation of σ, the population standard deviation. This is not the case, however, and with small samples, $s_{\bar{x}}$ will tend to underestimate σ more than half of the time. The distribution of the statistic based on sample means is thus more spread out than the normal distribution. This new distribution is called a t-distribution. Areas under the t-distribution can be used to estimate the probability of certain occurrence (Table A.2). The t-table is similar to the table of z-scores discussed earlier, except that information on the sample size is necessary to evaluate a t-score. This information is linked to the concept of

TABLE A.2. The t-Distribution

	Level of significance for one-tailed test					
	.10	.05	.025	.01	.005	.0005
	Level of significance for two-tailed test					
df	.20	.10	.05	.02	.01	.001
1	3.078	6.314	12.706	31.821	63.657	636.619
2	1.886	2.920	4.303	6.965	9.925	31.598
3	1.638	2.353	3.182	4.541	5.841	12.941
4	1.533	2.132	2.776	3.747	4.604	8.610
5	1.476	2.015	2.571	3.365	4.032	6.859
6	1.440	1.943	2.447	3.143	3.707	5.959
7	1.415	1.895	2.365	2.998	3.499	5.405
8	1.397	1.860	2.306	2.896	3.355	5.041
9	1.383	1.833	2.262	2.821	3.250	4.781
10	1.372	1.812	2.228	2.764	3.169	4.587
11	1.363	1.796	2.201	2.718	3.106	4.437
12	1.356	1.782	2.179	2.681	3.055	4.318
13	1.350	1.771	2.160	2.650	3.012	4.221
14	1.345	1.761	2.145	2.624	2.977	4.140
15	1.341	1.753	2.131	2.602	2.947	4.073
16	1.337	1.746	2.120	2.583	3.921	4.015
17	1.333	1.740	2.110	2.567	2.898	3.965
18	1.330	1.734	2.101	2.552	2.878	3.922
19	1.328	1.729	2.093	2.539	2.861	3.883
20	1.325	1.725	2.086	2.528	2.845	3.850
21	1.323	1.721	2.080	2.518	2.831	3.819
22	1.321	1.717	2.074	2.508	2.819	3.792
23	1.319	1.714	2.069	2.500	2.807	3.767
24	1.318	1.711	2.064	2.492	2.797	3.745
25	1.316	1.708	2.060	2.485	2.787	3.725
26	1.315	1.706	2.056	2.479	2.779	3.707
27	1.314	1.703	2.052	2.473	2.771	3.690
28	1.313	1.701	2.048	2.467	2.763	3.674
29	1.311	1.699	2.045	2.462	2.756	3.659
30	1.310	1.697	2.042	2.457	2.750	3.646
40	1.303	1.684	2.021	2.423	2.704	3.551
60	1.296	1.671	2.000	2.390	2.660	3.460
120	1.289	1.658	1.980	2.358	2.617	3.373
∞	1.282	1.645	1.960	2.326	2.576	3.291

(After Runyon and Haber, *Fundamentals of Behavioral Statistics*, 1972:293). Reprinted by permission of McGraw-Hill.

degrees of freedom (*df*) that is very important in statistical analysis. Degrees of freedom refer to the number of freely varying quantities in a sample. If, as in the *t*-distribution, our sample must have a mean of a particular value, then the last case we add to the sample must have a value that results in our sample having the necessary mean. All other cases may vary freely, so long as the last one takes whatever value is necessary to attain the mean. In this case, we say that we have $n - 1$ degrees of freedom because all but one case vary freely.

One of the most common applications of the *t*-distribution is in the comparison of two sample means when σ is unknown through a test known as the student *t*-test. Suppose we have samples of ceramic vessels from two different sites. From Site A, we have 26 bowls with a mean rim diameter of 18.0 cm ($s_A = 3.2$). From Site B, we have 35 bowls with a mean rim diameter of 15 cm ($s_B = 3.6$). We want to be able to evaluate the relationship between bowl size at the two sites, in particular, to test the hypothesis that bowls from Site A are significantly larger than bowls from Site B. The differences in mean rim diameter that we observe between the bowls from the two sites may result from a variety of factors. These differences may be the function of sampling error resulting from the relatively small sample sizes from each site. Or they may reflect a true difference in vessel size between sites, as a result of factors such as variation in norms, in molds used in bowl production, or the association of vessel size with other factors, such as household size. Phrased another way, the bowls may come from a single statistical population or from two distinct statistical populations.

We do not know the population variances of our samples and therefore cannot rely on the properties of the standard normal distribution to solve this problem. Rather, we must develop an estimate of the population variance and standard deviation, using the available data from our samples. To do this, we assume that the two populations have identical variances. The discrepancies between the two samples, if any, therefore result from differences in their central tendencies, or means, rather than to differences in distributions about the mean. By assuming identical variances, we can pool the individual sample variances into a single estimate of population variance:

$$s_p^2 = \frac{\displaystyle\sum_{i=1}^{n}(x_i - \bar{x})^2 + \sum_{i=1}^{n}(y_i - \bar{y})^4}{n_x + n_y - 2}$$

This provides an estimator of the total variability in the population. We can then use this estimate to calculate a *t*-score for the differences between two sample means:

$$t = \frac{(\bar{x} - \bar{y}) - (\mu_x - \mu_y)}{s_{x-y}}$$

where: df equals $n_x + n_y - 2$; $\mu x - \mu y$ equals the expected values stated in the null hypothesis; and s_{x-y} equals the standard error of the differences between the two sample means.

More detailed discussions of the derivations of these formulae can be found in statistical texts. Now, however, we can turn to an example of the application of the student t-distribution in the analysis of archaeological data.

In this example, we will consider samples of ceramic bowls from two houses within a site. Rim-diameter measures have been recorded in each sample as follows:

House A: 10, 11, 12, 12, 10, 8, 13 cm

$n = 7$, $\bar{x}_A = 10.86$, $s_A = 1.68$

House B: 15, 13, 14, 14, 13, 12, 12, 13, 14

$n = 9$, $\bar{x}_B = 13.33$, $s_B = 1.00$

We want to test whether the residents of House B can be said to have used larger bowls than the residents of House A at the .05 level of significance. The hypotheses we are evaluating are $H_0 : \mu_a > \mu_b$ and $H_1 : \mu_a < \mu_b$. We will reject H_0 if our t value is less than or equal to -1.761, as found on our table of t-scores for a one-tailed test with 14 degrees of freedom ($7 + 9 - 2$). To compute t, we must first compute the pooled estimate of variance:

$$s_p^2 = \frac{18.86 + 8.00}{14} = 1.919$$

and the standard error of the differences between the sample variances:

$$s_{x-y} = \frac{1.919}{7} + \frac{1.919}{9} = .274 + .2132 = .6979$$

Then:

$$t = \frac{10.86 - 13.33}{.6979} = -3.54$$

The value for t, -3.54, lies far outside of the -1.761 that defines the region of rejection. We therefore must reject our null hypothesis at the .05 level, and can, in fact, reject it at the .005 level of significance. The bowls from the two houses can be said to differ significantly in size or, put another way, the samples from each house do not appear to have been selected from the same statistical population of bowl size.

The two-sample student t-test permits comparisons of sample means from independent samples that may or may not be derived from a single population. We can use this test to compare samples from two proveniences, such as sites or locations within sites, as in the example presented. Chronological distinctions between samples from two stratigraphic layers could be similarly examined. In addition, the student t-test might be useful in the definition and evaluation of ceramic typologies. If, for example, we divide vessels into distinct classes on the basis of a bimodal histogram of a particular variable distribution, we can use the student t-test to evaluate this and other variable distributions to aid in assessing the legitimacy and usefulness of this division.

Two assumptions are critical prerequisites to the use of the student t-statistic. We must be able to assume that our samples are random samples from populations that are approximately normally distributed and that they have equal variances. If these assumptions cannot be met for particular data sets, then other nonparametric tests must be used to compare the sample means.

The student t-test is an important technique for comparing two samples. Often, however, we wish to examine and compare more than two sample means; we may wish to look at samples from several different sites or areas within sites. An alternate test, called the *analysis of variance* test or "anova," must be used when dealing with more than two samples. The analysis of variance technique permits the simultaneous comparison of two or more sample means. It can be used in the comparison of two or more independent variables or, as we will consider here, in the analysis of a single variable over several samples. The analysis of variance technique is somewhat more complex than the student t-technique discussed. It is extremely useful in that we often wish to compare more than two samples, such as when looking at the frequency distribution of a quantitative variable among three or more provenience units, or differences between three or more types.

The analysis of variance technique involves the estimation of two independent measures of variance—one based on the variability between the groups and the other based on the variability within groups. The *F-ratio* provides a measure for assessing the differences between two variances. The *F*-ratio is three-dimensional; we must, therefore, consider the degrees of freedom of each variance and a ratio of the two variances. The columns of the *F*-table refer to the *df* of the numerator in our variance ratio, whereas the rows refer to the degrees of freedom of the denominator. In the analysis of variance technique, the numerator is the estimated variance between samples, whereas the denominator is the estimate of the variance within samples. If the between-group variance is large relative to the within-group variance, the F-ratio will be large. If the converse holds, and the between-group variance is small relative to the within-group variance, then the F-ratio will be small. A large F-ratio implies that differences between the groups are greater than differences within any group, and therefore the differences between the groups may be statistically significant. Table A.3 presents F-ratios values at the .05 and .01 level of significance.

An important concept in the analysis of variance is the *sum of squares*. The sum of squares is, simply, the numerator in the formula for variance (Runyon and Haber 1972:217):

$$\sum_{i=1}^{n} \bar{x}^2 = \sum X^2 - \frac{(\sum X^2)}{N}$$

In the analysis of variance technique we can divide the total sum of squares into its two components: the within-group sum of squares and the between-group sum of squares.

The total sum of squares is computed by subtracting the overall mean of all samples from each individual score, squaring that value, and summing the resultant values over all cases:

$$\sum_{i=1}^{n} X^2_{tot} = \sum_{i=1}^{n} (x_i - \bar{x}_{tot})^2 = \sum_{i=1}^{n} x^2_{tot} - \frac{\sum_{i=1}^{n} x_{tot}^2}{n}$$

The within-group sum of squares is the sum of the sum of squares obtained within each group. That is:

$$\sum_{i=1}^{n} x^2_w = \sum_{i=1}^{n} x^2_1 + \sum_{i=1}^{n} x^2_2 + \sum_{i=1}^{n} x^2_n$$

The sum of squares for each group is computed by the formula:

$$\sum_{i=1}^{n} x^2 = \sum_{i=1}^{n} x_i^2 - \left(\sum_{i=1}^{n} x\right)^{2/n}$$

The between-group sum of squares is obtained by subtracting the overall mean from each group mean, squaring that value, and multiplying by the number of cases (n) in each group, and summing across all groups:

$$\sum_{i=1}^{n} x_b^2 = \sum_{i=1}^{n} n_i(\bar{x}_i - \bar{x}_{tot})^2$$

TABLE A.3. The F-Distribution

df denominator	1	2	3	4	5	6	7	8	9	10	11	12	20	50	100
1	161	200	216	225	230	234	237	239	241	242	243	244	248	252	252
	4052	**4999**	**5403**	**5625**	**5764**	**5859**	**5928**	**5981**	**6022**	**6056**	**6082**	**6106**	**6208**	**6302**	**6334**
2	18.51	19.00	19.25	19.16	19.30	19.33	19.36	19.37	19.38	19.39	19.40	19.41	19.44	19.47	19.49
	98.49	**99.01**	**99.17**	**99.25**	**99.30**	**99.33**	**99.34**	**99.36**	**99.39**	**99.40**	**99.41**	**99.42**	**99.45**	**99.48**	**99.49**
3	10.13	9.55	9.28	9.12	9.01	8.94	8.88	8.84	8.81	8.78	8.76	8.74	8.66	8.58	8.56
	43.12	**30.81**	**29.46**	**28.71**	**28.24**	**27.91**	**27.67**	**27.49**	**27.34**	**27.23**	**27.13**	**27.05**	**26.69**	**26.30**	**26.23**
4	7.71	6.94	6.59	6.39	6.26	6.16	6.09	6.04	6.00	5.96	5.93	5.91	5.80	5.70	5.66
	21.20	**18.00**	**16.69**	**15.98**	**15.52**	**15.21**	**14.98**	**14.80**	**14.66**	**14.54**	**14.45**	**14.37**	**14.02**	**13.69**	**13.57**
5	6.61	5.79	5.41	5.19	5.05	4.95	4.88	4.82	4.78	4.74	4.70	4.68	4.56	4.44	4.40
	16.26	**13.27**	**12.06**	**11.39**	**10.97**	**10.67**	**10.45**	**10.27**	**10.15**	**10.05**	**9.96**	**9.89**	**9.55**	**9.24**	**9.13**
6	5.99	5.14	4.76	4.53	4.39	4.28	4.21	4.15	4.10	4.06	4.03	4.00	3.87	3.75	3.71
	13.74	**10.92**	**9.78**	**9.15**	**8.75**	**8.47**	**8.26**	**8.10**	**7.98**	**7.87**	**7.79**	**7.72**	**7.39**	**7.09**	**6.99**
7	5.59	4.74	4.35	4.12	3.97	3.87	3.79	3.73	3.68	3.63	3.60	3.57	3.44	3.32	3.28
	12.25	**9.55**	**8.45**	**7.85**	**7.46**	**7.19**	**7.00**	**6.84**	**6.71**	**6.62**	**6.54**	**6.47**	**6.15**	**5.85**	**5.75**
8	5.32	4.46	4.07	3.84	3.69	3.58	3.50	3.44	3.39	3.34	3.31	3.28	3.15	3.03	2.98
	11.26	**8.65**	**7.59**	**7.01**	**6.63**	**6.37**	**6.19**	**6.03**	**5.91**	**5.82**	**5.74**	**5.67**	**5.36**	**5.06**	**4.96**
9	5.12	4.26	3.86	3.63	3.48	3.37	3.29	3.23	3.18	3.13	3.10	3.07	2.93	2.80	2.76
	10.56	**8.02**	**6.99**	**6.42**	**6.06**	**5.80**	**5.62**	**5.47**	**5.35**	**5.26**	**5.18**	**5.11**	**4.80**	**4.51**	**4.41**
10	4.96	4.10	3.71	3.48	3.33	3.22	3.14	3.07	3.02	2.97	2.94	2.91	2.77	2.64	2.59
	10.04	**7.56**	**6.55**	**5.99**	**5.64**	**5.39**	**5.21**	**5.06**	**4.95**	**4.85**	**4.78**	**4.71**	**4.41**	**4.12**	**4.01**
11	4.84	3.98	3.59	3.36	3.20	3.09	3.01	2.95	2.90	2.86	2.82	2.79	2.65	2.50	2.45
	9.65	**7.20**	**6.22**	**5.67**	**5.32**	**5.07**	**4.88**	**4.74**	**4.63**	**4.54**	**4.46**	**4.40**	**4.10**	**3.80**	**3.70**
12	4.75	3.88	3.49	3.26	3.11	3.00	2.92	2.85	2.80	2.76	2.72	2.69	2.54	2.40	2.35
	9.33	**6.93**	**5.95**	**5.41**	**5.06**	**4.82**	**4.65**	**4.50**	**4.39**	**4.30**	**4.22**	**4.16**	**3.86**	**3.56**	**3.46**
20	4.35	3.49	3.10	2.87	2.71	2.60	2.52	2.45	2.40	2.35	2.31	2.28	2.12	1.96	1.90
	8.10	**5.85**	**4.94**	**4.43**	**4.10**	**3.87**	**3.71**	**3.56**	**3.45**	**3.37**	**3.30**	**3.23**	**2.94**	**2.63**	**2.53**
50	4.03	3.18	2.79	2.56	2.40	2.29	2.20	2.13	2.07	2.02	1.98	1.95	1.78	1.60	1.52
	7.17	**5.06**	**4.20**	**3.72**	**3.41**	**3.18**	**3.02**	**2.88**	**2.78**	**2.70**	**2.62**	**2.56**	**2.26**	**1.94**	**1.82**
100	3.94	3.09	2.70	2.46	2.30	2.19	2.10	2.03	1.97	1.92	1.88	1.85	1.68	1.48	1.39
	6.90	**4.82**	**3.98**	**3.51**	**3.20**	**2.99**	**2.82**	**2.69**	**2.59**	**2.51**	**2.43**	**2.36**	**2.06**	**1.73**	**1.59**

(After Runyon and Haber, *Fundamentals of Behavioral Statistics*, 1972: 294–296). Reprinted by permission of McGraw-Hill.
Note. The obtained F is significant at a given level if it is equal to or *greater than* the value shown in the table (0.05 [light row] and 0.01 [bold row]).

As an example, let us examine three ceramic samples from three chronologically related sites in a region. Our samples are composed of five small jars from each site, and we have measured the variable vessel height on each jar:

We wish to test the hypothesis that these three samples are drawn from a single statistical population of vessel height. Our null hypothesis, H_0, is $\mu_a = \mu_b = \mu_c$. Our alternative hypothesis, H_1, is that the three samples are not equal (μ_a not equal to μ_b is not equal to μ_c).

Analysis of Variance Test:
Vessel Height from Three Sites

	Site A		Site B		Site C	
	x_i	x_i^2	x_i	x_i^2	x_i	x_i^2
	7	49	9	81	4	16
	8	64	10	100	5	25
	9	81	11	121	6	36
	10	100	12	144	7	49
	11	121	13	169	8	64
Sum	45	415	55	615	30	190

$$n_a = 5 \qquad n_b = 5 \qquad n_c = 5$$
$$x_a = 9.00 \qquad x_b = 11.00 \qquad x_c = 6.00$$
$$n_{tot} = 15 \qquad x_{tot} = 8.67 \qquad \Sigma x^2_{tot} = 130 \qquad \Sigma x^2 = 1220$$

To compute the total sum of squares we use the formula:

$$\sum_{i=1}^{n} X^2_{tot} = \sum_{i=1}^{n} x^2_{tot} - \sum_{i=1}^{n} x^2/N = 1220 - (130)^2/15 = 93.33$$

The within-group sum of squares equals:

$$\sum_{i=1}^{n} X^2_w = \sum_{i=1}^{5} X^2_A + \sum_{i=1}^{5} X^2_B + \sum_{i=1}^{5} X^2_C$$

$$= (415 - 45^2/5) + (615 - 55^2/5) + 190 - 30^2/5)$$

$$= 10 + 10 + 10 = 30$$

The between-group sum of squares equals:

$$\sum_{i=1}^{n} x_b^2 = \sum_{i=1}^{3} n_i(\overline{x}_i - \overline{x}_{tot})^2$$

$$= 5(9 - 8.67)^2 + 5(11 - 8.67)^2 + 5(6 - 8.67)^2$$

$$= .5445 + 27.1445 + 35.6445 = 63.333$$

(Note that the between-group sum of squares and the within-group sum of squares add up to the total sum of squares value.)

To arrive at variance estimates from the within- and between-group sum of squares, we must divide each by the appropriate number of degrees of freedom. For the between-group value, the degrees of freedom equal the number of groups (k) minus 1. With three groups, our $df = 3 - 1 = 2$. Our estimate of between-group variance (σ_b^2), then, is equal to $63.33/2 = 31.667$.

The within-group degrees of freedom is equal to the total number of cases minus the number of groups, in this case $15 - 3 = 12$. Our within-group variance estimate ($\sigma^2 w$) is therefore equal to $30/12 = 2.500$.

Next we must calculate the F-ratio and determine whether our variance estimates could have been reasonably derived from the same statistical population at the significance level of .05. The F-ratio is computed by dividing the between-group variance estimate by the within-group variance estimate.

$$F = \frac{\sigma^2_b}{\sigma^2_w} = 31.667/2.5 = 12.66$$

Our degrees of freedom are 2/12. We next use the F-ratio table for 2 (column—numerator) and 12 (row—denominator) degrees of freedom and the .05 level of significance to define our region of rejection. We will reject the null hypothesis when F is greater than 3.88. We therefore reject the null hypothesis in this example and can say that the samples of vessels from Sites A, B, and C represent statistically significant-sized classes, that is, they were not drawn from the same statistical population.

The analysis of variance technique requires the assumptions that the samples are random samples from populations that are normally distributed and that the sample variance of each group is approximately equal. In the example presented, the sample size of each group is relatively small ($n = 5$), and sampling biases could dramatically alter the results. Ideally, one would want to use much larger sample sizes in the analysis of variance (and student t) tests. The complexity of calculations clearly increases dramatically as sample size increases; hence this limited example. The calculation of the necessary values becomes very involved and time consuming and can be significantly aided by computer assistance, with prepackaged statistical programs (like SPSS—the Statistical Package for the Social Sciences, and SAS).

QUALITATIVE DATA: DESCRIPTIVE STATISTICS

Qualitative variables can take two forms: variables measured on nominal or ordinal scales. These two measurement scales share the characteristic that no absolute quantitative values are assigned to attribute states and can be treated similarly in descriptive summaries. A useful means of displaying qualitative data is the bar graph (see Figure A.7 a,b). Bar graphs differ from histograms in that there is no necessary relation between the classes being graphed. The y-axis of the bar graph can employ either raw count data or frequency data on the proportion of cases in each variable state. A circle graph or pie chart provides another graphical technique for representing the frequency distributions of nominal data. In a circle graph, the relative frequencies of each variable state are illustrated such that each is represented by an appropriately sized arc of the circle (see Figure A.7c). Ogives, or cumulative frequency curves, have been discussed previously and are commonly used with qualitative data (see Figure A.7d). The absence of necessary ordering between variable states is a problem in cumulative frequency charts, and manipulation of the ordering can result in a distortion of the data to achieve particular results.

Numerical summaries of single qualitative variables are restricted to counts per variable state or a statement of the relative frequencies of each variable state, for example, 40% or .40 red, 30% or .30 black, and so on. Numerical summaries such as the mean, standard deviation, mode, and variance are not relevant to qualitative data.

Under many circumstances we may wish to look at the relation between two nominal variables and the co-occurrence of variable states. For example, we may wish to consider if there is a relation between vessel shape and vessel color, between shape and time period, between size and shape, and so on. An inferential method for doing this is the chi-square statistic, which will be discussed later. This statistic is dramatically effected by sample size. An alternative descriptive approach to assessing the relation between categorical or nominal variables is the *phi coefficient of correlation*. The phi coefficient is independent of sample size, though it is applicable only to assessing the relation between two variables that each have two attribute states. These variables can be expressed in a contingency table:

	Variable A State 1	Variable B State 2	Total
Variable B State 1	a	b	$a + b$
Variable B State 2	c	d	$c + d$
Total	$a + c$	$b + d$	$a + b + c + d$

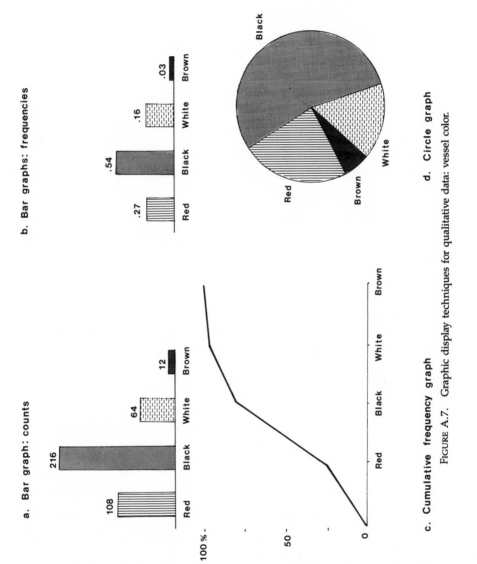

FIGURE A.7.   Graphic display techniques for qualitative data: vessel color.

When each variable has only two attribute states, the contingency table produced is called a 2 by 2 contingency table. The phi coefficient is calculated by the formula:

$$\Phi = \frac{ad - bc}{(a + b)(a + c)(b + d)(c + d)}$$

Phi, then, equals the difference between the products of the diagonals, divided by the square root of the product of the row and column totals. Like the Pearson rho correlation coefficient presented earlier, the value of phi can range between -1.00 and 1.00. A high negative value for phi indicates an inverse relation between the two variables, such that State 1 of Variable A co-occurs with State 2 of Variable B, and State 2 of Variable A co-occurs with State 1 of Variable B. When the opposite relation holds, then phi will have a high positive value. A phi of 0.00 indicates no association between the two variables.

Another measure of correlation, the *Tau-b* (*T*) *coefficient*, can be used to assess the correlations between two nominal variables when two or more attribute states exist. The Tau-b coefficient considers the probability of incorrectly assigning an individual to a particular state of one variable, under conditions when the other variable state is known and unknown. This will be illustrated in an example. Our data consist of measurements on two nominal variables: decoration (Variable A) and vessel shape (Variable B). The variable states for the first are decorated and undecorated; the variable states for the second are bowls and jars:

	Decoration		
Shape	Decorated	Undecorated	Total
Bowls	5	36	41
Jars	22	12	34
Total	27	48	75

To compute Tau-b we must calculate the probability of incorrectly assigning an individual vessel to a state of the shape variable when the state of the decoration variable is unknown and when it is known. In this example, we have a total of 41 bowl sherds and 34 jar sherds. If we lined up these 75 sherds on a table and randomly assigned them to bowl and jar piles, what would be the probability that we would incorrectly assign any individual sherd to the bowl category, if we knew the total number of bowls and jars we wanted to end up with (i.e., 41 bowls and 34 jars)? The probability that an individual sherd would be incorrectly placed in the class bowl (B_1) is equal to 34/75 or .45. Because, in the long run, 41 individuals must be assigned to Class B_1, we can expect $41 \times 34/75$ or 18.6 incorrect assignments, and $41 - 18.6$ or 22.4 correct assignments of individuals to class B_1. Similarly, the probability of incorrectly assigning a sherd to the class jars (B_2) is equal to 41/75 or .55. We would expect, therefore, that $34 \times 41/75$ or 18.6 sherds would be incorrectly assigned to class B_2, and $34 - 20.4$ or 18.6 individual sherds will be correctly assigned to class B_2. We therefore estimate a total of $18.6 + 18.6$ or 37.2 errors, if individual sherds are randomly assigned to states of Variable B.

Now, if we repeated this procedure, taking into account what we know about Variable A, that is, that 5 of the 41 bowls are decorated and 36 undecorated, and 22 of the 34 jars are decorated and 12 undecorated, what would be the probability of incorrectly assigning a decorated sherd to the class of decorated bowls? In this case, the probability would be equal to the number of decorated bowls divided by the total number of decorated sherds: 5/27 or .19. If we randomly sort the vessels into four piles, knowing in advance how many sherds must end up in each pile, we could expect to incorrectly assign $22 \times .19$ or 4.07 sherds to the pile of decorated bowls.

Similarly, when assigning sherds to the decorated jar class, we would expect to make $5 \times 22/27$ or 4.07 incorrect assignments. The probability that we would incorrectly randomly assign an individual undecorated sherd to the class undecorated bowls would be equal to 12/48 or .25. In assigning 36 undecorated sherds to the class undecorated bowls, we would expect to make $36 \times .25$ or 9.0 errors. The probability of incorrectly assigning an undecorated sherd to the class undecorated jars is equal to the number of undecorated bowls divided by the total number of undecorated sherds, or $36/48 = .75$. In randomly selecting 12 undecorated sherds to be placed in the pile of undecorated jars, we would expect to make $12 \times .75$, or 9.0 errors. The total number of errors that we would make when randomly sorting sherds into this piles, with the total number of decorated and undecorated of bowl and jar sherds known, would be equal to $4.07 + 4.07 + 9.0 + 9.0 = 26.14$ errors.

The formula for computing the Tau-b coefficient is:

$$\text{Tau-b} = \frac{(\text{\# of errors in B w/unknown A}) - (\text{\# of errors in B w/known A})}{(\text{\# of errors in B w/unknown A})}$$

$$= \frac{37.2 - 26.14}{37.2} = .297$$

We can claim that with a knowledge of the distribution of Variable A we will make about $37.20 - 26.14$ or 11.06 fewer errors than we would in the absence of that knowledge and that therefore, there is a positive relation of .297 between states of the variable decoration and states of the variable vessel form. Tau-b can be similarly computed when more than two variable states are recorded. We can reverse the computations to consider the number of errors in assignments to Variable A when Variable B is known and unknown (Tau-a).

QUALITATIVE DATA: INFERENTIAL STATISTICS

The class of inferential statistics relevant to nominal or ordinal data is known as nonparametric statistics. Unlike the parametric tests presented earlier, "a nonparametric test of significance is defined as one which makes no assumptions concerning the shape of the parent distribution or population, and accordingly is commonly referred to as a distribution-free statistic" (Runyon and Haber 1972:229). Such tests are often less powerful than their parametric counterparts but are useful and necessary in a wide variety of cases when we are dealing with qualitative data or cannot assume normal distributions. In this section, I will first consider tests for nominal qualitative data and then examine tests for ordinal qualitative data.

Nominal Data

The most common and important inferential statistic for the analysis of nominal data is the *chi-square statistic* (χ^2). The chi-square test evaluates the independence of categorical variables in order to answer the question: Is there a statistically significant relationship between variable states of nominal Variables A and B? The counts of occurrences of each combination of Variable A and B states can be charted in a contingency tables of r rows $\times$ c columns, where r equals the number of possible variable states of Variable B and c equals the number of possible variable states of Variable A.

As an example, let us examine the numbers of red and black vessels recovered in stratigraphic excavations at a two-component site. Variable A in this example is color, and Variable B is chronological period. In Period I, 45 of 195 recovered sherds are red in color, and the remaining 150 sherds are black. In Period II, 65 of the 95 recovered sherds are red, and 30 are black. Phrased another way, 45 of the 110 red sherds date to Period I, with 65 from Period II, and 150 of the 180 black sherds date to Period I, with 30 from Period II.

These can be illustrated in a 2 × 2 contingency table:

	Red	Black	Row total
Period I	45	150	195
Period II	65	30	95
Total	110	180	290

We wish to test if there is a statistically significant relationship between color and chronological period in this sample and if our sample is a random sample of a population in the population of sherds of this site. Our null hypothesis states that there is no significant relation between the variables color and chronological period, whereas our alternative hypothesis states that there is a significant relation between the two variables. We will evaluate these hypotheses at the .01 level of significance.

If no relation exists between the two variables, we would expect that the number of cases in each cell of our contingency table would be proportional to the marginal totals of each class for that cell. We can compute these *expected frequencies* (E) by multiplying column totals times row totals and dividing this product by the total number of cases. In the present example our expected frequencies are:

	Red	Black	Row total
Period I	$110 \times 195/290 = 74$	$180 \times 195/290 = 121$	195
Period II	$110 \times 95/290 = 36$	$180 \times 95/290 = 59$	95
Total	110	180	290

If the *observed frequencies* (O) are very different from the frequencies we would expect if no relation existed between the two variables, then we will reject our null hypothesis. The statistic we use for evaluating the relation between the two variables, the chi-square statistic, is computed by the following formula:

$$\chi^2 = \frac{\sum_{i=1}^{n} (O - E)^2}{E}$$

In our example,

$$\chi^2 = \frac{(45 - 74)^2}{74} + \frac{(150 - 121)^2}{121} + \frac{(65 - 36)^2}{36} + \frac{(30 - 59)^2}{59}$$

$$= 11.365 + 6.950 + 23.361 + 14.254 = 55.930$$

The degrees of freedom for the chi-square statistic equal the number of rows minus 1 times the number of columns minus 1 $(R - 1)(c - 1)$. The chi-square statistic sums the deviations for each case from the expected frequencies. Dividing each product by the expected frequency for that cell produces the standardized value for the chi-square statistic, similar to a z-score. The probability of a particular value of chi-square under conditions of no relationship between two variables varies with different degrees of freedom. The proportion of area under the curve of the chi-square distribution (which is asymmetrical) for different degrees of freedom is presented in Table A.4.

In our example, we have 1 degree of freedom, $(2 - 1)(2 - 1)$. With 1 df and a significance of .01, we would reject the null hypothesis when our chi-square value is greater than 6.63490. Because our chi-square value of 55.930 is greater than our level of rejection, we will reject the null hypothesis at the .01 level and could, in fact, reject it at the .001 level ($\chi^2 = 10.828$). We can therefore state that there is a statistically significant relation between vessel color and chronological period. In particular, Period I is dominated by black vessels, whereas during Period 2, red vessels predominate. Chi-square statistics are computed in the same manner when more than two states exist for each variable (3×3 tables, 4×6 tables, and so on).

As noted earlier, the chi-square statistic is dramatically affected by sample sizes. As an example, if we were to double the number of cases in each cell, which preserves the same relative frequencies of each case, we also would double our expected values. The value of the computed chi-square statistic would also double, making the relation appear even more significant than in the original example. When sample sizes are very small, the chi-square statistic is not a reliable measure of the relation between two variables. As a general rule, in the 1 degree of freedom case (a 2×2 contingency table), each cell should contain 5 or more members. With more than 1 degree of freedom, 80% of the cells should contain 5 or more members. If these conditions are not met, other statistical tests, such as the maximum likelihood statistic, can be applied (see Siegel 1956, for discussion of other tests of independence for nominal variables).

Ordinal Data

In this section we will consider some statistical tests appropriate to the analysis of ordinal data. Ordinal variables are those that are recorded along an ordered scale rather than being measured. Somewhat more information is provided than with nominal variables, though less than with quantitative measures. The techniques appropriate to the analysis of ordinal data

TABLE A.4. The Chi-Square Distribution

df	p = .99	.98	.95	.90	.80	.70	.50	.30	.20	.10	.05	.02	.01
1	.000157	.000628	.00393	.0158	.0642	.148	.455	1.074	1.642	2.706	3.841	5.412	6.635
2	.0201	.0404	.103	.211	.446	.713	1.386	2.408	3.219	4.605	5.991	7.824	9.210
3	.115	.185	.352	.584	1.005	1.424	2.366	3.665	4.642	6.251	7.815	9.837	11.341
4	.297	.429	.711	1.064	1.649	2.195	3.357	4.878	5.989	7.779	9.488	11.668	13.277
5	.554	.752	1.145	1.610	2.343	3.000	4.351	6.064	7.289	9.236	11.070	13.388	15.086
6	.872	1.134	1.635	2.204	3.070	3.828	5.348	7.231	8.558	10.645	12.592	15.033	16.812
7	1.239	1.564	2.167	2.833	3.822	4.671	6.346	8.383	9.803	12.017	14.067	16.622	18.475
8	1.646	2.032	2.733	3.490	4.594	5.527	7.344	9.524	11.030	13.362	15.507	18.168	20.090
9	2.088	2.532	3.325	4.168	5.380	6.393	8.343	10.656	12.242	14.684	16.919	19.679	21.666
10	2.558	3.059	3.940	4.865	6.179	7.267	9.342	11.781	13.442	15.987	18.307	21.161	23.209
11	3.053	3.609	4.575	5.578	6.989	8.148	10.341	12.899	14.631	17.275	19.675	22.618	24.725
12	3.571	4.178	5.226	6.304	7.807	9.034	11.340	14.011	15.812	18.549	21.026	24.054	26.217
13	4.107	4.765	5.892	7.042	8.634	9.926	12.340	15.119	16.985	19.812	22.362	25.472	27.688
14	4.660	5.368	6.571	7.790	9.467	10.821	13.339	16.222	18.151	21.064	23.685	26.873	29.141
15	5.229	5.985	7.261	8.547	10.307	11.721	14.339	17.322	19.311	22.307	24.996	28.259	30.578

(continued)

TABLE A.4. (*Continued*)

df	p = .99	.98	.95	.90	.80	.70	.50	.30	.20	.10	.05	.02	.01
16	5.812	6.614	7.962	9.312	11.152	12.624	15.338	18.418	20.465	23.542	26.296	29.633	32.000
17	6.408	7.255	8.672	10.085	12.002	13.531	16.338	19.511	21.615	24.769	27.587	30.995	33.409
18	7.015	7.906	9.390	10.865	12.857	14.440	17.338	20.601	22.760	25.989	28.869	32.346	34.805
19	7.633	8.567	10.117	11.651	13.716	15.352	18.338	21.689	23.900	27.204	30.144	33.687	36.191
20	8.260	9.237	10.851	12.443	14.578	16.266	19.337	22.775	25.038	28.412	31.410	35.020	37.566
21	8.897	9.915	11.591	13.240	15.445	17.182	20.337	23.858	26.171	29.615	32.671	36.343	38.932
22	9.542	10.600	12.338	14.041	16.314	18.101	21.337	24.939	27.301	30.813	33.924	37.659	40.289
23	10.196	11.293	13.091	14.848	17.187	19.021	22.337	26.018	28.429	32.007	35.172	38.968	41.638
24	10.856	11.992	13.848	15.659	18.062	19.943	23.337	27.096	29.553	33.196	36.415	40.270	42.980
25	11.524	12.697	14.611	16.473	18.940	20.867	24.337	28.172	30.675	34.382	37.652	41.566	44.314
26	12.198	13.409	15.379	17.292	19.820	21.792	25.336	29.246	31.795	35.563	38.885	42.856	45.642
27	12.879	14.125	16.151	18.114	20.703	22.719	26.336	30.319	32.912	36.741	40.113	44.140	46.963
28	13.565	14.847	16.928	18.939	21.588	23.647	27.336	31.391	34.027	37.916	41.337	45.419	48.278
29	14.256	15.574	17.708	19.768	22.475	24.577	28.336	32.461	35.139	39.087	42.557	46.693	49.588
30	14.953	16.306	18.498	20.599	23.364	25.508	29.336	33.530	36.250	40.256	43.773	47.962	50.892

are referred to as *rank-order statistics*. As noted earlier, descriptive techniques for summarizing ordinal data are identical to those used with nominal data. The inferential tests relevant to ordinal data are, however, very different.

One of these inferential tests is the *Wilcoxon Two Sample Test*. Like the *t*-test, the Wilcoxon test examines the distribution of a variable in two independent random samples to consider whether they could be derived from a single population. Whereas the *t*-test relies on sample means, the Wilcoxon test considers sample medians. The median is defined as the central value of a sample, such that half of the cases fall above that value and half below.

Suppose, for example, that we have a sample of 6 complete vessels from Site A and 6 complete vessels from Site B and we want to compare differences in vessel height between the two samples. We could measure the height of each vessel and use a *t*-test to compare vessels from the two sites or class the vessels into nominal classes, such as short, medium, or tall, and use the chi-square statistic to compare sample distributions (though our sample sizes in this instance are much too small to permit the use of the chi-square test). Or we could rank all of the vessels into an ordered set and use the Wilcoxon two-sample test. The first step, then, is to order all the vessels according to height and assign a rank to each vessel, with a value of 1 assigned to the shortest vessel and 12 to the tallest.

Vessel	Rank	Vessel	Rank
A1	5	B1	10
A2	7	B2	12
A3	2	B3	9
A4	1	B4	6
A5	4	B5	11
A6	3	B6	8

Next, we sum the ranks for each sample. The sum of Sample A ranks is equal to 22 = W_a; the sum of sample B ranks equals 56 = W_b. We want to test whether vessels from Site B are taller than vessels from Site A. Our null hypothesis is that W_a is greater than or equal to W_b, whereas our alternative hypothesis states that W_a is less than W_b. The Wilcoxon statistic allows us to test whether these two samples have equal distributions by considering the probability that W_a will be less than or equal to a particular value if both samples come from the same population.

In probabilistic terms, we can think of this case as 12 independent trials. The probability that with a sample of 6, W_a will be less than or equal to 22 can be computed by determining the total number of possible outcomes and experimentally discovering how many of these have a value of 22 or less. Even in this relatively limited example, there are 924 possible outcomes. If we were to examine each of these outcomes, we would find that W_b equals 22 or less in only two cases, $W_a = 1 + 2 + 3 + 4 + 5 + 6$ or $W_a = 1 + 2 + 3 + 4 + 5 + 7$. In this case, the probability that W_a is less than or equal to 22 in two samples of 6 drawn from the same population is equal to $2/924 = .002$. We would therefore reject our null hypothesis. The probability of a particular W_a can be calculated in a much simpler fashion, by using the table of the Wilcoxon distribution (Table A.5) and a statistic called the *Wilcoxon U*:

$$U = W_a - \frac{n_1(n_1 + 1)}{2}$$

In our example,

$$22 - \frac{6(7)}{2} = 1$$

The leftmost columns of the Wilcoxon table are the sample sizes of Sample 1 (n_1) and Sample 2 (n_2), in this example 6 and 6. The column labeled $c_{n_1 n_2}$ tells us the number of possible outcomes for these samples. We look under the U value of 1, which we have computed, and see the value 2. This means that there are two possible outcomes that could produce a value of W_a less than 22. We can compute the probability of this occurrence by dividing 2 into 924, the total number of possible outcomes (equals .002). We will therefore reject the null hypothesis and can say that vessels from Site B are taller than vessels from Site A.

When comparing ordinal data, it may happen that there is a tie in ranking, that is, two vessels may have the same height. When this occurs, each of those cases should be ordered and assigned a rank that is the mean of their ordering. If, for example, cases ranked 9, 10, 11 are all the same size, then they would each be assigned the value of 10 or $(9 + 10 + 11)/3$. If cases ranked 5 and 6 are identical, they would each be assigned a rank of 5.5. When the sample sizes exceed those on the Wilcoxon-U table, the probability of a particular outcome may be estimated by assuming that when sample sizes are large the distribution of W_1 approaches a normal distribution with a mean of $\mu_w = n_1(n+1)/2$ and a standard deviation of

$$\sigma_w = \sqrt{n_1 n_2(n + 1)/12}$$

where $n = n_1 + n_2$. These values can be used to convert the sample value of

TABLE A.5. Wilcoxon Distribution[a]

n_1	n_2	$Cn.n_1$	0	1	2	3	4	5	6	7	8	9	10	11	12	13	14	15	16	17	18	19	20
3	3	20	1	2	4	7	10	13	16	18	19	20											
3	4	35	1	2	4	7	11	15	20	24	28	31	33	34	35								
4	4	70	1	2	4	7	12	17	24	31	39	46	53	58	63	66	68	69	70				
3	5	56	1	2	4	7	11	16	22	28	34	40	45	49	52	54	55	56					
4	5	126	1	2	4	7	12	18	26	35	46	57	69	80	91	100	108	114	119	122	124	125	126
5	5	252	1	2	4	7	12	19	28	39	53	69	87	106	126	146	165	183	199	213	224	233	240
3	6	84	1	2	4	7	11	16	23	30	38	46	54	61	68	73	77	80	82	83	84		
4	6	210	1	2	4	7	12	18	27	37	50	64	80	96	114	130	146	160	173	183	192	198	203
5	6	462	1	2	4	7	12	19	29	41	57	76	99	124	153	183	215	247	279	309	338	363	386
6	6	924	1	2	4	7	12	19	30	43	61	82	111	143	182	224	272	323	378	433	491	546	601
3	7	120	1	2	4	7	11	16	23	31	40	50	60	70	80	89	97	104	109	113	116	118	119
4	7	330	1	2	4	7	12	18	27	38	52	68	87	107	130	153	177	200	223	243	262	278	292
5	7	792	1	2	4	7	12	19	29	42	59	80	106	136	171	210	253	299	347	396	445	493	539
6	7	1716	1	2	4	7	12	19	30	44	63	87	118	155	201	253	314	382	458	539	627	717	811
7	7	3432	1	2	4	7	12	19	30	45	65	91	125	167	220	283	358	445	545	657	782	918	1064
3	8	165	1	2	4	7	11	16	23	31	41	52	64	76	89	101	113	124	134	142	149	154	158
4	8	495	1	2	4	7	12	18	27	38	53	70	91	114	141	169	200	231	264	295	326	354	381
5	8	1287	1	2	4	7	12	19	29	42	60	82	110	143	183	228	280	337	400	466	536	607	680
6	8	3003	1	2	4	7	12	19	30	44	64	89	122	162	213	272	343	424	518	621	737	860	994
7	8	6435	1	2	4	7	12	19	30	45	66	93	129	174	232	302	388	489	609	746	904	1080	1277
8	8	12870	1	2	4	7	12	19	30	45	67	95	133	181	244	321	418	534	675	839	1033	1254	1509

(After Thomas 1986: 500). Reprinted by permission.
[a]With no pairing.

W_1 to a z-score and the probability estimated from the table of the areas under a standard normal curve. Where ties exist in the data, the following formula must be used to estimate the standard deviation:

$$\sigma_w = \sqrt{\frac{n_1 n_2 - n(n^2 - 1) - \Sigma T_i}{12n(n - 1)}}$$

where T_i equals $(t_i - 1)t_i(t_i + 1)$, in which t_i equals the number of ties at rank i.

STATISTICS AND CERAMIC ANALYSIS: DISCUSSION

This appendix has examined some basic descriptive and inferential techniques useful in the statistical analysis of archaeological ceramics. These relatively simple descriptive and inferential techniques should be the first step in any data analysis, assessing the distribution of individual variables, of pairs of variables, and variability between samples. As discussed earlier, many of the dimensions of ceramic variability that archaeologists are interested in are not directly measurable and can only be assessed by considering the interaction of a number of variables. Where the relevant variables are highly correlated, the analysis of only one variable may be sufficient to summarize and assess these dimensions.

In other cases, several variables must be considered simultaneously in order to accurately assess the variability in the data. Multivariate statistical analyses, such as principal components analysis, factor analysis, and cluster analysis, may be appropriate in these cases. A discussion of these techniques lies outside the scope of the present work, although some of the techniques have been illustrated in the discussion of particular problem-oriented examples of ceramic studies. Detailed discussions of some multivariate techniques relevant to archaeological analysis can be found in Doran and Hodson (1975), Orton (1980), Whallon and Brown (1981), Kintigh and Ammerman (1982), Binford and Binford (1972), Cowgill (1968, 1977), Hodson (1970), Leonard and Jones (1989), and Shennan (1988).

References

Akkermans, P. M. M. G.
   1987   A late Neolithic and early Halaf village at Sabi Abyad, Northern Syria. *Paleòrient* 13:23–40.
Allen, J.
   1984   Pots and poor princes: A multidimensional approach to the role of pottery trading in Papua. In *The Many Dimensions of Pottery: Ceramics in Archaeology and Anthropology.* Ed. by S. E. van der Leeuw and A. C. Pritchard, pp. 407–464. University of Amsterdam, Amsterdam.
Appadurai, A., Ed.
   1986   *The Social Life of Things.* Cambridge University Press, New York.
Arnold, D. E.
   1975   Ceramic ecology of the Ayacucho Basin. *Current Anthropology* 16:183–205.
   1976   Ecological variables and ceramic production: Toward a general model. In *Primitive Art and Technology.* Ed. by J. S. Raymond, B. Loveseth, C. Arnold, and G. Reardon, pp. 92–108. University of Calgary, Canada.
   1978   Ceramic variability, environment and culture history among the Pokom in the Valley of Guatemala. In *The Spatial Organization of Culture.* Ed. by Ian Hodder, pp. 39–59. University of Pittsburgh Press, Pittsburgh.
   1985   *Ceramic Theory and Cultural Process.* Cambridge University Press, Cambridge.
   1989   Patterns of learning, residence and descent among potters in Ticul, Yucatan, Mexico. In *Archaeological Approaches to Culture Identity.* Ed. by S. J. Shennan, pp. 174–184. Unwin Hyman, London.
Balfet, H.
   1966   Ethnographical observations in North Africa and archaeological interpretation. In *Ceramics and Man.* Ed. by F. R. Matson, pp. 161–177. Viking Fund Publications in Anthropology, Chicago.
   1981   Production and distribution of pottery in the Maghreb. In *Production and Distribution: A Ceramic Viewpoint.* Ed. by H. Howard and E. L. Morris, pp. 257–269. BAR International Series, 120, Oxford.
Benco, N. L.
   1985   *Ceramic diversity and political centralization: A case study from North Africa.* Paper presented at the 50th Annual Meeting of the Society for American Archaeology, Denver.

1987   *The Early Medieval Pottery Industry at al-Basra, Morocco*. BAR International Series, No. 341, Oxford.

Binford, L. R.
1962   Archaeology as anthropology. *American Antiquity* 28:217–225.
1976   Forty-seven trips: A case study in the character of some formation processes in the archaeological record. In *Contributions to Anthropology: The Interior Peoples of Northern Alaska*. Ed. by Edwin S. Hall. Ottawa National Museum of Man Mercury Series, 49.
1981   *Bones: Ancient Men and Modern Myths*. Academic Press, New York.
1989   The "New Archaeology," then and now. In *Archaeological Thought in America*. Ed. by C. C. Lamberg-Karlovsky, pp. 50–63. Cambridge University Press, Cambridge.

Binford, S. R., and L. R. Binford
1972   *New Perspectives in Archaeology*. Aldine, Chicago.

Binford, L. R., S. R. Binford, R. Whallon, and M. A. Hardin
1970   *Archaeology at Hatchery West*. Society for American Archaeology, Memoir 35.

Birmingham, J.
1975   Traditional potters of the Kathmandu Valley: An ethnoarchaeological study. *Man*(n.s.) 10:370–386.

Bishop, R. L.
1980   Aspects of ceramic compositional modeling. In *Models and Methods in Regional Exchange*. Ed. by R. E. Fry, pp. 47–65. Society for American Archaeology, Papers No. 1. Society for American Archaeology, Washington, D. C.

Bishop, R. L., R. L. Rands, and G. R. Holley
1982   Ceramic compositional analysis in archaeological perspective. In *Advances in Archaeological Method and Theory*, Volume 5. Ed. by M. B. Schiffer, pp. 275–330. Academic Press, New York.

Blanton, R. E.
1978   *Monte Albán: Settlement Patterns at the Ancient Zapotec Capital*. Academic Press, New York.

Blanton, R. E. *et al.*
1982   Monte Albán's Hinterland Part I. *Memoirs of the Museum of Anthropology, University of Michigan*, Number 23. Ann Arbor.

Boone, J. L.
1987   Defining and measuring midden catchment. *American Antiquity* 52:336–345.

Bondioli, L., M. Tosi, and M. Vidale
1984   Craft activity areas and surface surveys at Moenjodaro. In *Interim Reports* I. Ed. by M. Jansen and G. Urban, pp. 9–37. University of Aachen, Aachen.

Bordes, Francois
1972   *A Tale of Two Caves*. Harper & Row, New York.

Brainerd, G. W.
1951   The place of chronological ordering in archaeological analysis. *American Antiquity* 16:301–313.

Braun, D.
1977   *Middle Woodland — Early Late Woodland Social Change in the Prehistoric Central Midwestern U.S.* Unpublished Ph.D. Dissertation, Department of Anthropology, University of Michigan, Ann Arbor.
1980a   Experimental interpretations of ceramic vessel use on the basis of rim and neck formal attributes. In The Navajo Project. Ed. by D. C. Feiron *et al.*, pp. 171–231. *Museum of Northern Arizona Research Paper*, 1, Flagstaff.
1980b   *Neolithic regional cooperation, a midwestern example*. Paper presented at the forty-sixth annual meeting of the Society for American Archaeology, Philadelphia.

1983   Pots as tools. In *Archaeological Hammers and Theories*. Ed. by A. S. Keene and J. A. Moore, pp. 107–134. Academic Press, New York.

1985   Ceramic decorative diversity and Illinois Woodland regional interaction. In *Decoding Prehistoric Ceramics*. Ed. by B. A. Nelson, pp. 128–155. Southern Illinois University Press, Carbondale.

Brumfiel, E., and T. K. Earle, Eds.
1987   *Specialization, Exchange and Complex Societies*. Cambridge University Press, Cambridge.

Caso, A., I. Bernal, and J. Acosta
1967   *La Cerámica de Monte Albán*. Memorias del Instituto Nacional de Antropología e Historia, 13. Mexico City.

Clarke, D. L.
1970   *Beaker Pottery of Great Britain and Ireland*. Cambridge University Press, Cambridge.

1976   The Beaker network: Social and economic models. *Glockenbechersymposium Obereid 1974*. Ed. by J. N. Lanting, J. D. van der Waals, pp. 459–476. Haarlem, The Netherlands.

1979   The beaker network: Social and economic models. In *Analytical Archaeologist*, pp. 333–362. Academic Press, New York.

Conkey, M.
1978   Style and information in cultural evolution: Toward a predictive model for the Paleolithic. In *Social Archaeology: Beyond Subsistence and Dating*. Ed. by C. L. Redman, M. J. Berman, E. V. Curtin, W. T. Langhorne, Jr., N. M. Versaggi, and J. C. Wanser, pp. 61–85. Academic Press, New York.

1982   Boundedness in art and society. In *Symbolic and Structural Archaeology*. Ed. by I. Hodder, pp. 115–128. Cambridge University Press, Cambridge.

1989   The use of diversity in stylistic analysis. In *Quantifying Diversity in Archaeology*. Ed. by R. D. Leonard and G. T. Jones, pp. 118–129. Cambridge University Press, Cambridge.

Conkey, M. W., and J. D. Spector
1984   Archaeology and the study of gender. In *Advances in Archaeological Method and Theory*, Volume 7. Ed. by M. B. Schiffer, pp. 1–38. Academic Press, Orlando.

Costin, C. L.
1988   *Ceramic exchange among the prehispanic Wanka of highland Peru*. Paper presented at the 53rd Annual Meeting of the Society for American Archaeology, Phoenix.

Costin, C. L., and T. K. Earle
1989   Status distinction and legitimation of power as reflected in changing patterns of consumption in late prehispanic Peru. *American Antiquity* 54:691–714.

Costin, C. L. et al.
1989   The impact of Inca conquest on local technology in the Upper Mantaro Valley, Peru. In *What's New? A Closer Look at the Process of Innovation*. Ed. by S. E. van der Leeuw and Robin Torrence, pp. 107–139. Unwin Hyman, London.

Cowgill, G. L.
1968   Archaeological applications of factor, cluster, and proximity analysis. *American Antiquity* 33:367–375.

1972   Models, methods, and techniques for seriation. In *Models in Archaeology*. Ed. by D. L. Clarke, pp. 381–424. Methuen, London.

1977   The trouble with significance tests and what we can do about it. *American Antiquity* 42:350–368.

Cowgill, G. L., J. H. Altschul, and R. S. Sload
1984   Spatial analyses of Teotihuacan: A Mesoamerican metropolis. In *Intrasite Spatial*

Analysis in Archaeology. Ed. by H. Hietala, pp. 154–195. Cambridge University Press, Cambridge.

Dabagh, T.
1966   Halaf pottery. *Sumer* 22:23–43.

Dales, G. F., and J. M. Kenoyer
1988   Preliminary report on the third season (January–March 1988) of research at Harappa, Pakistan. Manuscript on file, University of California at Berkeley.

D'Altroy, T. N., and R. L. Bishop
1990   The provincial organization of Inka ceramic production. *American Antiquity* 55:120–137.

David, N.
1972   On the life span of pottery, type frequencies, and archaeological inference. *American Antiquity* 37:141–142.

David, N., and H. Hennig
1972   *The Ethnography of Pottery: A Fulani Case Seen in Archaeological Perspective*. McCaleb Modules in Anthropology, No. 21. Addison-Wesley, Reading, Mass.

David, N., J. Sterner, and K. Gavua
1988   Why pots are decorated. *Current Anthropology* 29:365–389.

Davidson, T. E., and H. McKerrel
1976   Pottery Analysis and Halaf period trade in the Khabur headwaters region. *Iraq* 38:45–56.

Deal, M.
1983   *Pottery Ethnoarchaeology among the Tzeltal Maya*. Ph.D. Dissertation, Department of Archaeology, Simon Frazer University.

DeBoer, W. R.
1974   Ceramic longevity and archaeological interpretation: An example from the Upper Ucayali, Eastern Peru. *American Antiquity* 39:335–343.

1984   The last pottery show: System and sense in ceramic studies. In *The Many Dimensions of Pottery: Ceramics in Archaeology and Anthropology*. Ed. by S. E. van der Leeuw and A. C. Pritchard, pp. 527–568. University of Amsterdam, Amsterdam.

1985   Pots and pans do not speak, nor do they lie: The case for occasional reductionism. In *Decoding Prehistoric Ceramics*. Ed. by B. A. Nelson, pp. 347–357. Southern Illinois University Press, Carbondale.

DeBoer, W. R., and D. Lathrap
1979   The making and breaking of Shipibo-Conibo ceramics. In *Ethnoarchaeology: Implications of Ethnography for Archaeology*. Ed. by C. Kramer, pp. 102–138. Columbia University Press, New York.

DeBoer, W. R., and J. A. Moore
1982   The measurement and meaning of stylistic diversity. *Ñawpa Pacha* 20:147–162.

Deetz, J.
1965   *The Dynamics of Stylistic Change in Arikara Ceramics*. University of Illinois Press, Chicago.

Doran, J. E., and F. R. Hodson
1975   *Mathematics and Computers in Archaeology*. Harvard University Press, Cambridge, Mass.

Douglas, M.
1971   Deciphering a meal. In *Myth, Symbol, and Culture*. Ed. by C. Geertz, pp. 61–82. W. W. Norton and Company, New York.

1982   Goods as a system of communication. In *In the Active Voice*, by Mary Douglas, pp. 16–33. Routledge & Kegan Paul, London.

Douglas, M., and B. Isherwood
1979   *The World of Goods.* Penguin, Middlesex.
Dunnell, R. C.
1978   Style and function: A fundamental dichotomy. *American Antiquity* 43:192–202.
1989   Aspects of the application of evolutionary theory in archaeology. In *Archaeological Thought in America.* Ed. by C. C. Lamberg-Karlovsky, pp. 35–49. Cambridge University Press, Cambridge.
Dunnel, R. C., and T. L. Hunt
1990   Elemental composition and inference of ceramic vessel function. *Current Anthropology* 31:330–336.
Dyson, S. L.
1976   *Cosa: The Utilitarian Pottery.* American Academy in Rome, Rome.
Earle, T. K.
1987   Specialization and the production of wealth: Hawaiian chiefdoms and the Inka empire. In *Specialization, Exchange and Complex Societies.* Ed. by E. M. Brumfiel and T. K. Earle, pp. 64–75. Cambridge University Press, New York.
Earle, T. K., and T. N. D'Altroy
1989   The political economy of the Inka empire: The archaeology of power and finance. In *Archaeological Thought in America.* Ed. by C. C. Lamberg-Karlovsky, pp. 167–182. Cambridge University Press, New York.
Earle, T., C. Costlin, and G. Russell
1986   Specialization and the Inka state. In *The Social and Economic Contexts of Technological Change.* The World Archaeological Congress, pp. 1–18. Allen & Unwin, London.
Ellen, R. F., and I. C. Glover
1974   Pottery manufacture and trade in central Moluccas, Indonesia: The modern situation and historical implications. *Man* (n.s.) 9:353–379.
Feinman, G. M.
1980   *The Relationship between Administrative Organization and Ceramic Production in the Valley of Oaxaca, Mexico.* Unpublished Ph.D. dissertation, Department of Anthropology, City University of New York.
1985   Changes in the organization of ceramic production in pre-hispanic Oaxaca, Mexico. In *Decoding Prehistoric Ceramics.* Ed. by B. A. Nelson, pp. 195–224. Southern Illinois University Press, Carbondale.
Feinman, G. M., S. A. Kowaleski, and R. E. Blanton
1984   Modelling archaeological ceramic production and organizational change in the pre-Hispanic valley of Oaxaca. In *The Many Dimensions of Pottery: Ceramics in Archaeology and Anthropology.* Ed. by S. E. van der Leeuw and A. C. Pritchard, pp. 295–334. University of Amsterdam, Amsterdam.
Feinman, G. M., S. Banker, R. F. Cooper, G. B. Cook, and L. M. Nicholas
1989   A technological perspective on changes in the ancient Oaxacan grayware ceramic tradition: Preliminary results. *Journal of Field Archaeology* 16:331–343.
Foster, G. M.
1960   Life expectancy of utilitarian pottery in Tzintzuntan, Michoacan, Mexico. *American Antiquity* 25:606–609.
1965   The sociology of pottery: Questions and hypotheses arising from contemporary Mexican work. *Ceramics and Man.* Ed. by F. R. Matson, pp. 43–61. Viking Fund Publications in Anthropology, No. 41, New York.
Frankel, D.
1979   *Archaeologists at Work: Studies on Halaf Pottery.* British Museum Publications, London.

Franken, H. J.
1971   Analysis of methods of potmaking in archaeology. *Harvard Theological Review* 64:227–255.
Friedrich, M. H.
1970   Design structure and social interaction. *American Antiquity* 35:332–343.
Gibbs, L.
1987   Identifying gender representation in the archaeological record: A contextual study. In *The Archaeology of Contextual Meanings*. Ed. by I. Hodder, pp. 79–89. Cambridge University Press, Cambridge.
Gifford, D. C.
1981   Taphonomy and paleoecology: A critical review of archaeology's sister disciplines. In *Advances in Archaeological Method and Theory*, Volume 4. Ed. by M. B. Schiffer, pp. 365–438. Academic Press, New York.
Gifford, J. C.
1960   The type-variety method of ceramic classification as an indicator of cultural phenomena. *American Antiquity* 25:341–347.
Gifford-Gonzales, D., D. B. Damrosch, D. R. Damrosch, J. Pryor, and R. L. Thunen
1985   The third dimension in site structure: An experiment in trampling with vertical dispersal. *American Antiquity* 50:803–818.
Gilman, P. A., and B. J. Mills
1984   Preliminary report on the Anderson site ceramics. In *Ladder Ranch Research Project: A Report of the First Season*. Ed. by M. C. Nelson, pp. 51–66. Technical Series of the Maxwell Museum of Anthropology, 1. Albuquerque, New Mexico.
Goody, J.
1982   *Cooking, Cuisine and Class*. Cambridge University Press, Cambridge.
Grace, V.
1961   *Amphoras and the Ancient Wine Trade*. American School of Classical Studies at Athens, Princeton.
Grim, R. E.
1968   *Clay Mineralogy*, second edition. McGraw–Hill Book Co., New York.
Guthe, C. R.
1925   Pueblo Pottery Making. *Papers of the Smithsonian Expedition*, No. 2. Yale University Press, New Haven.
Haaland, R.
1978   Ethnographical observations of pottery-making in Darfur, Western Sudan, with some reflections on archaeological interpretation. *New Directions in Scandinavian Archaeology*, Volume I. Ed. by K. Kristiansen and C. Paluden-Muller, pp. 47–61. National Museum of Denmark, Copenhagen.
Hall, G. D., S. M. Tarka, Jr., W. J. Hurst, D. Stuart, and R. E. W. Adams
1990   Cacao residues in ancient Maya vessels from Rio Azul, Guatemala. *American Antiquity* 55:138–143.
Hally, D. J.
1986   The identification of vessel function: A case study from northwest Georgia. *American Antiquity* 51:267–295.
Halim, M., and M. Vidale
1983   Kilns, bangles, and coated vessels: Ceramic production in closed containers at Moenjodaro. In *Report of Field Work Carried Out at Mohenjo Daro. Interim Reports Vol. 1, 1982–1983*. Ed. by M. Jansen and G. Urban, pp. 63–97. Forschungsprojekt "Moehnjo-Dar," Aachen.

Hardin, M. A.
1979   The cognitive basis of productivity in a decorative art style: Implications of ethnographic study for archaeologists' taxonomies. In *Ethnoarchaeology*. Ed. by C. Kramer, pp. 75–100. Columbia University Press, New York.
1984   Models of decoration. In *The Many Dimensions of Pottery: Ceramics in Archaeology and Anthropology*. Ed. by S. E. van der Leeuw and A. C. Pritchard, pp. 573–607. University of Amsterdam, Amsterdam.
Harrison, R. J.
1980   *The Beaker Folk: Copper Age Archaeology in Western Europe*. Thames and Hudson, London.
Hegmon, M. M.
1990   *Style as a Social Strategy: Dimensions of Ceramic Stylistic Variation in the Ninth Century Northern Southwest*. Ph.D. dissertation, The University of Michigan, Ann Arbor.
Henrikson, E., and M. McDonald
1983   Ceramic form and function: An ethnographic search and archaeological application. *American Anthropologist* 85:630–643.
Hill, J. N.
1970   *Broken K Pueblo: Prehistoric Social Organization in the American Southwest*. University of Arizona Anthropological Papers, 18, Tucson.
Hill, J. N., and R. K. Evans
1972   A model for classification and typology. In *Models in Archaeology*. Ed. by D. L. Clarke, pp. 231–274. Metheun, London.
Hill, J. N., and J. Gunn
1977   *The Individual in Prehistory*. Academic Press, New York.
Hodder, I.
1978   Simple correlations between material culture and society: A review. In *The Spatial Organization of Culture*. Ed. by I. Hodder, pp. 3–24. University of Pittsburgh Press, Pittsburgh.
1981   Pottery production and use: A theoretical discussion. In *Production and Distribution: A Ceramic Viewpoint*. Ed. by H. Howard and E. Morris, pp. 215–220. BAR International Series, 120.
1982a   Theoretical archaeology: A reactionary view. In *Symbolic and Structural Archaeology*. Ed. by I. Hodder, pp. 1–16. Cambridge University Press, Cambridge.
1982b   Sequences of structural change in the Dutch Neolithic. In *Symbolic and Structural Archaeology*. Ed. by Ian Hodder, pp. 162–177. Cambridge University Press, Cambridge.
1986   *Reading the Past*. Cambridge University Press, Cambridge.
1989   This is not an article about material culture as text. *Journal of Anthropological Archaeology* 8:250–269.
Hodges, H. W. M.
1964   *Artifacts: An Introduction to Primitive Technology*. Frederick A. Preager, New York.
Hodson, F. R.
1970   Cluster analysis and archaeology: Some new developments and applications. *World Archaeology* 1:299–320.
Hole, B. L.
1980   Sampling in archaeology: A critique. *Annual Review of Anthropology* 9:217–234.
Howard, H., and E. L. Morris, Eds.
1981   *Production and Distribution: A Ceramic Viewpoint*. BAR International Series, 120, Oxford.

Johnson, G. A.
1973   Local Exchange and Early State Formation in Southwestern Iran. *University of Michigan Museum of Anthropology Anthropological Papers*, No. 51. Ann Arbor.
1975   Locational analysis and the investigation of Uruk local exchange systems. In *Ancient Civilizations and Trade*. Ed. by J. Sabloff and C. C. Lamberg-Karlovsky, pp. 285–340. University of New Mexico Press, Albuquerque.
1977   Aspects of regional analysis in archaeology. *Annual Review of Anthropology* 6:479–508.
1987   The changing organization of Uruk administration on the Susiana Plain. In *The Archaeology of Western Iran: Settlement and Society from Prehistory to the Islamic Conquest.* Ed. by F. Hole, pp. 107–139. Smithsonian Institution Press, Washington, D.C.
Junker, L. L.
1985   Morphology, function and style in traditional ceramics: A study of contemporary pottery from Bellary District, Karnataka. In *Vijayanagara: Progress of Research, 1983–1984.* Ed. by M. S. Nagaraja Rao, pp. 144–151. Vijayanagara Research Centre Series 2, Department of Archaeology and Museums, Mysore.
Kendall, A.
1973   *Everyday Life of the Incas*. G. P. Putnam's Sons, New York.
Kenoyer, J. M.
1983   Shell industries at Moenjo Daro, Pakistan. In *Report of Field Work Carried Out at Mohenjo Daro. Interim Reports Vol. 1*, 1982–1983. Ed. by M. Jansen and G. Urban, pp. 99–116. Forschungsprojekt "Moehnjo-Dar," Aachen.
1989a   *Harappan craft specialization and the question of urban segregation and stratification.* Paper presented at the 54th Annual Meetings of the Society for American Archaeology, Atlanta.
1989b   Socio-economic structures of the Indus civilization as reflected in specialized crafts and the question of ritual segregation. In *Old Problems and New Perspectives in the Archaeology of South Asia*. Ed. by J. M. Kenoyer, pp. 171–182. Wisconsin Archaeological Reports, 2. Madison.
Kintigh, K. W.
1984   Measuring archaeological diversity by comparison with simulated assemblages. *American Antiquity* 49:44–54.
1985   Social structure, the structure of style, and stylistic patterns in Cibola pottery. In *Decoding Prehistoric Ceramics*. Ed. by B. A. Nelson, pp. 35–74. Southern Illinois Press, Carbondale.
Kintigh, K. W., and A. J. Ammerman
1982   Heuristic approaches to spatial analysis in archaeology. *American Antiquity* 47:31–63.
Kohler, T. A., and E. Blinman
1987   Solving mixture problems in archaeology: Analysis of ceramic materials for dating and demographic reconstruction. *Journal of Anthropological Archaeology* 6:1–28.
Kohler, T. A., and L. Wandsnider
1990   *Technology, quantification, theory, and archaeology: A.D. 2001.* Paper presented at "Archaeology in the Future" conference, Carbondale.
Kolb, C. C., Ed.
1988   *Ceramic Ecology Revisited, 1987: The Technology and Socioeconomics of Pottery.* BAR International Series, 436 (2 volumes). Oxford.
Kolb, C. C., and L. M. Lackey, Eds.
1988   *A Pot for All Reasons: Ceramic Ecology Revisited.* Laboratory of Anthropology, Temple University, Philadelphia.

Kowaleski, S. A., R. E. Blanton, G. Feinman, and L. Finsten
1983   Boundaries, scale, and internal organization. *Journal of Anthropological Archaeology*
         2:32–56.
Kowaleski, S. A., G. M. Feinman, L. Finsten, R. E. Blanton, and L. M. Nicholas
1989   Monte Albán's Hinterland, Part II. *Memoir of the Museum of Anthropology, University
         of Michigan*. No. 23. Ann Arbor.
Kramer, C.
1985   Ceramic ethnoarchaeology. *Annual Review of Anthropology* 14:77–120.
Kruskal, J. B.
1971   Multidimensional scaling in archaeology: Time is not the only dimension. In
         Mathematics in the Archaeological and Historical Sciences. Ed. by F. R. Hodson, D. G.
         Kendall, and P. Tautu, pp. 119–132. Edinburgh University Press, Edinburgh.
LeBlanc, S. A.
1975   Microseriation: A method for fine chronological differentiation. *American Antiquity*
         40:22–38.
Lekson, S. H.
1984   Prehistoric settlement in the Middle Palomas drainage: Southern New Mexico. In
         Ladder Ranch Research Project: A Report of the First Season. Ed. by M. C. Nelson, pp.
         15–23. Technical Series of the Maxwell Museum of Anthropology, 1. Albuquer-
         que, New Mexico.
Leonard, R. D., and G. T. Jones, Eds.
1989   *Quantifying Diversity in Archaeology*. Cambridge University Press, Cambridge.
Longacre, W. A.
1968   Some aspects of prehistoric society in East-Central Arizona. In *New Perspectives in
         Archaeology*. Ed. by L. R. and S. Binford, pp. 89–102. Aldine, Chicago.
1970   Archaeology as Anthropology: A Case Study. *Anthropological Papers of the Univer-
         sity of Arizona*, 17. Tucson.
1985   Pottery use-life among the Kalinga, Northern Luzon, The Philippines. In *Decoding
         Prehistoric Ceramics*. Ed. by B. A. Nelson, pp. 334–346. Southern Illinois University
         Press, Carbondale.
Mabry, J., J. M. Skibo, M. B. Schiffer, and K. Kvamme
1988   Use of a falling-weight tester for assessing ceramic impact strength. *American
         Antiquity* 53:829–839.
Mackay, E. J. H.
1943   Chanhu-daro excavations 1935–1936. *American Oriental Series*, 20. American Ori-
         ental Society, New Haven.
Mallowan, M. E. L.
1936   The excavations at Tall Chagar Bazar and an archaeological survey of the Habur
         region. *Iraq* 3:1–86.
Mathur, K.
1964   *Caste and Ritual in a Malwa Village*. Asia Publishing House, Bombay.
Mayer, A.
1960   *Caste and Kinship in Central India*. University of California Press, Berkeley.
Mercer, R., Ed.
1977   *Beakers in Britain and Europe*. BAR Supplementary Series 26. Oxford.
Michaels, J. W.
1973   *Dating Methods in Archaeology*. Seminar Press, New York.
Miller, D.
1981   The relationship between ceramic production and distribution in a Central Indian

village. In *Production and Distribution: A Ceramic Viewpoint*. Ed. by H. Howard and E. Morris, pp. 221–228. BAR International Series 120.

1982   Structures and strategies: An aspect of the relationship between social hierarchy and cultural change. In *Symbolic and Structural Archaeology*. Ed. by I. Hodder, pp. 89–98. Cambridge University Press, Cambridge.

1985   *Artefacts as Categories*. Cambridge University Press, Cambridge.

Mills, B. J.

1984   Functional analysis of ceramics from the Anderson Site. In *Ladder Ranch Research Report: A Report of the First Season*. Ed. by M. C. Nelson, pp. 67–81. Technical Series of the Maxwell Museum of Anthropology, 1. Albuquerque, New Mexico.

1989   Integrating functional analyses of vessels and sherds through models of ceramic assemblage formation. *World Archaeology* 21:133–147.

Mills, B. J., E. L. Camilli, and L. Wandsnider

1990   Spatial patterning in ceramic vessel distributions. In *Piecing Together the Past: Refitting Studies in Archaeology*. Ed. by J. L. Hoffman and J. G. Enloe. BAR, International Series (forthcoming).

Mueller, J. W.

1975   *Sampling in Archaeology*. University of Arizona Press, Tucson.

Mughal, M. R.

1972   *Present State of Research on the Indus Valley Civilization*. Directorate of Archaeology and Museums, Government of Pakistan, Karachi.

1980   *Archaeological Survey in Bhawalapur*. Department of Archaeology and Museums, Government of Pakistan, Karachi.

1982   Recent archaeological research in the Cholistan Desert. In *Harappan Civilization*. Ed. by G. Possehl, pp. 85–95. Oxford University Press, New Delhi.

Myers, J. E.

1984   *The Political Economy of Ceramic Production: A Study of the Islamic Commonware Pottery of Medieval Osar es-Seghir*. Unpublished Ph.D. dissertation, Department of Anthropology, State University of New York at Binghamton.

Nagaraja Rao, M. S., Ed.

1983   *Vijayanagara: Progress of Research 1979–1983*. Vijayanagara Research Centre Series 1. Directorate of Archaeology and Museums, Mysore.

1985   *Vijayanagara: Progress of Research 1983–1984*. Vijayanagara Research Centre Series 2. Directorate of Archaeology and Museums, Mysore.

Nelson, B. A., Ed.

1985   *Decoding Prehistoric Ceramics*. Southern Illinois University Press, Carbondale.

Nelson, M. C., Ed.

1984   *Ladder Ranch Research Project: Report of the First Season*. Technical Series of the Maxwell Museum of Anthropology, 1. Albuquerque, New Mexico.

Nicklin, K.

1971   Stability and innovation in pottery manufacture. *World Archaeology*. 3:13–48.

Olin, J. S., and A. D. Franklin, Eds.

1982   *Archaeological Ceramics* Smithsonian Institution Press, Washington, D. C.

Orton, C.

1980   *Mathematics in Archaeology*. Collins, London.

Owen, B., G. Russell, and C. Costin

1988   *The impact of Inka policy on the Wanka populace*. Paper presented at the 53rd Annual Meeting of the Society for American Archaeology, Atlanta.

Parsons, J. R.

1972   Archaeological settlement patterns. *Annual Review of Anthropology* 1:127–250.

Pastron, A. G.
  1974   Preliminary ethnoarchaeological investigations among the Tarahumara. In *Ethno-archaeology: Archaeological Survey Monograph* IV. Ed. by C. B. Donnan and C. W. Clewlow, Jr. University of California, Los Angeles.
Patrick, M., A. J. de Koning, and A. B. Smith
  1985   Gas liquid chromatographic analysis of fatty acids in food residues from ceramics found in the southwestern Cape, South Africa. *Archaeometry* 27:231–236.
Peacock, D. P. S.
  1971   Roman amphorae in pre-Roman Britain. In *The Iron Age and Its Hill Forts*. Ed. by M. Jesson and D. Hill, pp. 161–188. Southampton Monograph Series, South Hampton.
  1981   Archaeology, ethnology, and ceramic production. In *Production and Distribution: A Ceramic Viewpoint*. Ed. by H. Howard and E. L. Morris, pp. 187–194. BAR International Series, N. 120. Oxford.
Peacock, D. P. S., Ed.
  1977   *Pottery and Early Commerce*. Cambridge University Press, Cambridge.
Peebles, C. S.
  1978   Moundville: The form and content of a Mississippian society. To appear in *Reviewing Mississippian Development*. Ed. by S. Williams, University of New Mexico Press, Albuquerque.
  1987   Moundville from 1000 to 1500 A.D. as seen from 1840 to 1985 A.D. In *Chiefdoms in the Americas*. Ed. by R. D. Drennan and C. A. Uribe, pp. 21–42. University Press of America, Lanham, M.D.
Phillips, P.
  1970   Archaeological survey in the Lower Yazoo Basin, Mississippi, 1949–1955. *Papers of the Peabody Museum of Archaeology and Anthropology, 25*.
Plog, S.
  1976   The inference of prehistoric social organization from ceramic design variability. *Michigan Discussions in Anthropology* 1:1–47.
  1980   *Stylistic Variation in Prehistoric Ceramics*. Cambridge University Press, New York.
  1983   Analysis of style in artifacts. *Annual Review of Anthropology* 12:125–142.
Pollock, S. M.
  1983a   Style and information: An analysis of Susiana ceramics. *Journal of Anthropological Archaeology* 2:354–390.
  1983b   *The Symbolism of Prestige: An Archaeological Example from the Royal Cemetery of Ur.* Ph.D. Dissertation, Department of Anthropology, University of Michigan. University Microfilms, Ann Arbor.
Pracchia, S., M. Tosi, and M. Vidale
  1985   On the type, distribution, and extent of craft industries at Moenjo-daro. In *South Asian Archaeology 1983*. Ed. by J. Schotsmans and M. Taddei, pp. 207–247. Instituto Universitario Orientale, Naples.
Ragir, S.
  1972   A review of techniques for archaeological sampling. In *Contemporary Archaeology*. Ed. by Mark P. Leone, pp. 178–192. Southern Illinois University Press, Carbondale.
Rappaport, R. A.
  1971   Ritual, sanctity, and cybernetics. *American Anthropologist* 73:59–76.
Redman, C. L.
  1973   Multistage fieldwork and analytical techniques. *American Antiquity* 38:61–79.
Redman, C. L., and P. J. Watson
  1970   Systematic intensive surface collection. *American Antiquity* 35:279–290.

Reina, R. E., and R. M. Hill II
  1978   *Traditional Pottery of Guatemala.* University of Texas Press, Austin.
Rice, P. M.
  1981   Evolution of specialized pottery production: A trial model. *Current Anthropology* 22:219–240.
  1984a   The archaeological study of specialized pottery production: Some aspects of method and theory. In *Pots and Potters: Approaches in Ceramic Archaeology.* Ed. by P. M. Rice, pp. 45–54. Institute of Archaeology, University of California, Los Angeles.
  1984b   Change and conservatism in pottery-producing systems. In *The Many Dimensions of Pottery: Ceramics in Archaeology and Anthropology.* Ed. by S. E. van der Leeuw and A. C. Pritchard, pp. 231–288. University of Amsterdam, Amsterdam.
  1987   *Pottery Analysis: A Sourcebook.* University of Chicago Press, Chicago.
  1989   Ceramic diversity, production, and use. In *Quantifying Diversity in Archaeology.* Ed. by R. D. Leonard and G. T. Jones, pp. 109–117. Cambridge University Press, Cambridge.
Rice, P. M., Ed.
  1984   Pots and Potters: Current Approaches in Ceramic Archaeology. *Institute of Archaeology Monograph 24.* University of California, Los Angeles.
Riley, J. A.
  1981   The late Bronze Age Aegean and the Roman Mediterranean: A case for comparison. In *Production and Distribution: A Ceramic Viewpoint.* Ed. by H. Howard and E. L. Morris, pp. 133–144. BAR International Series, No. 120. Oxford.
  1984   Pottery analysis and the reconstruction of ancient exchange systems. In *The Many Dimensions of Pottery: Ceramics in Archaeology and Anthropology.* Ed. by S. E. van der Leeuw and A. C. Pritchard, pp. 55–74. University of Amsterdam, Amsterdam.
Ritchie, W. A.
  1944   *The Pre-Iroquoian Occupations of New York State.* Rochester Museum of Arts and Sciences, Rochester.
Ritchie, W. A., and R. S. MacNeish
  1949   The pre-Iroquoian pottery of New York State. *American Antiquity* 15:97–124.
Rothschild-Boros, M. C.
  1981   The determination of amphora contents. In *Archaeology and Italian Society: Prehistoric Roman and Medieval Studies.* Ed. by G. Barker and R. Hodges, pp. 79–89. BAR International Series, 102. Oxford.
Rouse, I.
  1967   Seriation in archaeology. In *American Historical Anthropology: Essays in Honor of Leslie Spier.* Ed. by C. L. Riley and W. W. Taylor, pp. 153–195. Southern Illinois University Press, Carbondale.
Roux, V.
  1989   *The Potter's Wheel: Craft Specialization and Technical Competence.* Oxford and IBH Publishing, New Delhi.
Runyon, P. P., and A. Haber
  1972   *Fundamentals of Behavioral Statistics.* Addison-Wesley, Reading, Mass.
Rye, O. S.
  1976   Keeping your temper under control: Materials and the manufacture of Papuan pottery. *Archaeology and Physical Anthropology in Oceania* 11:106–137.
  1981   *Pottery Technology: Principles and Reconstruction.* Taraxacum, Inc., Washington, D. C.
Rye, O. S., and C. Evans
  1976   *Traditional Pottery Techniques of Pakistan.* Smithsonian Institution Publications in Anthropology, No. 21. Washington, D.C.

Sackett, J. R.
1982   Approaches to style in lithic archaeology. *Journal of Anthropological Archaeology* 1:59–112.
Santley, R. S., P. J. Arnold III, and C. A. Pool
1989   The ceramics production system at Matacapan, Veracruz, Mexico. *Journal of Field Archaeology* 16:107–132.
Saraswati, B.
1978   *Pottery Making Cultures and Indian Civilization*. Abhinav Publications, New Delhi.
Saraswati, B., and N. K. Behura
1966   *Pottery Techniques in Peasant India*. Memoirs of the Anthropological Survey of India, 13. Calcutta.
Scarry, M. M.
1981   The University of Michigan Moundville Excavations: 1978–1979. *Southeastern Archaeological Conference Bulletin* 24:87–90.
Scheans, D. J.
1977   *Filipino Market Potteries*. National Museum of the Philippines, Manilla.
Schiffer, M. B.
1976   *Behavioral Archaeology*. Academic Press, New York.
1985   *Formation Processes of the Archaeological Record*. University of New Mexico Press, Albuquerque.
Schreiber, K. J.
1987   Conquest and consolidation: A comparison of the Huari and Inka occupations of a highland Peruvian valley. *American Antiquity* 52:229–248.
Shanks, M., and C. Tilley
1987   *Reconstructing Archaeology: Theory and Practice*. Cambridge University Press, Cambridge.
Shar, G. M., and M. Vidale
n.d.   Surface evidence of craft activity at Chanhu-daro. *Annali dell'Instituto Universitario Orientale di Napoli*, Naples (forthcoming).
Shennan, S.
1988   *Quantifying Archaeology*. Academic Press, Orlando.
Shepard, A. O.
1961   *Ceramics for the Archaeologist*. Carnegie Institution of Washington, Publication 609. Washington, D. C.
Siegel, S.
1956   *Nonparametric Statistics for the Behavioral Sciences*. McGraw-Hill, New York.
Sinopoli, C. M.
1986   *Material Patterning and Social Organization: The Archaeological Ceramics of Vijayanagara, South India*. Ph.D. Dissertation, Department of Anthropology, University of Michigan, Ann Arbor.
1988   The organization of craft production at Vijayanagara, South India. *American Anthropologist* 90:580–597.
1991   *Pots and Palaces: The Earthenware Ceramics of the Noblemen's Quarter of Vijayanagara*. American Institute of Indian Studies and Manohar Press, New Delhi.
in press The ceramics of the Noblemen's Quarter of Vijayanagara. In *South Asian Archaeology, 1987*. Ed. by M. Taddei. Institute of Oriental Studies, Naples, Italy.
Sinopoli, C. M., and T. R. Blurton
1986   Modern pottery production in rural Karnataka. In *Dimensions of Indian Art: Pupul Jayaka Seventy*. Ed. by L. Chandra and J. Jain, pp. 439–456. Agam Kala Prakashan, New Delhi.

Smith, M.
   1985   Toward an economic interpretation of ceramics: Relating vessels size and shape to
          use. In *Decoding Prehistoric Ceramics*. Ed. by B. A. Nelson, pp. 254–309. Southern
          Illinois University Press, Carbondale.
Spaulding, A. C.
   1982   Structure in archaeological data: Nominal variables. In *Essays on Archaeological
          Typology*. Ed. by R. J. Whallon and J. A. Brown, pp. 1–22. Center for American
          Archaeology, Evanston.
Srinivas, M. N.
   1967   *Social Change in Modern India*. University of California Press, Berkeley.
Stanislawski, M. B.
   1969   What good is a broken pot? An experiment in Hopi-Tewa ethnoarchaeology.
          Southwestern Lore 35:11–18.
   1973   Review of "Archaeology as Anthropology: A Case Study." *American Antiquity*
          38:117–122.
   1978   If pots were mortal. In *Explorations in Ethnoarchaeology*. Ed. by R. A. Gould, pp.
          201–228. University of New Mexico Press, Albuquerque.
Stark, B. L.
   1985   Archaeological identification of pottery production locations: Ethnoarchaeo-
          logical and archaeological data in Mesoamerica. In *Decoding Prehistoric Ceramics*.
          Ed. by B. A. Nelson, pp. 158–194. Southern Illinois University Press, Carbondale.
Steponaitis, V.
   1983   *Ceramics, Chronology, and Community Patterns: An Archaeological Study at Moundville*.
          Academic Press, New York.
   1984   Technological studies of prehistoric pottery from Alabama: Physical properties
          and vessel function. In *The Many Dimensions of Pottery: Ceramics in Archaeology and
          Anthropology*. Ed. by S. E. van der Leeuw and A. C. Pritchard, pp. 79–122.
          University of Amsterdam, Amsterdam.
Steward, J. H.
   1942   The direct historical approach to archaeology. *American Antiquity* 7:337–344.
Thomas, D. H.
   1976   *Figuring Anthropology*. Holt, Rinehart & Winston, New York.
   1978   The awful truth about statistics in American archaeology. *American Antiquity*
          43:231–244.
   1986   *Refiguring Anthropology*. Waveland Press, Prospect Heights, IL.
Trigger, B. G.
   1989   *A History of Archaeological Thought*. Cambridge University Press, Cambridge.
van der Leeuw, S. E.
   1976   *Studies in the Technology of Ancient Pottery*. University of Amsterdam, Amsterdam.
   1977   Toward a study of the economics of pottery making. In *Ex Horreo*. Ed. by B. L. Van
          Beek, R. W. Brandt, and W. Goeman-van Waateringe, pp. 68–76. University of
          Amsterdam, Amsterdam.
   1984   Dust to dust: A transformational view of the ceramic cycle. In *The Many Dimensions
          of Pottery: Ceramics in Archaeology and Anthropology*. Ed. by S. E. van der Leeuw and
          A. C. Pritchard, pp. 707–774. University of Amsterdam, Amsterdam.
van der Leeuw, S. E., and A. C. Pritchard, Eds.
   1984   *The Many Dimensions of Pottery: Ceramics in Archaeology and Anthropology*. Univer-
          sity of Amsterdam, Amsterdam.
Vandiver, P. B., O. Soffer, B. Klima, and J. Svoboda
   1989   The origins of ceramic technology at Dolni Vestoniçe, Czechoslovakia. *Science*
          246:1002–1008.

Vidale, M.
1987   Some observations and conjectures on a group of steatite-debitage concentration on the surface of Moenjodaro. In *Annali dell'Instituto Universitario Orientale*, Naples.
1989   Specialized producers and urban elites: On the role of craft industries in Mature Harappan urban contexts. In *Old Problems and New Perspectives in South Asian Archaeology*. Ed. by J. M. Kenoyer, pp. 171–181. Wisconsin Archaeological Reports, 2. Madison.

Vitelli, K. D.
1989   Were pots first made for foods? Doubts from Francthi. *World Archaeology* 21:17–29.

Washburn, D.
1977   *A Symmetry analysis of Upper Gila Area Ceramic Design*. Papers of the Peabody Museum 68. Harvard University, Cambridge, Mass.
1989   The proper of symmetry and the concept of ethnic style. In *Archaeological Approaches to Cultural Identity*. Ed. by S. J. Shennan, pp. 157–173. Unwin Hyman, London.

Watson, P. J.
1977   Design analysis of painted pottery. *American Antiquity* 42:381–393.

Watson, P. J., and S. A. LeBlanc
1973   A comparative statistical analysis of painted pottery from seven Halafian sites. *Paleorient* 1:119–133.

Welbourn, A.
1984   Endo ceramics and power strategies. In *Ideology, Power and Prehistory*. Ed. by D. Miller and C. Tilley, pp. 17–24. Cambridge University Press, Cambridge.

Welch, P. D.
1986   *Models of Chiefdom Economy: Prehistoric Moundville as a Case Study*. Ph.D. dissertation, Department of Anthropology, University of Michigan, Ann Arbor.

Whallon, R. J., Jr.
1968   Investigations of late prehistoric social organization in New York State. In *New Perspectives in Archaeology*. Ed. by L. and S. Binford, pp. 223–244. Aldine, Chicago.
1969   Reflections of social interaction in Owasco ceramic decoration. *Eastern States Archaeological Federation Bulletins* 26 and 27.
1971   Type: A computer program for monothetic subdivisive classification. *University of Michigan Museum of Anthropology, Technical Reports*, 1. Ann Arbor.
1972   A new approach to pottery typology. *American Antiquity* 37:13–33.
1983   Methods of surface collection in archaeological survey. In *Archaeological Survey in the Mediterranean Area*. Ed. by D. R. Keller and D. W. Rupp, pp. 73–83. BAR International Series, 155.

Whallon, R. J., and J. A. Brown, Eds.
1982   *Essays on Archaeological Typology*. Center for American Archaeology Press, Evanston, Illinois.

Wheat, J., J. Gifford, and W. Wasley
1958   Ceramic variety, type cluster, and ceramic system in Southwestern pottery analysis. *American Antiquity* 24:34–47.

Wheeler, R. E. M.
1947   Harappa 1946: The defences and cemetery R37. *Ancient India* 3:58–130.

Wiessner, P.
1983   Style and social information in Kalahari San projectile points. *American Antiquity* 48:253–276.
1984   Reconsidering the behavioral basis for style: A case study among the Kalahari San. *Journal of Anthropological Archaeology* 3:190–234.

Williams, D. F.
1981   The Roman amphorae trade with late Iron Age Britain. In *Production and Distribution: A Ceramic Viewpoint*. Ed. by H. Howard and E. Morris, pp. 123–132. BAR International Series, No. 120.
Wobst, H. M.
1977   Stylistic behavior and information exchange. In *For the Director: Essays in Honor of James B. Griffin*. Ed. by C. Cleland, pp. 317–342. Anthropological Papers of the University of Michigan, 61. Ann Arbor.
Wright, H. T., and G. Johnson
1975   Population, exchange and early state formation in southwestern Iran. *American Anthropologist* 77:267–289.
Wright, H. T., Ed.
1981   An Early Town on the Deh Luran Plain: Excavations at Tepe Farukhabad. *Memoir of the Museum of Anthropology, University of Michigan*, 13. Ann Arbor.
Wright, R. P.
1989   The Indus Valley and Mesopotamian civilizations: A comparative view of ceramic technology. In *Old Problems and New Perspectives in the Archaeology of South Asia*. Ed. by J. M. Kenoyer, pp. 145–156. Wisconsin Archaeological Reports, 2. Madison.
Wylie, A.
1985   The reaction against analogy. In *Advances in Archaeological Method and Theory*, Vol. 8. Ed. by M. B. Schiffer, pp. 63–111. Academic Press, Orlando.
Yellen, J.
1977   *Archaeological Approaches to the Present*. Academic Press, New York.

Glossary

ACTIVITY AREA. Location where specific past human activities took place that can be identified with archaeological evidence.

AMPHORA. Large narrow jar, with long neck, vertical strap handles, and round or conical base, used by Romans in long-distance trade.

APPLIQUÉ. Decorative technique, addition of molded clay to vessel surface.

BEAKER. Tall slender vessel with hourglass shape, characteristic form of the European Neolithic.

BREAKAGE RATE. Rate at which vessels of different functional classes are broken.

BURNISHING. Finishing technique, rubbing leather-hard vessel with hard tool, such as a stone or potsherd, to produce glossy surface, with irregular luster and polishing marks visible.

CARINATION. Sharp angular turn in vessel profile.

CENTERING. Phase in wheel-building, in which a ball of clay is placed in throwing platform and shaped so that it revolves concentrically with the wheel.

CLAY. Fine-grained sediment, with particle size less than two-thousandths of a millimeter, becomes plastic when wet.

COILING. Hand-building technique, involves forming and joining narrow coils of clay to build up vessel walls.

CORE. Interior portion of vessel wall, often different in color than interior or exterior surface.

DESIGN CONFIGURATION. Grouping of design elements into a structured set.

DESIGN ELEMENT. Smallest portion of a design that can stand alone.

DOWNDRAFT KILN. Kiln in which fuel chamber is adjacent to vessel chamber and heat passes into vessel chamber over a wall or barrier from above.

EARTHENWARE. Ceramic vessels fired to temperatures of 900–1200 degrees centigrade, porous, often brown or red in color.

EFFIGY VESSELS. Vessels shaped like animals, humans, or other naturalistic forms.

FINISHING TECHNIQUES. Secondary techniques that alter shape of formed vessel or affect its surface appearance.

GLAZE. Composed of silica, fluxes, and metallic oxides, becomes vitrified or glasslike when fired at high temperatures.

GROG. Fragments of fired ceramics ground to small size and added to clays as temper.

HEARTH FIRING. Open-air firing technique, fuels and vessel placed together, sometimes in shallow depression.

HOUSEHOLD INDUSTRY. Pottery production system involving production within household for external and internal consumption, often associated with part-time specialization.

HOUSEHOLD PRODUCTION. Pottery production system involving production within household, primarily for internal consumption.

ILLITE. Three-layer clay mineral, often used for paints or slips.

INFLECTION. Point on vessel profile where vessel wall changes direction.

INTUITIVE TYPOLOGY. Classification of artifacts on basis of perceived similarities and differences, variables often defined *post facto*.

KAOLINITES. Common clay mineral, three-layer clay, used in manufacture of porcelain vessels.

KILN. Firing facility, fuel and vessel placed in separate chambers linked by flues.

LARGE-SCALE INDUSTRY. Pottery production system, involving massive production in highly specialized workshops or factories.

LEATHER HARD. Clay that has dried to the point that it has lost most of its plasticity but is still soft enough to be carved or altered.

LEVIGATION. Process of separating fine-grained particles from coarse particles by mixing earth with water and forming a suspension that is passed through a series of traps to sort particles.

LIP. The edge of the vessel orifice.

MOLDS. Hand-building techniques, permanent forms into or over which clay is impressed to form vessels.

NECK. Part of jar or restricted vessel between body and rim, marked by constriction and change in orientation of vessel walls.

OVEN. Firing facility, vessel and fuel placed together inside of permanent stone or clay enclosure.

OXIDIZING ATMOSPHERE. Oxygen-rich firing atmosphere.

PADDLE AND ANVIL TECHNIQUE. Finishing technique; involves beating exterior of vessel with wooden paddle against stone or ceramic anvil held on vessel interior; thins and shaped vessels.

PAINTED DESIGNS. Inorganic or organic pigment applied to vessel surface to form decorative pattern.

PASTE. Clay or mixture of clay and added materials.

PINCHING. Hand-building technique, involves forming vessel by opening clay ball and pulling vessel walls up between fingers.

PIT FIRING. Firing technique, fuel and vessel placed together in an excavated pit, sometimes covered with stones or earth.

PLASTICITY. The ability of clay to be molded and maintain its shape.

POLISHING. Finishing technique, rubbing vessel with hard tool, such as stone or potsherd, to produce uniform and very glossy surface.

PORCELAINS. Ceramic vessels fired to temperatures above 1350 degrees centigrade, with vitrified bodies, usually white and translucent.

POROSITY. Number and size of pores or voids in a fired vessel.

PRIMARY CLAY. Clay found in close proximity to its parent rock source.

QUANTITATIVE TYPOLOGY. Ceramic typology based on statistical distribution of two or more variables.

REDUCING ATMOSPHERE. Oxygen-poor firing atmosphere.

RESIDUE ANALYSIS. The study of the remains of vessel contents, usually through chemical analysis.

RESTRICTED VESSEL. Vessel form, or profile, characteristic by narrowing or constricting of vessel form in between base and rim.

RIM. Upper part of vessel, near orifice.

SCRAPING. Finishing technique, involves scraping leather-hard vessel with tool held perpendicular to vessel to thin or shape vessel.

SECONDARY CLAY. Clay that has been transported some distance from its parent rock source.

SERIATION. Relative dating technique, based on changes in relative frequencies of types or variables over time.

SHERD (SHARD). Fragment or piece of broken vessel.

SLAB BUILDING. Hand-building technique, involves forming flat slabs of clay and connecting them to form vessel.

SLIP. Liquid mixture of clay and water applied over surface of vessel to affect color and texture.

SMECTITE. Three-layer clay mineral, often used for paints or slips.

SMOOTHING. Finishing technique, lightly rubbing leather-hard vessel with hard tool, such as a stone or potsherd, to produce smooth but non-glossy surface.

STONEWARES. Ceramic vessels fired to temperatures of 1200–1350 degrees Centigrade, partially vitrified bodies, usually brown, gray or white.

TEMPER. Nonplastic inclusions deliberately added to clays to improve workability and affect other characteristics of fired vessels.

TERRACOTTA. Ceramic vessel fired to temperature of less than 900 degrees centigrade, coarse and porous, usually red.

THERMAL STRESS RESISTANCE. Ability of vessel to withstand repeated expansion and contraction as a result of heating and cooling.

THROWING FROM THE HUMP. Wheel-building technique in which several vessels are formed from single large mass or hump of clay placed on rotating wheel.

TRACE ELEMENTS. Elements found in very small quantities in clays and vessels.

TRADITION. Consistent approach to vessel manufacture that persists over relatively long time period.

TRIMMING. Finishing technique, involves cutting vessel with hard tool held at acute angle to vessel to thin body.

TURNING. Finishing technique, thinning vessel with cutting tool while inverted vessel rotates on potter's wheel.

TYPE–VARIETY METHOD. Method of ceramic typology in which vessels are grouped into successively finer categories on basis of some combination of variables, including: paste, decorative treatment, surface finish, and location.

UNRESTRICTED VESSEL. Vessel form or profile characterized by open form with no narrowing or constrictions between base and rim.

UPDRAFT KILN. Fuel chamber directly below chamber holding vessels.

USER LIFE. Length of time that vessel is used for primary function.

USE WEAR. Traces on vessel formed as result of use, for example, charring on cooking vessels.

VARIABLE. Scale along which variation in artifacts may be assessed, can be nominal, ordinal, or quantitative.

WARE. Class of pottery characterized by similar technology, material, and surface treatment.

WASTER. Blistered or deformed vessel, formed as result of firing errors.

WORKSHOP INDUSTRY. Pottery production system involving production by specialists in permanent workshop facilities, often family workshops.

Index